THE WALL STREET JOURNAL.

Book of International Investing

Everything You Need to Know
About Investing in Foreign Markets

JOHN A. PRESTBO AND DOUGLAS R. SEASE

New York

To our wives,
Darlene and Jane,
who richly diversify our lives

Library of Congress Cataloging-in-Publication Data

Prestbo, John A.
The Wall Street journal book of international investing :
everything you need to know about investing in foreign markets /
by John A. Prestbo and Douglas R. Sease.
p.   cm.
ISBN 0-7868-6092-8
1. Investments, Foreign.   2. Investment analysis.
I. Sease, Douglas R.   II. Title.
HG4538.P675   1997
332.6'73—dc20   96-35266
CIP

Paperback ISBN: 0-7868-8310-3

Designed by Paul Chevannes

FIRST PAPERBACK EDITION
2 4 6 8 10 9 7 5 3

Contents

Contents

Introduction

International travel is such hard work. First, you have to decide where you want to go and when. Then, you must deal with travel agents or ticket clerks, make hotel reservations, arrange for transportation to the airport, get your visa (or renew your passport if, like us, you didn't notice until two weeks before departure that it had expired), and pack your bags. You sit jammed in uncomfortable seats, breathing bad air and eating worse food while being whisked through the sky at 450 miles an hour.

But then comes the good stuff. The sights, sounds, and smells of a foreign country. The fascinating new culture. The great food (assuming you aren't in Great Britain). The wonderful people. Just the sheer experience of it. Of course, you are probably glad to return home, where things are familiar and comfortable. But you're glad you went, too. For all the trouble, foreign travel is immensely rewarding.

Foreign investing is a lot like foreign travel. It's expensive, time-consuming, and sometimes frustrating, but in the end it is highly rewarding. We wrote this book in the hope that we can make it easier and more rewarding for you to put at least some of your money to work abroad. The fact you have picked up the book at all tells us that you are at least thinking about foreign investing, perhaps after hearing or reading about some of the spectacular fortunes to be made in emerging markets. But don't expect us to give you the inside skinny on which obscure little foreign stock market is going to rise 400% this year. We don't know and neither does anyone else.

What we are going to do is explain clearly why you should have some money abroad, where you might want to put it, and how to get it there. To some extent we encourage you to make overseas investments because we think it's the right thing to do. But, like the best guidebooks, we basically presume you want to go; you want us to help you get there and get the most out of it. Keep in mind, though, that this is only a guidebook. We won't plan every aspect of your trip. If you want that kind of advice we can help you find the right people to provide it; but be prepared to pay sometimes steep prices for this service.

Just as there are innumerable kinds of tourists—ranging from the packaged-tour, gratuities-included retiree to the just-graduated back-packer—there are many different kinds of investors. We try to accommodate the entire spectrum in this book. If, like many of us, you have decided that you're a better executive, teacher, doctor, or mother than you are an investor, that's fine. We can help you select money managers or mutual funds that will do the hard work of investing abroad for you. But if the excitement and intellectual challenge of investing have captured you, we're here to help you find the foreign markets and stocks that you can buy and sell with minimal expense and hassle.

Whatever your investment style, we are making certain assumptions about you. One is that you understand the fundamentals of investing. You know that stock prices don't always rise, that brokers make money whether or not you do, that bonds are not risk-free, and that Uncle Sam wants his cut of your profits.

Another assumption is that you have developed—or, maybe, discovered—your own philosophy about investing. We assume you know how much you have to invest, what your investment goals are, and how much risk you are willing to take. Mainly, we assume that you know how much time and effort you are willing to devote to your investments. The biggest single problem we find with individual investors is that they build high-maintenance portfolios, then don't do the maintenance. The frequent result is a financial disaster.

The four sections of this book walk you through the entire international investing sequence. Even though we assume that you already are interested in adding a foreign flavor to your portfolio, we devote Part One to grounding you in the reasons for doing so. Racking up a huge bonanza this year or next isn't one of those reasons. Achieving good returns, over time, is. Because we don't want you to have any unpleasant surprises in your foreign forays, we lay out the risks. Many of them are the same risks you face already with your U.S. portfolio. Others—coups and currencies, for example—might not spring readily to a U.S. investor's mind.

The second part gives you a complete rundown on the vehicles for your investment journey. You will almost certainly notice that we devote considerable space to mutual funds and their close cousins, closed-end funds. That emphasis springs from our conviction that for many individual investors, mutual funds are the most practical method of investing abroad. With mutual funds you can select any of several levels of involvement. There's the "leave-the-driving-to-us" approach of global and international funds (yes, there is a difference). Then there are regional and country funds for investors who have a good feeling about a particular part of the globe. And there are even industry and sector funds that put you into certain types of stocks wherever on earth they may be.

But for all the emphasis on mutual funds, we don't slight those of you with the time, ability, and willingness to do it yourself. If you really want to own some international stocks without leaving the good old U.S. of A., American depositary receipts are for you. These are, in essence, stocks issued by foreign companies that are traded on U.S. stock exchanges in dollars, not Japanese yen or Mexican pesos. If you really are adventurous, a growing number of U.S. brokerage firms are willing and able to rustle up shares of companies that aren't traded in this country at all. At the same time, an increasing number of foreign stock and bond markets welcome individual investors. You just have to understand that they don't always—in fact, hardly ever—handle things the way we do here.

Some of you may think we don't pay enough to attention to foreign bonds. But we have a rather firm position on bonds: We think you buy bonds for safety; and if you are taking a currency risk—which you automatically do with almost any foreign investment—you really aren't buying something that's safe. Ipso facto, we don't recommend foreign bonds. Period. We elaborate on this position, briefly, in the short chapter on bonds.

For those of you who want a little hand-holding on the way to building a foreign portfolio, help is out there in the form of money managers. But beware! Not all money managers—in fact, relatively few—know much about or have much experience in investing abroad. We'll explain how you pick the right management firm to help you meet your financial goals.

The third section is the real tour guide. This is where you get a look at the investment potential of different countries and regions. While the allure of exotic locations such as Indonesia or Argentina is undeniable for adventurous investors, there is plenty to be said in favor of such long-established markets as the United Kingdom. We put a nation's financial markets in the context of the country's culture. In most cases, we'll name some typical companies that you should at least keep an eye on as potential holdings or as barometers of a market's health.

We start the tour close to home, with Mexico and Canada. To

many of us, Canada is familiar; indeed, too familiar as a potential foreign investment destination. We explain why investing in Canada is not, in many ways, foreign investing. On the other hand, Mexico, which is just as close in a different direction, is a perfect example of the ideal foreign investment location, notwithstanding the market meltdown of late 1994. Indeed, for the savviest and bravest investors, the peso collapse that year provided a golden opportunity to get into Mexican stocks at what will almost certainly prove to be bargain levels years from now. The real value of Mexico, though, is that its economy, while becoming more closely tied to that of the United States, nevertheless moves in a different cycle.

Mundane as it may seem, we think the smart international investor needs to keep a portion of his or her funds in the major European markets: Great Britain, France, and Germany. Ranking among the most politically and economically developed nations in the world, these three countries provide markets that are nearly as regulated, transparent, and efficient as our own. Yet they also provide economic and market cycles that aren't precisely synchronized with the United States. Each of the three also has its own peculiarities, such as the deep-seated German distrust of stocks.

There was a time not so long ago that Japan was seen as the world's economic juggernaut, a vast production line that cranked out sleek and reliable cars and top-notch electronics. Today it's another story. Japanese automakers are having to fight hard to maintain their gains against U.S. competitors, and semiconductor manufacturers have never caught up to their U.S. counterparts. The ups and downs of the Japanese economy and stock market have been written about extensively. Yet there remains vast investment potential in Japan. After all, one of the basic rules of investing is to buy low and sell high. And by many measures Japanese assets remain cheap, especially considering Japan's pre-eminent position in Asia.

You can't talk about Asia without talking about the Asian Tigers: Hong Kong, Taiwan, Singapore, and South Korea, plus the up-and-comers, Malaysia, Thailand, Indonesia, and the Philippines. Some, such as Korea and Taiwan, offer limited investment opportunities. But the others are open to anyone willing to risk a buck. Hong Kong will be especially important in coming years as it is reintegrated—for better or worse—into China.

Next we visit the world's two most populous nations, China and

India. Why, do you suppose, investors have such a liking for the world's largest Communist dictatorship, yet until recently have shied away from making investments in the world's largest democracy? We try to answer that question, but maybe the majority of investors are wrong. In any case, these two countries have tremendous unrealized potential for investors. Just remember that it may stay unrealized for a long while to come.

Among the world's markets there are several that, while not very big and in some cases unsophisticated, can't exactly be classified as emerging, either. We call them the Second Tier, and they include such markets as Italy, Australia, New Zealand, Spain, Portugal, Switzerland, Sweden, and Finland. There are good reasons to seek out some of these markets. Finland, for example, turned in a startlingly good performance in 1994, rising nearly 50%. But there are some unusual risks, too, such as Austria's and Greece's exposure to the rebuilding nations of Central and Eastern Europe. We'll give you a quick rundown on the strengths and weaknesses of these markets and what caveats to keep in mind if you want to invest there.

South America is a major playing field for the emerging markets gurus. And rightly so. Brazil, Argentina, Chile, and even Peru are moving forward rapidly with economic development and trade liberalization programs. They have a long way to go and the road will be bumpy. But they offer a classic chance to get in, if not at the bottom any longer, at least before the air becomes too thin to breathe. The important thing to remember about these markets is that they have been, by and large, the investment targets of American investors. European and Asian investors are just beginning to catch on, and as they come piling in over the next few years, the liquidity they provide should help underpin these fledgling markets.

We know that as an investor you are willing to take some risks for improved returns. And there are some markets that will be happy to accommodate the thrill seekers among investors. Poland, Israel, and Turkey, for example, are somewhat akin to the Wild West of investing. You may make a lot of money, but you may lose a lot, too. Then there are places that simply aren't worth the risk at any cost. Russia and the other republics of the former Soviet Union haven't put their economies, much less their markets, into good enough shape to be hospitable for the average investor. Sure, you will hear about the intrepid investors making early forays into these markets. Let them go. You probably wouldn't have enjoyed being among the crew on Columbus's voyage to the New World, and you probably won't enjoy the experience you will have in these markets for the next few years. Let somebody else do the pioneering work. There will be plenty of opportunity later. If you do want to try it now, wear a seat belt. Things happen fast.

Where it is appropriate and useful in our survey of the various foreign markets, and where sufficient data exists to make comparisons valid, we'll show you how various countries' stock markets behave in relation to the U.S. market. That should give you an idea not only about how effective diversification into a given country's stocks will be but also about how much volatility—that means risk—you will encounter. We also take note of currency values against the dollar. All things being equal—and we always point out that they never are—it would be better to buy stocks in a country whose currency is rising against the dollar than vice versa. If it looks like the foreign currency is nearing its cyclical peak against the dollar, beware! A strengthening dollar can hurt returns from any given market.

Finally, in the fourth section of the book, we pull it all together. In the first of the two chapters in this last section we look at the various strategies that the pros use to invest internationally. We aren't suggesting that you ape any one of these managers or that you take your investment business to any of them. We just want to show you how people who do this all the time think about it. Some of their techniques will probably fit well with your own philosophy and objectives in investing abroad. Others may appear ludicrous to you, but they should spur you at least to think about your own views more carefully. We have found over the years that it's dangerous to reject any point of view out of hand without considering its merits.

In the final chapter of the book we present some hypothetical portfolios of both domestic and foreign investments constructed to accommodate different circumstances. There is, for example, the "don't-bother-me-and-make-it-cheap" portfolio, which consists entirely of index funds. Set up one of these and you can go sailing in the South Pacific for five years and not have to make a single phone call to check up on your portfolio. At the other end of the spectrum is the "stock-pickers-full-employment" portfolio, a demanding aggregation of foreign stocks from around the world that will require the kind of careful tending that only an investment fanatic will be willing to undertake.

More than likely your own portfolio will lie between those extremes. The main point is, it needs to be one with which you can be comfortable, because it will help provide the returns you need to meet your goals.

Have a good trip.

PART ONE

The Rewards and Risks of Global Investing

We don't think anyone should rush headlong into an investment decision. This is money we're talking about, after all. You probably worked hard to earn and save the money in your investment portfolio, and you shouldn't squander it on a whim or the advice of someone who doesn't have your long-term interests at heart. You should know your own risk tolerance, your financial goals, and the time you have to reach those goals before embarking on any investment program. Above all, you should have a thorough understanding of the potential risks and probable rewards of any particular investment.

Foreign investing can be confusing, and confusion can lead to poor decisions. We see the results of such decisions frequently. One of our close friends has amassed nearly $1 million in his profit-sharing retirement plan at work. Though he has access through that plan to a mutual fund specializing in overseas investments, he refuses to put even a few thousand dollars in that fund. "Too risky," he says, citing the modest loss the fund sustained in 1994. He chooses to ignore the fact that over the past ten years—and he is at least ten years away from retirement—that same fund has outperformed every other fund to which he has access. At the same time, we know others who have their entire investment portfolio—granted, not as large as our friend's million-dollar nest egg—invested in emerging-market stocks. They are gambling that the occasional big plunges sweeping these markets from time to time will be more than offset over the long haul by enormous gains fostered by fast-growing economies.

We think there's a solid middle ground that avoids both extremes, and we make the argument for that approach in the first two chapters of this book. In Chapter 1 we tell you why you need to have some of your money invested abroad—not for the big killings that might be made in some emerging markets but for the *protection* that comes with diversification. In Chapter 2 we discuss the very real risks of investing abroad. Some of them are the same risks we worry about with our domestic investments. Others, such as political and currency risks, are inherent to venturing beyond our own shores in search of diversification.

We hope you finish these two chapters firmly convinced that for the long-term investor, the rewards of international investing are well worth the risks.

CHAPTER I

The Rewards

W E figure you bought this book for one of two reasons. Either you want to make a killing in some hot emerging market, or you're scared to invest abroad.

Let's deal first with those of you who want to make a killing. You've been tempted by those stories in *The Wall Street Journal* or other publications about the fantastic profits that investors reap in one foreign market or another. People still talk about the 115% gain that Hong Kong posted in 1993. In 1994 little Finland racked up a second consecutive big windfall for investors. Had you jumped into the Finnish stock market headfirst at the beginning of 1994 you would have had a 48.5% gain in dollar terms at the end of the year. And that would have come on the heels of a stunning 73% gain in dollar terms in 1993.

If that's what you're looking for here, well, sorry, you just threw away the price of this book. We can't tell you what the next hot market will be, and neither can anybody else. How do we know that? As editors in *The Wall Street Journal*'s Money and Investing section, we are constantly bombarded by money managers, strategists, analysts, and countless newsletters, all telling us what the next hot stock or market will be. We do our best to listen to or read as much of this stuff as possible. How many times do you think we heard or read, late in 1993 and early in 1994, that Finland was going to be one of the hottest markets of 1994?

Zero. Zip. None. Nada. That's right. Nobody we talked to, none of the sophisticated analysts' reports, and none of the "hot tip" newsletters we read late in 1993 or early in 1994 even mentioned Finland, despite its 1993 gain, much less predicted it would produce a second consecutive year of spectacular returns. Hong Kong was probably touted the most, followed by Mexico. So, if you followed the advice that many of the pundits were giving as 1994 opened, you would have sunk your money in Hong Kong, destined to fall 32% in dollar terms in 1994, and Mexico, which plunged a stunning 41.5% in dollar terms.

Unfortunately, such occurrences are all too common. Here, in an overly simplistic scenario, is what happens: Some investment pros—seldom the same ones in case after case—recognize that a particular beaten-down market offers an unusual investment opportunity. They put several million dollars to work in the market, which boosts prices perceptibly. More money managers see the effects of that initial investment and decide the market is getting "hot." They pump in more millions, sending prices even higher. The locals, who probably know more about the real value of their own market, jump in to take advantage of all that foreign money heading their way, and the cycle gains a momentum of its own. Even the dumbest money managers know enough to realize their clients want to see that they, too, are in the hot market, so even more foreign money pours in, pushing prices still higher.

Of course, the savvy investors who recognized the opportunity in the first place probably recognize equally well when a market is overvalued. They start to get out even as the chumps are flocking to get in. The word that the "smart money" is beginning to sell leaks out among insiders at the stock exchange, which prompts the local money to start abandoning ship, too. Prices fall a little, perhaps enough to convince the chumps that they have a new "buying opportunity." But eventually the efficiency of the market asserts itself and prices retreat to a more rational level. Often that rational level is far below the market's peak, and many investors are stuck with sizable losses. You never hear about them. It's a truism of the market that only the successful tend to talk.

None of this is to say that you shouldn't have some of your investable money at work in places known generally as "emerging markets." Many of these countries' economies, both small and large, will grow at considerably faster rates over the coming years than the economies of industrialized nations. Their stock markets will reflect that growth. But the ride is apt to be very uncomfortable. Hong Kong is a prime example of the risks and rewards we're talking about. An investor who put $10,000 in Hong Kong 15 years ago now has a portfolio valued at about $100,000—a tenfold increase. Yet that nervy soul has also endured nine bear markets in Hong Kong stocks, by which we mean drops of more than 20%. Two of those declines exceeded 50%. How comfortable will you be if you sink your entire portfolio into a market like that at the top and see it plunge 60% in a matter of months? How happy will you be if the kids' college tuition is coming due, but it's all invested in a market that just fell 45%? Of course, those of us with long-term views can look on the bright side: If you are determined to play the hot markets, don't rush in and buy your favorite when it is already up 80%. You will almost certainly get another chance to buy it cheap in coming years.

SPREADING THE RISK

Those of you who have been scared to get into international investing can relax. We don't think international investing should be about hot markets or losing your shirt. Rather, it should be about diversification. We all know that if you pick the right stock here at home you can double or triple your money in a matter of weeks or months. We also know, however, that it's almost impossible to pick that single right stock. That's why we usually buy several stocks for our portfolios. Or, many of us buy a mutual fund, where we get an instant portfolio of several hundred stocks. In short, we're not willing to gamble everything on one throw of the dice, no matter how attractive a company's stock looks. A diversified portfolio doesn't rise as much as the best-performing single stock on the New York Stock Exchange in any given year. But it also doesn't fall as far as the worst-performing stock. By selecting several stocks you have reduced the volatility of your portfolio while, we hope, maximizing its return.

Many investors aren't comfortable having their portfolios entirely in stocks. They hold some bonds, probably keep some of their assets in cash, and maybe dabble in real estate. That way, if stocks overall are declining, their bond portfolio might be rising in value. Or perhaps their real estate holdings are appreciating while the returns on short-term cash are falling. That's another layer of diversification—lowering risks while maximizing returns. It's just common sense. Money managers who want to charge you for that kind of common sense call it "tactical asset allocation."

Consider that when many of us were coming of investing age 10—okay, 20 to 25—years ago, the U.S. stock market was far and away the world's largest. In 1970 the value of all U.S. listed shares represented a commanding 66% of the total $929 billion in world stock market capitalization. There simply didn't seem to be much need to look beyond our own borders for possible investments. But that picture has changed remarkably in 20 years. Today the U.S. stock market represents a little more than a third of the total stock market equity in the world. Simply put, that means there are more potential stock investments outside the United States than there are here at home. Would a smart investor dare set an arbitrary rule that he or she would consider only a third of all the stocks listed on the New York Stock Exchange as potential in-

The Changing World Stock Market

Markets ranked by total capitalization, in millions of U.S. dollars

	1980				1995		
		Market Cap.	% of Total			Market Cap.	% of Total
1	United States	$1,448,120	53%	1	United States	$6,857,622	39%
2	Japan	379,679	14%	2	Japan	3,667,292	21%
3	United Kingdom	205,200	7%	3	United Kingdom	1,407,737	8%
4	Canada	118,300	4%	4	Germany	577,365	3%
5	South Africa	100,000	4%	5	France	622,053	3%
6	Germany	71,700	3%	6	Switzerland	433,621	2%
7	Australia	59,700	2%	7	Canada	366,344	2%
8	France	54,600	2%	8	Netherlands	356,481	2%
9	Hong Kong	39,104	1%	9	Hong Kong	303,705	2%
10	Switzerland	37,600	1%	10	South Africa	280,526	2%
11	Netherlands	29,300	1%	11	Australia	245,218	1%
12	Italy	25,600	1%	12	Malaysia	222,729	1%
13	Singapore	24,418	1%	13	Italy	209,522	1%
14	Spain	16,600	1%	14	Spain	197,788	1%
15	Mexico	12,894		15	Taiwan	187,206	1%
16	Sweden	12,900		16	Korea	181,955	1%
17	Malaysia	12,395		17	Sweden	178,049	1%
18	Belgium	10,000		18	Singapore	148,004	1%
19	Chile	9,400		19	Brazil	147,636	1%
20	Brazil	9,160		20	Thailand	141,507	1%
21	India	7,585		21	India	127,199	1%
22	Taiwan	6,082		22	Belgium	104,960	1%
23	Denmark	5,400		23	Mexico	90,694	1%
24	Israel	4,828		24	Chile	73,860	

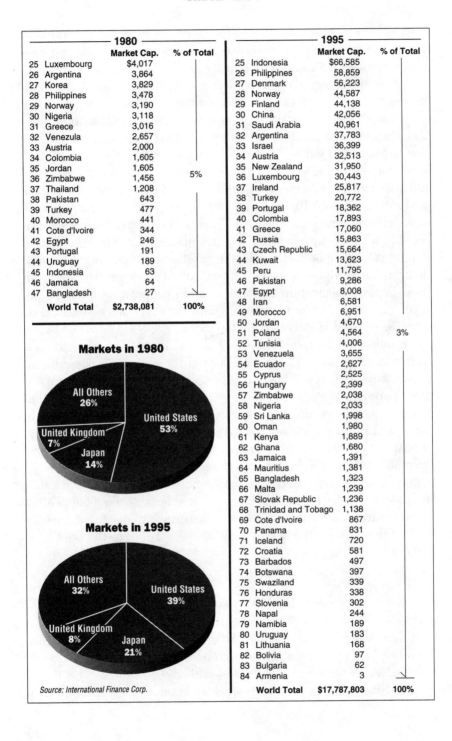

1980		
	Market Cap.	% of Total
25 Luxembourg	$4,017	
26 Argentina	3,864	
27 Korea	3,829	
28 Philippines	3,478	
29 Norway	3,190	
30 Nigeria	3,118	
31 Greece	3,016	
32 Venezula	2,657	
33 Austria	2,000	
34 Colombia	1,605	
35 Jordan	1,605	
36 Zimbabwe	1,456	5%
37 Thailand	1,208	
38 Pakistan	643	
39 Turkey	477	
40 Morocco	441	
41 Cote d'Ivoire	344	
42 Egypt	246	
43 Portugal	191	
44 Uruguay	189	
45 Indonesia	63	
46 Jamaica	64	
47 Bangladesh	27	
World Total	**$2,738,081**	**100%**

Markets in 1980

All Others 26%
United States 53%
United Kingdom 7%
Japan 14%

Markets in 1995

All Others 32%
United States 39%
United Kingdom 8%
Japan 21%

Source: International Finance Corp.

1995		
	Market Cap.	% of Total
25 Indonesia	$66,585	
26 Philippines	58,859	
27 Denmark	56,223	
28 Norway	44,587	
29 Finland	44,138	
30 China	42,056	
31 Saudi Arabia	40,961	
32 Argentina	37,783	
33 Israel	36,399	
34 Austria	32,513	
35 New Zealand	31,950	
36 Luxembourg	30,443	
37 Ireland	25,817	
38 Turkey	20,772	
39 Portugal	18,362	
40 Colombia	17,893	
41 Greece	17,060	
42 Russia	15,863	
43 Czech Republic	15,664	
44 Kuwait	13,623	
45 Peru	11,795	
46 Pakistan	9,286	
47 Egypt	8,008	
48 Iran	6,581	
49 Morocco	6,951	
50 Jordan	4,670	
51 Poland	4,564	3%
52 Tunisia	4,006	
53 Venezuela	3,655	
54 Ecuador	2,627	
55 Cyprus	2,525	
56 Hungary	2,399	
57 Zimbabwe	2,038	
58 Nigeria	2,033	
59 Sri Lanka	1,998	
60 Oman	1,980	
61 Kenya	1,889	
62 Ghana	1,680	
63 Jamaica	1,391	
64 Mauritius	1,381	
65 Bangladesh	1,323	
66 Malta	1,239	
67 Slovak Republic	1,236	
68 Trinidad and Tobago	1,138	
69 Cote d'Ivoire	867	
70 Panama	831	
71 Iceland	720	
72 Croatia	581	
73 Barbados	497	
74 Botswana	397	
75 Swaziland	339	
76 Honduras	338	
77 Slovenia	302	
78 Napal	244	
79 Namibia	189	
80 Uruguay	183	
81 Lithuania	168	
82 Bolivia	97	
83 Bulgaria	62	
84 Armenia	3	
World Total	**$17,787,803**	**100%**

vestments? Of course not. But many investors, by shunning non-U.S. stocks, put themselves in the equally dubious position of placing two-thirds of the world's stocks off limits.

Many of the world's best companies—and potentially the world's best stock buys—aren't in the United States. In the past year or two, for example, there has been great debate among automobile buffs about which auto company turns out the best products, Chrysler or Ford. (Nobody is willing to stick up for General Motors.) Yet all that arguing is about the second string. We suspect that any intelligent automobile executive, if painfully candid, would tell you that the world's best automakers are Toyota and Honda. Even when their currency penalizes them fiercely, and even as Ford and Chrysler have made noticeable advances in design and quality, Japanese automakers still have managed to hang on to their U.S. market share. And when the yen-dollar relationship goes in their favor, both Toyota and Honda make more headway against their American and European competitors. So, if you are thinking about owning an auto stock, you must at least consider Toyota and Honda as potential picks.

Another advantage of investing abroad is that you have the opportunity to get in on the ground floor of some amazing possibilities. How many of us would love to be in the position that our parents or grandparents were in many years ago when they bought stock in that fledgling company called American Telephone & Telegraph? Well, more and more governments in developing countries are deciding, wisely, that private enterprise can run telecommunications systems, and railroads and airlines, better than the government can. As these huge enterprises are "privatized," the international investor will have a shot at becoming a charter stockholder. Isn't it at least a little bit appealing to own shares of a telephone company in a growing country where only 15% of the population currently has phones? The growth potential is enormous.

BREAKING THE CYCLE

But there's much more to this whole international investing picture than just having a bigger menu from which to choose. You're doubtless familiar—perhaps painfully so—with the economic cycle in the United States and how it affects stock and bond values. In a booming economy, cyclical stocks do well. Then early signs of inflation set in, interest rates rise, and things start slowing down. That's when growth stocks tend to shine and cyclical stocks start to decline. Eventually, we slip into recession, inflation fades, interest rates come down, and the whole process starts again. If you choose to be invested only in the United States, you will be entirely at the mercy of that cycle. Investing outside the United States will expose you to economies at differing points on the cycle. Escaping the economic and investment cycle—or at least muting its effect on your portfolio—is one of the primary aims of investing outside this country.

The accompanying charts help illustrate what we are talking about. First, look at the Dow Jones Industrial Average going back ten years. Those of you who have been investors for some time no doubt recall how your own portfolios performed during the ups and downs depicted here, including the disaster of October 1987.

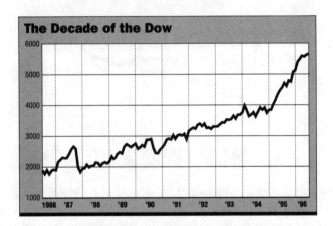

Let's overlay the Dow Industrials with the performance of the French stock market over the same decade. Obviously the U.S. market and the French market don't move in lockstep, although there are worldwide events, such as the 1987 crash, that tend to be reflected in both markets.

Now look at the Dow and the Canadian stock market. They look pretty similar, don't they? As we'll explain later in more detail, those similar stock market charts suggest that Canada might not be the ideal investment site for someone looking to offset the U.S. stock market cycle.

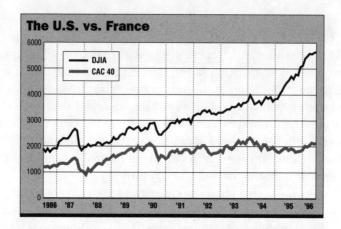

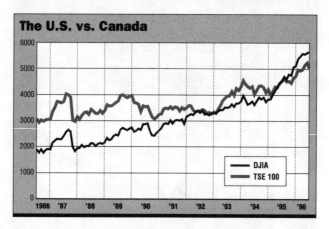

Next, we dump a few more markets onto the Dow, including a couple of hot emerging markets. Don't be fooled if the chart looks like chaos. What you're really seeing is the smoothing effect of a diversified international portfolio of stocks. The presence of the Mexican market in the ten-year example clearly widens the band in which prices fluctuate, as the Hong Kong market does in the five-year chart. That's an example of how increased risk—defined here as the size of price swings—can also produce increased rewards. (Note that in 1992 and 1993, both Mexico and Hong Kong outperformed the more developed markets.) This is what we call the merry-go-round effect: Just as not all the wooden horses rise or plunge together, there usually are some markets rising while others are falling. Therefore, the risk that a portfolio of stocks from different countries will be substantially lower on

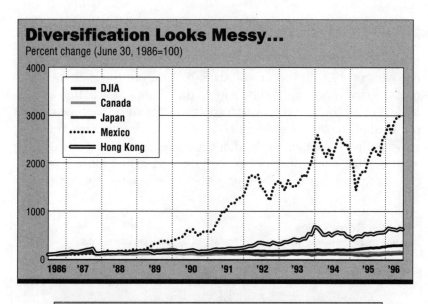

Diversification Looks Messy...

Percent change (June 30, 1986=100)

- ——— DJIA
- ——— Canada
- ——— Japan
- ········ Mexico
- ═══ Hong Kong

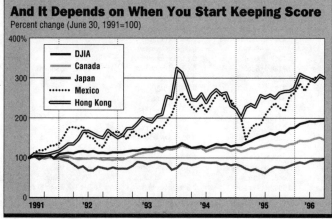

And It Depends on When You Start Keeping Score

Percent change (June 30, 1991=100)

- ——— DJIA
- ——— Canada
- ——— Japan
- ········ Mexico
- ═══ Hong Kong

any given date is considerably less than for a portfolio of stocks from any one country. That's what diversification is all about.

The investment pros—the ones who want to charge you for their advice—have a name for all this: "the correlation coefficient of markets." That's just a $100-an-hour phrase for the extent to which one market moves in lockstep with another. A correlation coefficient of 1, the highest number, means that two markets move exactly alike. Hypothetically, if one market rose 10%, the other would rise 10%, too. Note in the table on the following page the countries with correlation coefficients of more than 0.9000; they come closer than any other markets to moving in lockstep with the United States. A correlation coefficient of -1 means that two markets would move exactly opposite. If one went up 10%, the other would fall 10%. Interestingly, there are no markets that move exactly opposite to the United States. Right in the middle of all that is a correlation coefficient of zero. That means that one market's moves have absolutely no effect on the other market. They move entirely independently of one another. A zero coefficient is the ideal goal for a diversified portfolio, but too ideal to achieve except accidentally, and then only fleetingly. About the best we can do with sin-

Market Correlations
How Stock Markets in the Dow Jones Global Indexes Compare with the U.S.
(A correlation of 1 is perfect; 0 means uncorrelated, and -1 is negatively correlated)

In Local Currencies				In U.S. Dollars			
In Alphabetical Order		High to Low		In Alphabetical Order		High to Low	
Australia	0.8019	Ireland	0.9418	Australia	0.8547	Netherlands	0.9536
Austria	0.1032	Switzerland	0.9172	Austria	0.4794	Sweden	0.9523
Belgium	0.8392	Canada	0.9121	Belgium	0.9272	Switzerland	0.9508
Canada	0.9121	Netherlands	0.9075	Canada	0.8856	Ireland	0.9360
Denmark	0.6360	Sweden	0.9017	Denmark	0.8436	Belgium	0.9272
Finland	0.6634	United Kingdom	0.8846	Finland	0.7204	United Kingdom	0.9078
France	0.4350	South Africa	0.8483	France	0.8265	Germany	0.8866
Germany	0.7967	Belgium	0.8392	Germany	0.8866	Canada	0.8856
Hong Kong	0.7617	Mexico	0.8116	Hong Kong	0.7588	Australia	0.8547
Indonesia	0.6138	Spain	0.8068	Indonesia	0.4560	Denmark	0.8436
Ireland	0.9418	Australia	0.8019	Ireland	0.9360	Norway	0.8325
Italy	0.3716	Germany	0.7967	Italy	0.2955	Spain	0.8294
Japan	0.3483	Singapore	0.7681	Japan	0.4922	France	0.8265
Malaysia	0.6632	Hong Kong	0.7617	Malaysia	0.6950	Singapore	0.8166
Mexico	0.8116	Norway	0.7457	Mexico	-0.4869	New Zealand	0.7817
Netherlands	0.9075	Philippines	0.6958	Netherlands	0.9536	Hong Kong	0.7588
New Zealand	0.6267	Finland	0.6634	New Zealand	0.7817	Finland	0.7204
Norway	0.7457	Malaysia	0.6632	Norway	0.8325	South Africa	0.7002
Philippines	0.6958	Denmark	0.6360	Philippines	0.6997	Philippines	0.6997
Singapore	0.7681	New Zealand	0.6267	Singapore	0.8166	Malaysia	0.6950
South Africa	0.8483	Indonesia	0.6138	South Africa	0.7002	Thailand	0.5743
South Korea	0.5092	Thailand	0.5886	South Korea	0.5163	South Korea	0.5163
Spain	0.8068	South Korea	0.5092	Spain	0.8294	Japan	0.4922
Sweden	0.9017	Taiwan	0.4361	Sweden	0.9523	Austria	0.4794
Switzerland	0.9172	France	0.4350	Switzerland	0.9508	Indonesia	0.4560
Taiwan	0.4361	Italy	0.3716	Taiwan	0.3714	Taiwan	0.3714
Thailand	0.5886	Japan	0.3483	Thailand	0.5743	Italy	0.2955
United Kingdom	0.8846	Austria	0.1032	United Kingdom	0.9078	Mexico	-0.4869

gle markets would be to buy Austria or Japan. Their coefficients indicate that they seldom move in tandem with the United States.

One reason that a zero correlation can't be achieved is that there are certain events so important on a worldwide scale that every market responds to them to one degree or another. That's particularly evident if you look at October 1987. The U.S. market crash was literally a crash heard around the world, and nearly every other market was affected by it. Notice, too, the big jump in most markets in early 1992. That was the beginning of the Persian Gulf War, another shot heard—or at least felt—by markets around the world.

Some analysts are beginning to suggest that achieving diversification through international investing will become more difficult in coming years. The occurrence of "global events" like the Persian Gulf War will certainly continue and possibly increase in number. What's more, global trade is inexorably linking nations closer to one another. Europe's move in recent years toward more unity in the Common Market, for example, is likely to tie together those economies so closely that a significant event in one country will have more of a spillover effect on neighboring nations.

Certainly such ideas are worth thinking about. But concerns that the value of international diversification will erode anytime soon are premature. We're convinced that for long-term investors, a diversified international portfolio will liberate you from any one country's economic and market ups and downs and, in the end, achieve a superior return with less risk.

SAFETY IN DIVERSITY

Several studies over the years have demonstrated pretty conclusively that not being tethered to a single market cycle has a very salutary effect on the performance of a portfolio. Here we're duplicating two charts that money managers often use to show clients the value of diversification. Basically the charts show risk versus reward, risk being the tendency of returns to vary over time and reward being the amount of those returns. The horizontal axis of the charts is the standard deviation, a statistical measure of volatility or risk. The further left you move on the scale, the less risk is involved. The vertical axis measures annualized percentage returns in U.S. dollars. The higher you go, the better your return.

Look first at the chart that graphs risks and rewards during the period from 1981 until 1987. At the lower right hand corner is a stock portfolio composed entirely of big U.S. stocks. On this chart that's the worst of all worlds: high risk and low returns. Now follow the line to the left and up a bit. We're moving into more attractive territory now.

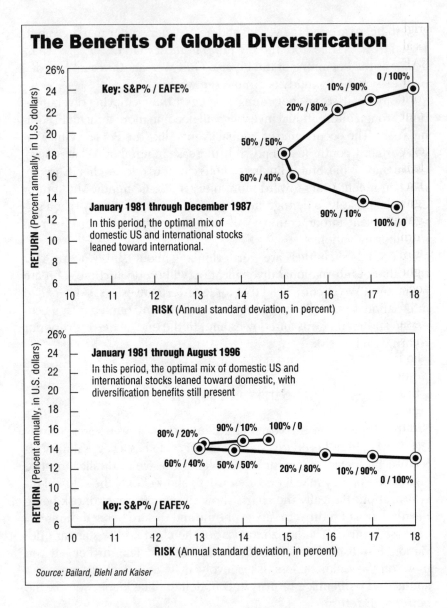

The Benefits of Global Diversification

Source: Bailard, Biehl and Kaiser

Returns are somewhat higher, risks are a little lower. All we have done to get to that point is divert 10% of that U.S. stock portfolio to foreign stocks, specifically Morgan Stanley's Europe, Austral-Asia, Far East Index (EAFE), an unmanaged index of 1,000 foreign stocks.

Keep moving left on the line and the world becomes a much

brighter place. Risks are still falling and, voila! Returns are rising. And it's all being accomplished simply by diverting more of our portfolio to EAFE and less to the U.S. stocks.

Finally, at the left edge of the chart we hit the best of all possible worlds: the risk/reward ratio is at its optimum. We've reached this point with a 50-50 mix of U.S. and foreign stocks.

Notice now that the return line is continuing to rise as we add bigger and bigger chunks of foreign stocks to our portfolio. But the trouble is, as it rises it begins to move to the right. The significance of that turn to the right is that we can boost our returns by adding more foreign stocks, but only by increasing our risks. The line ends in the upper right hand corner, with a portfolio that contains only foreign stocks. During the 1980s, investors who held foreign stocks had much better returns than almost anyone else. And their risk level was actually no higher than investors with portfolios that contained only domestic stocks.

But that was the 1980s. Look now at the second chart that plots the same risk-reward scenario based on what has happened since 1988. The situation has almost completely reversed itself. The foreign portfolio has produced the lowest returns with the highest risks. The domestic portfolio has, on the other hand, produced the highest rewards with substantially less risk. What gives? Basically, the 1990s to date have been a period of massive changes worldwide. Foreign stocks have been hurt by two events that have crippled Germany and Japan, the two massive engines of foreign economic growth. Certainly no one mourns the end of the Cold War, but the reunification of Germany has been enormously costly to that country. And Japan's high-flying real estate and financial sectors finally ran out of fuel and the wreckage is still being sorted out. Meanwhile, here at home, companies have been through a binge of "restructuring" aimed at becoming more efficient and productive and they've accomplished those goals. Earnings have exploded over the past several years and the U.S. stock market, reflecting that explosion, has soared. The world has been turned topsy turvy.

So, you say, isn't this a powerful argument *against* investing abroad? Why not stick with the winner for the long haul?

Sorry, it isn't that easy. Here's where smart investing takes guts. Remember the single most important lesson of investing: buy low and sell high. Here we'll use an analogy from the world of automobiles, with which most of us are familiar. Today you have to decide between buying one of two automobiles. The first is a foreign model. It's very stylish, goes fast, handles well and gets great gas mileage. The other is a domestic model. It's a little stodgy, doesn't go as fast, and isn't as efficient. If the two were priced the same, it wouldn't be much of a choice, would it? But get this: the foreign model is priced several thousand dollars *less* than the domestic car. Talk about a no-brainer!

That's exactly the situation facing an investor today. Over the long haul—we're talking the very long haul—foreign stocks have tended to outperform U.S. stocks. That's the go-fast part of our car analogy. And with the amazing runup in U.S. stock prices so far this decade, we think the domestic market is pretty expensive. Especially compared to foreign stocks. That's the price part of our analogy. Germany is going to come through its reunification just fine and Japan is fixing its financial mess. Don't underestimate the ability of either country to come back very strong over the next decade. And meanwhile there are dozens of other younger, smaller, but rapidly growing economies and stock markets out there.

We'll go into much more detail in the fourth section of this book about what all this means for an investment strategy and the structure of a portfolio. Right now it's just important to remember that we're talking about two of the most critical concepts in investing: diversification and time. Without one or the other, you're putting yourself at needless risk. With both at your disposal, you're doing what every smart investor should be doing: getting maximum returns with the lowest possible risk.

THE TIME IS RIGHT

John Templeton, one of the most respected pioneers of global investing, had a wonderful answer to the age-old question "When should I invest?"

His stock answer (you should pardon the pun): "The best time to invest is when you have the money."

Assuming you have the money, there are powerful arguments that now is as good a time as there has ever been to undertake a global investment program. There are forces at work that, taken together, will almost certainly result in an increasingly more attractive environment for cross-border investing in coming years. And the sooner you put your

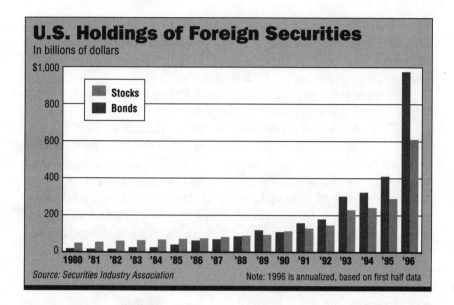

U.S. Holdings of Foreign Securities
In billions of dollars

Legend: Stocks, Bonds

Source: Securities Industry Association   Note: 1996 is annualized, based on first half data

money to work in that environment, the more likely you will be to enjoy the fruits of international investing.

An important element of the changing environment is the swift collapse of many centrally directed economies. The most notable example, of course, is the Soviet Union. Out of the chaos that currently blurs the economic picture in the old Soviet Republics will emerge some kind of market economies. It might not be next year or even by the end of the century. And we're quick to caution investors that they probably don't want to be the trailblazers in such uncharted territory. But eventually functioning markets will exist in places like Russia. And once they have been tested and found workable, they'll be important, albeit perhaps small, components of global portfolios in the 21st century.

Other governments, especially in many of the emerging nations, are coming to the conclusion that functioning capital markets are a critical element to the success of development programs. The most interesting case to watch is that of Hong Kong as it is reintegrated back into China. Will the Chinese, already embarked on an ambitious, though flawed, approach to a market economy allow Hong Kong to continue as the freewheeling money center that it became under British colonial rule? Or will the Chinese government, which still demonstrates fairly frequently that it is at heart a ruthless Communist dictatorship, give in to its urge to bring Hong Kong to heel? The answer, which should be obvious by the end of this decade, will tell us a lot about China's long-term chances of joining the rest of the world as a full and equal partner in the 21st century.

There are demographic trends at work that also bode well for the future of international investing, the most important of which is education. The developed countries have made education a high priority for most of this century. But it has been only in the last few decades that many of the developing nations have undertaken to educate the majority of their citizens. The progress has been astounding. A World Bank report recently showed that in Turkey, for example, adult literacy has soared to 81%, compared to just 38% in 1960. India's literacy rate is 48%, compared to 28% in 1960. South Korea has achieved a phenomenal 95% literacy rate, the equivalent of most major industrialized nations.

Education is important because it results in economic change. An educated population can learn new techniques for farming and manufacturing, attracting or creating new industries, jobs, and income. By and large, entrepreneurialism is related to literacy levels, and an informed public is better able to select a government that will pursue policies aimed at the overall benefit of a nation rather than of only privileged classes. As literacy rates continue to rise throughout the developing world, we can expect to see more investment opportunities opening for those willing to venture beyond the U.S. borders.

Modern technology is contributing to the boom in international investing, too. Communications among the industrialized nations are virtually instantaneous. Powerful desktop computers can crunch vast quantities of data in a matter of seconds. It would have been nearly impossible just ten years ago for Dow Jones to construct its World Stock Index. Today it can provide investors with up-to-the-second readings of more than two dozen markets. It allows investors anywhere in the world to compare the movement of markets and industry groups not only in dollar terms but also in local currencies. While there still remains a risk in many emerging markets of having too little information on which to base investment decisions, the time is rapidly approaching when the risk in developed markets will be information overload.

Another factor favoring international investment is the steady breaking down of trade barriers. There is a sign posted in the foreign department here at *The Wall Street Journal*'s New York headquarters that says, "I Never Want to Hear the Word GATT Again." That plain-tive moan is the result of the more than seven-year negotiations that finally produced a new General Agreement on Tariffs and Trade in 1994. The drawn-out negotiations were marked by much petty squab-bling, deadlines set and missed, and lengthy debates over such arcane issues as vegetable oil subsidies. Yet for all that, world trade will ben-efit mightily from the result of that treaty. Tariffs are falling, protec-tionism has been reduced, and everyone will benefit, not least the international investor. As world trade flows increase, investors will be given new opportunities for investment.

You Can't Get There without Going There

At some point in your investing career you're going to run across an advisor, a friend, or a neighbor who will argue that you needn't sink money into all those risky stocks and markets overseas to get global ex-posure for your portfolio. Just buy companies like General Motors, Deere, Procter & Gamble, or Merck, they'll tell you. They all have big operations and sales outside the United States, so they benefit when foreign economies are booming; their stock prices rise, and you get all the benefits of foreign investing without any of the risks.

Sorry. It isn't that easy.

With very few exceptions, the stocks of domestic companies traded on domestic stock exchanges behave more like other domestic stocks than like foreign stocks. It is true that GM has large European opera-tions and that in a good year for European economies GM's European car sales go up and its profit from European operations jumps. Those European profits either help offset losses in the United States, if it's a bad year for car sales here, or push the company's total profits even higher if it's a good year for car sales here. But the stock, which is what we're really interested in, behaves like a U.S. stock, specifically a cycli-cal U.S. stock.

There's another variation on this theme, too, that you should be aware of, though it doesn't come up nearly as often. Some mutual fund operators claim that an investor using their funds can get into some not-yet-emerged markets. The most egregious recent example is a closed-end mutual fund that is trying to lure investors into getting in on the ground floor (actually, the basement) of what they hope will be major market opportunities in Cuba. While it uses the euphemistic name of the Herzfeld Caribbean Basin Fund, the fund's Nasdaq trading symbol—CUBA—tells the whole story. The trouble is, Cuba doesn't have a stock market or even a free market, and the Caribbean Basin Fund, which was grandly announced in 1994 as "the first fund to invest in Cuba" didn't, at the end of that year, have a cent invested in Cuba. Instead, the fund operator invests in U.S. companies that may, one day, have some tenuous link to Cuba. In 1994 the fund's biggest holding was Florida East Coast Industries, a railroad and land owner based in St. Augustine, Florida. The company claims that it is planning a rail-barge operation between Cuba and South Florida once that trade route opens. Another holding was Royal Caribbean Cruises, which, should Cuba be opened up to U.S. tourism, might make a port call or two there. That, to us, is a far cry from investing in Cuba, but plenty of investors bought the curious logic. The fund soared to $8 a share on its first day of trading from an initial offering price of $5.20.

Oh well.

GLOBAL BONDS? WE'LL PASS

We have extensively discussed the merits of international stock investing. The alert reader by this time may well be saying, "But what about bonds?"

Well, what about them? We have a long-standing view that bonds are bought for security, for the assured payment of a known amount of money at regular intervals. That may be an old-fashioned view, and certainly Wall Street's bond moguls—the cocky characters who called themselves "Masters of the Universe" in Tom Wolfe's wonderful Wall Street satire *Bonfire of the Vanities*—will ridicule us for taking it. But we don't much care what Wall Street salespeople think. If you want to bet on something, we figure you should bet on stocks, where each company has a different management, product line, financial profile, and so on. When you buy bonds for any reason other than to hold them until maturity, you are doing nothing but placing a bet on interest rates. And predicting interest rates is about as close to shooting craps as we know.

We're talking about U.S. Treasury bonds here, the absolute safest investment in the world. We certainly don't recommend that anyone gamble with corporate bonds, where you face not only the unknown risk of interest-rate action but also the risk of corporate misfeasance, malfeasance, or just plain screwups that result in defaults or debt downgrades. So you can imagine how we feel about foreign bonds, government or otherwise. Any government bond that you buy—British, German, Japanese—has at least some measure of additional credit risk beyond a U.S. government bond. Add to that the currency risk, and it simply doesn't make any sense to buy a foreign bond. Unless, of course, you still want to bet on interest-rate moves. If it's well-nigh impossible to predict interest rates at home, we don't think you have a chance of doing it consistently well abroad. We deal with this subject in a little more detail later in the book, but don't bother turning to that chapter if you're looking for help on how to build a foreign bond portfolio. You aren't going to get any encouragement or help from us.

SUMMARY

There. Now you have our case for investing abroad. We don't know where the next hot market is going to be that will make you rich overnight. About all we can do in that regard is advise you not to waste your time and money trying to find it. If you insist, then put everything you've got in whatever market has fallen the furthest in the past 12 months. You should have the courage of your convictions to buy low and sell high.

Okay, so you're not that courageous. Or foolish. You will want to read the rest of this book. You already know that diversification of a stock portfolio is a good thing. All we want you to recognize is that diversifying your portfolio outside the United States is a better thing. Historically, portfolios with some component of foreign stocks—up to 50%—have enjoyed extra rewards with less risks. Given the long-term forces at work in the world, it seems to us that foreign investing will only become more rewarding over the years.

What are you waiting for?

CHAPTER II

The Risks

WHEN we began doing the research for this book, Mexico was the darling of the international investing set. Through the late 1980s and early 1990s, the government had engineered an economy with low inflation and low debt, and it had successfully privatized many state-owned industries. As 1994 approached, the economy was beginning to show signs of recovering from a slowdown, corporate earnings were improving, and the overall outlook was bright. In short, Mexico was—and had been for several years—the classic emerging-market "story."

In 1993 the Mexican stock market climbed nearly 50%. An investor could buy big, blue-chip stocks such as Telefonos de Mexico, the telecommunications concern that had long been a favorite of international investors. The more adventuresome could pick and choose among a host of smaller stocks of fast-growing companies. Americans flocked to buy shares of mutual funds with holdings in Mexico, prompting a spurt in the number of such funds and the assets they had invested south of the border. In 1992 there were only two Latin American mutual funds available in the United States, and they had total assets of $250 million. By 1994 there were at least a dozen Latin American funds with more than $4 billion invested. Telmex was so popular that an estimated 400 U.S. mutual funds had a dollop or two in their portfolios. Even mundane money market funds in the United States had taken a big stake in Mexico by investing heavily in the country's high-yielding short-term government bonds.

Then came the Chiapas revolt in January 1994. Peasants in the region, suffering under the government's tight monetary policies, rebelled, bringing to the attention of foreign investors for the first time the failure of the government to address pressing social issues. The Chiapas revolt, which continued to simmer, was followed a few months later by the assassination of presidential candidate Luis Donaldo Colosio Murrieta, handpicked to succeed Carlos Salinas de Gortari. His violent death immediately raised questions about the safety of investments in Mexico. American money managers, panic-stricken, flooded the Ministry of Finance with telephone calls demanding to know what was happening. The Dow Jones Mexico Index fell 2% the day after the assassination and another 3% in the four days following. Yet as tragic as Mr. Colosio's death was, Mexico's investment story survived it. Ernesto Zedillo Ponce de León was chosen to succeed Mr. Colosio as the presidential candidate of the long-ruling Institutional Revolutionary Party, known as PRI, and he won an impressive victory on promises to create jobs and attend more closely to the social needs of poor Mexicans.

During all of this, though, few investors had taken heed of yet another danger signal. Through most of 1994, Mexico had been running a staggeringly high trade deficit, at least partly the result of its policy of trying to peg the peso to the dollar—a policy that in turn made Mexico so attractive to foreign investment. But the new administration, which took office early in December, realized that the peso's stability and the resulting trade deficit threatened any government effort to stimulate growth, because Mexico needed to finance its imports with dollars attracted by high interest rates. Besides, maintaining the peso's link to the dollar was enormously costly, as more and more Mexican and foreign investors tried to avoid the currency. With no warning, the Mexican government on December 20, 1994, devalued the peso by 12.7%. The reaction at home and abroad was swift and bloody. Interest rates soared, the Mexican stock market plunged. When it became evident that the government would not be able to defend the peso even at its new, lower level, the Mexican government cut the currency loose and it tumbled even further. The combination of falling share prices and the crashing peso left U.S. investors with a 41.5% loss on their Mexican holdings for 1994, coming close to wiping out the nearly 50% gains of the previous year.

Mexico's trials in 1994 capture neatly many of the risks that confront any international investor:

• **Political risk:** The Chiapas rebellion and the assassination of Mr. Colosio both threatened to sour the investment climate in Mexico. Many investors envision political risk associated with assassinations and coups, but the reality is that it seldom takes anything so dramatic to upset international investors.

• **Currency risk:** The peso's sharp devaluation at the end of 1994 brought home as nothing has in years the fact that currency matters when you're investing outside the United States. Despite the various crises that swept the country in 1994, the Mexican Bolsa fell only 8.6% in 1994 in peso terms. But American investors converting their Mexican portfolios into dollars would have lost 42%.

• **Market risk:** We all live with this one, even here in the United States. It is simply the chance that something as ephemeral as investor sentiment—or as concrete as purposefully raising interest rates—will upset an otherwise healthy stock market. At the extreme, you get the stock market crash of 1987; in less spectacular cases, you get a bear market.

• **Information risk:** This is the lack of information that makes international investing somewhat more risky than investing at home. It's simply harder to find out what is going on in another country, whether in politics, economics, markets, or individual companies.

The only real risk that isn't illustrated by Mexico's problems in 1994 is the seemingly mundane one known as custody risk, or the question of how efficiently a market executes trades and keeps track of who owns what. It, too, is a very real risk, albeit one mostly associated with the more primitive emerging markets.

We aren't going to soft-pedal the risks of investing abroad, especially in emerging markets like Mexico. If you are accustomed to investing in the United States, get ready for a big change. You're leaving the world's safest haven for a walk on the wild side. Yet as we examine more carefully the nature of the various risks that worry potential international investors, we think you will see why you should still want to invest abroad. We think you also will see why we keep harping on the two essential ingredients of investing, especially international investing: time and diversification.

POLITICAL RISK

Assassinations and coups are the most extreme and violent example of what most analysts call political risk. Politics is the exercise of power, and the global investor is vitally interested in how a government exercises the power vested in it, as well as in how it transfers that power from time to time. Living as we do in a nation that has a long history of vigorous but orderly debate and transfer of power, we tend to view assassination as one of the most abhorrent and cowardly means of challenging power, a risk mostly found in emerging markets. Yet many of us can still remember exactly where we were and what we were doing when we first heard that John Kennedy had been shot and killed in Dallas on November 22, 1963. We've seen the television footage of his brother Robert, a candidate for the presidency, gunned down in the midst of his campaign. We remember the grimace on President Ronald Reagan's face when he was struck by a bullet fired by a would-be assassin outside a Washington, D.C., hotel. In 1994 alone, several shots were fired at the White House and a small airplane was intentionally crashed into the official residence.

Despite that violent record of death and attempted murder—a much worse modern-day record than those of other major industrialized nations such as Japan, Great Britain, Germany, and France—the United States is still regarded as the most politically safe country in the world. Transfers of power have been orderly. The closest we have ever come to the threat of a coup was a little wild speculation among some pundits about what Richard Nixon might do to avoid losing his presidency in the face of Watergate. The fact is that in times of international turmoil, the U.S. dollar rises more often than not as investors abroad seek a safe haven for their money. U.S. Treasury bonds are esteemed as the world's safest investment. And the U.S. stock market is far and away the world's best regulated, most efficient, and most transparent—that is, you can see prices move tick-by-tick, and there is easy access to an abundance of market data—stock market. In short, despite the horrific impact of an assassination on a nation's reputation and psyche, there are other, far more important factors that go into assessing the political risk of investing in any country.

To put political risk in its proper context for the international investor, we suggest a change in terminology. Rather than be concerned about political risk, we think it is better to worry about economic risk. Often they are the same thing for no other reason than that governments are the single largest factor influencing any nation's economy. The government sets monetary policy, which influences the value of a nation's currency. It is the government that decides trade policy, which determines the industries that will grow and those that will fail. Taxes are levied by the government. Securities laws and regulations are mandated by government. While assassinations, coups, and declarations of war are the events we hear about because they grab the headlines, it is these other manifestations of government that ultimately matter more to international investors.

There are, of course, certain countries or pseudo-countries where the political situation is so unstable that an investor has no business risking money there. Many of the nations of Africa and the emerging nations that once comprised the Soviet Union are cases in point. Some haven't even devised a lasting system for determining who is in power, much less how power will be exercised and transferred. The economic risk that flows out of that political situation is extreme and should be avoided.

Once we eliminate these basket cases from our list of potential investment markets, we can make another quick decision about political risk: There are some countries that we simply don't have to worry about. What's the chance, for instance, that there will be political upsets in Great Britain, France, or Germany that pose serious threats to those nations' powerful economies? Nil, or at least the next thing to it. The governments may change, and one party may emphasize social programs or tax hikes that investors might not like. But those kinds of policy changes are merely fine tuning. Italy seems to have a new government every few months, yet it still remains on practically everybody's list as an inviting investment haven—provided, as always, you do your homework on specific investments. We have learned much more about how Japan's government works in recent years, including the pervasive presence of scandal and bribery in high places; as a result, many of us view Japan with considerably less awe and respect these days. Yet it, too, is highly unlikely to undergo any wrenching political change that will make it less desirable or important as an investment target. Even scanning what we call the "second tier" of foreign markets—Spain, Portugal, the Scandinavian nations, for instance—reveals little that should concern an investor about those markets. The message is that for most established democracies with modern economies, there really isn't much to worry about on the political front.

But now we come to the hard part, which is assessing political and economic risk in the emerging markets. As we pointed out at the beginning of this chapter, Mexico underwent a wrenching devaluation of its currency late in 1994. The devaluation was a government action, taken intentionally to respond to an economic crisis. It hurt American investors badly, especially those who had begun only recently to invest in emerging markets. They had enjoyed none of the big gains in previous years to offset the sudden loss of 30% or 40% of their portfolios' value.

A lot of smart people were caught by that sudden move, including many Latin American investment fund managers who thought they were especially well informed about Mexico. Could they have seen it coming? It's hard to say. With benefit of hindsight, plenty of analysts say it should have been obvious that Mexico's burgeoning trade deficit would lead to some kind of problem. Could the hit they took have been lessened somehow? Certainly. For whatever reasons, many fund managers had concluded that of all the Latin American countries, Mexico was the most stable. So, they put an inordinate amount of money into Mexican investments while cutting back on the amount they invested in other Latin American countries. That was a mistake. At the end of 1994, Morgan Stanley Capital International EMF Latin American Index, a widely used benchmark that weights Latin American markets according to their size and availability to U.S. investors, gained 0.64%, while most of the funds that had overweighted Mexico were down anywhere from 6.64% to 23.73%. That relative performance demonstrates very clearly the benefits of adequate diversification.

Still, the bottom-line truth is that investors in emerging markets are taking more political risks than they do at home or in the major markets of the industrialized world. There are all sorts of ideas about how to minimize that risk. Some investment advisers, inviting the "politically incorrect" label, suggest that dictatorships, to be blunt about it, make better emerging-market investment bets than do democracies. They argue that democracies in developing nations are inherently unstable and subject to voter whim, which prevent them from taking the tough measures required to launch an infant economy into the modern world. Singapore, Taiwan, and South Korea are often cited as shining examples of authoritarian control leading to economic growth and prosperity. This kind of thinking also explains why many investors would rather put money into China, the world's largest dictatorship, than in India, the world's largest democracy. The trouble is, those arguing this position forget to mention Cuba, an economic disaster by any measure, and the old Soviet Union, which collapsed under the weight of its economic mismanagement. They also forget to mention the economic successes of functioning democracies including Poland, Brazil, and even India.

We'll take a closer look at India later in the book, but it's worth considering what changes have occurred there to make it an appealing market. After decades of socialism, which followed India's independence in 1947, the country is moving inexorably toward free markets. Since the beginning of this decade, the Indian government has enacted several measures that will help drive India's economic growth at a rapid clip during the next several years. Tariff barriers have been slashed, restrictions on currency transactions are being lifted, privatization of some government holdings is underway, and the financial markets are being opened to foreign investment. If that all seems very attractive, it is. But given a scenario like this—and there are several others around the world that resemble it—the global investor has to ask, "What can go wrong, and how likely is it to happen?"

In India's case, there are several things that could go wrong. For example, there is considerable ethnic tension within India, marked by occasional riots and communal killing. That tension was brought home to international investors very clearly in 1993 when terrorists exploded a bomb in the Bombay stock market. It was reassuring that trading was resumed within hours, even as the rubble was still smoking. As upsetting as such events can be, though, few analysts looking at India today expect it to be torn by the widespread violence that resulted in the partitioning of India and Pakistan in the late 1940s.

It is also possible that the government could backtrack on many of the steps that it has taken to liberalize the economy and the markets. Onerous import duties, restrictions on exports, new currency regulations, and limitations on foreign participation in India's financial markets all could badly disrupt the economic progress the country has made to date.

But how likely are such steps? The better question is, why would such steps be taken? For ten years India has been embarked on a liberalization program that has gathered speed. Some of that speed was imparted after the collapse of the Soviet Union, one of India's major trading partners. Without that source of trade, the government quickly stepped up efforts to make India more attractive to other partners, including the United States. India now has a burgeoning middle class, and the benefits of the economic programs are becoming widely known and enjoyed. In the last elections, each party vied to outdo the others in its commitment to continued economic reform and growth. Thus, while it is possible that economy-stifling things could happen, it is unlikely that they will. Therefore, the potential political risk in India is far offset by the potential rewards.

A final point needs to be made about the nature of political risk as it relates to Mexico. The peso devaluation that the Mexican government engineered was a painful surprise to American investors. Yet in retrospect it was also a necessary step. Mexico could not have continued to pursue the economic policies it had been following. But the pain aside, the steps that were taken will ultimately contribute to a firmer economic foundation. There is no reason to think that Mexico won't continue to grow and that the 1994 debacle was anything more than a temporary setback. For the investors who saw their Mexican stocks beaten down in 1994, we would once again point to the example of Hong Kong, which has undergone two market crashes in 20 years. The long-term investor who had the nerve and discipline to ride through those shocking retreats is well off today. And the really smart investors who bought heavily into Hong Kong in the midst of all the gloom are even better off. If you were in Mexico in 1994, be patient, the story is far from over. If you weren't in Mexico in 1994, we hope you got in during 1995. The gains since then have been impressive.

On balance, recent history indicates to us that overall political risk is declining as democracies and free markets are growing. That general trend, coupled with intelligent investors' efforts to diversify their portfolios to limit exposure to any one country, convince us that political risks need not be a barrier to international investing.

CURRENCY GIVETH AND CURRENCY TAKETH AWAY

While most new global investors worry too much about the political or economic risks we just discussed, the overseas veterans probably over-fret about currency risk—the chance that a foreign investment will go sour not because of business fundamentals or collapsing stock markets but because the currency in which that investment is held has fallen in value compared to the U.S. dollar.

We don't want to sound like Pollyannas, but why all the worry? First, there is little that an individual investor can do about currency risk. It's much too expensive for an individual to do what some professionals do: hedge against adverse currency moves in derivatives markets. Further, it is about as likely over the long haul that currency translations will help you as hurt you. This kind of "help" happens when the U.S. dollar weakens against other currencies.

Let's run through a quick refresher course on how currency values affect investments. Foreign stocks or bonds are usually purchased in the currency of the country where they are listed. (Some people think American depositary receipts, which we will explain later, allow a U.S. investor to buy foreign stocks in dollars without any currency risk, but it simply isn't so.) The mechanics of investing overseas requires that you exchange your dollars for zlotys or marks or rials, and only then can you buy that foreign stock. And when you sell the foreign stock weeks, months, or years later (we vote for years), you have to exchange the foreign currency you are paid for your stock and turn it back into dollars. If, during the period you held that foreign stock, the currency of that country has weakened against the dollar, you will get back fewer dollars for each unit of the foreign currency. In some cases, the currency translation could wipe out tidy gains on the stock. In the absolute worst case, a loss on the stock could be made even worse by a loss on the currency, too. But don't forget the positive side. The sharp decline of a foreign-stock investment could be minimized or even neutralized by a currency that gained against the dollar—the proceeds would be exchanged into more dollars than previously. In the absolute best case, you could have a big gain in the stock as well as a big gain from the currency—a win-win situation of impressive proportions.

Here's an example of how it works: You have $100,000 to invest in a German stock selling for 40 marks a share. On the day you make your investment, the dollar is valued at 1.8000 marks. First, you convert your dollars to marks and wind up with 180,000 marks (1.8000 times $100,000). With that you buy 4,500 shares of the German company. Fortunately, you made a great pick and the stock rises in two years to 60 marks, an impressive 50% gain. You sell and receive 270,000 marks. Now comes the moment of truth. You must convert your marks back to dollars, and everything hinges on how the German currency has fared against the dollar.

Let's take the worst case first. During the two years that you watched your German stock price climbing, the mark has been falling. On the day you sell your stock and convert to dollars, the mark is quoted at 2.800 marks to the dollar. In other words, you get 1 dollar for every 2.8 marks you hold. The clerk at the bank tallies it all up and hands you a check for $96,428.57. Ouch! Your $100,000 bought a stock that did very well, yet you lost nearly $4,000 on the deal.

Now let's look on the bright side. The day of reckoning comes and you find that during the two years you held that German stock the mark has risen against the dollar and now is quoted at 1.4 marks to the dollar. In other words, you get 1 dollar for every 1.4 marks you hold. The friendly bank clerk totes it up this time and hands you a check for $192,857.14, a $42,857.14 gain on currency values alone. You're a genius!

So, all you have to do now is go out and find good investments in countries whose currencies will appreciate sharply against the dollar for the next ten years. Sorry, but that's a wild-goose chase that will end in disaster. Not that plenty of people don't try. Wall Street, London, Frankfurt, Tokyo, and other financial capitals are full of highly paid, sharp-witted currency traders trying to figure out which way currencies are going to go in the next few minutes, maybe hours at the outside. The best of them make a few more right decisions than wrong decisions and keep their jobs until the relentless pressure overwhelms them and they quit. Most make more mistakes than good bets and lose their jobs before they have had time to burn out.

Now let's look briefly at how some professional money managers deal with currency risk. It's called hedging. They basically use the futures markets to lock in a certain exchange rate at some point in the future. They know, without a doubt, what their mark or yen holdings will be worth in dollars at that future date. It doesn't matter whether these currencies rise or fall against the dollar in the intervening period. The trouble is, this kind of protection costs money, which happens to be what you're trying to make.

Suppose we have two portfolio managers, one a cautious, worry-wart type who hedges all his foreign exchange risk, and the other a little more prone to take a risk, especially over the long run. If they bought the same portfolio of foreign stocks on the same day and currencies remained at the same values for the period of the investment, the hedged manager's returns in the end would be lower than the unhedged manager. If the foreign currencies, on balance, rose against the dollar, the unhedged portfolio would show a far greater return. Only if the currencies, on average, fell against the dollar would the hedged manager produce the superior return.

But if you are investing abroad on your own, none of this matters. The costs of hedging for individual portfolios are so high that it would make no sense. If you're that afraid of currency risk, you have three choices: Stay home; buy only mutual funds that hedge their currency exposures, or buy stocks only in countries whose currencies are directly linked to the dollar. (One of these is Hong Kong, up 115% in 1993 and down 62% in 1994. Need we say more about how foolish all this worrying is?)

THE MARKETS ALSO GIVETH AND TAKETH AWAY

You can't escape market risk by staying home. The U.S. stock market is subject to unexplained ups and downs just like any other market. In fact, one of the main reasons you should invest abroad is to minimize the risk of a retreat in the U.S. stock market. Granted, some of your foreign investments may be caught in a sudden downdraft or endure the agonizing pain of a sustained bear market. But if you are sufficiently diversified, you can enjoy returns from other markets that are rising.

Diversification assumes you already have money at work in various markets. But how about those times when you're just getting started or when you want to reinvest profits you have made somewhere else? As simplistic as it seems, our only advice with regard to market risk is that old saw, "buy low, sell high." If you are sitting on a pile of investable money and are scanning the world's markets for a place to put it, chances are you will be tempted to sink most of it into the hottest market in the past quarter or the past year. After all, you're hearing nothing but good things: The government is encouraging foreign investment, inflation is low, economic growth is strong, the locals are standing in line at brokerage offices to place their orders.

It's too late.

When all you hear is good news, the next new thing you're likely to hear is bad news: Inflation is rising, the government is worried about too much speculation and is clamping down on local investments, taxes are rising. You name it. Something will send your hot little market directly into the tank, and you would be along for the ride.

Instead, why don't you scan *The Wall Street Journal* for a little disaster news? Make a list of the ten worst-performing markets around the world and put 10% of your money into each one of those. Then go play golf, get better at your job, take a vacation, anything that will divert your mind from your foreign investments for a few years. After that, take another look at them. Sell the four markets that have risen the most. Make another list of the ten worst-performing markets. Put your winnings to work in those, and then go away again. You get the picture. Buy the losers, stick with them, take some profits, and reinvest in some more losers. That's one way to minimize market risk. Admittedly, it takes guts, but you'll be doing what the smart investors do. More important, you aren't doing what the chumps are doing.

We often recommend to novice investors that they use an investment technique called dollar cost averaging. It's very simple: You commit a predetermined amount of money to an investment class (stocks are one investment class, bonds are another) at periodic intervals, say $500 a month or $200 a week. Over time, that steady inflow of money will buy some shares when the stock price is low and some when it's high. But overall, it will buy more shares at low prices than it buys at high prices. The net result is a portfolio with a lower average cost than might be obtained by committing a large amount of money at precisely the wrong time. You can do the same thing with an international portfolio, whether you buy foreign stocks directly, through American depositary receipts, or via mutual and closed-end funds.

The point is, of course, that you can't and shouldn't try to avoid market risk. Without risk, there would be no rewards. Again, diversification is the key. The more markets you are in, the less likely you will suffer big losses when one or two take a dive.

WHAT'S GOING ON?

Information risk, more than any other of the risks we have dealt with so far, is going to be a limiting factor in setting up your foreign investment plan. It is simply more difficult to find out what's going on in a foreign country, whether it's information about the government, the economy, or a specific stock. We think far too many investors make ill-advised decisions based on something other than information, even in their domestic portfolios. They'll sometimes invest thousands in a stock on the basis of a dinner conversation with a friend, a tip from a cousin, or a rumor in a newspaper column. A good investor is extremely un-comfortable not knowing everything he or she can about an investment. Information risk is what ultimately convinces thousands of investors that they're better off letting a mutual fund or professional money manager handle their investments. But it's also important to recognize that if you have special knowledge about a country or a foreign company, you have a significant advantage over most other investors, professional or otherwise.

If you aren't a voracious reader, the chances are good that you won't be a well-informed global investor. The broadcast media become interested in foreign coverage only when a war or scandal is breaking. To stay up to date on what's happening abroad will require daily reading of newspapers, not just *The Wall Street Journal* but also one of the big-league city newspapers nearest you: the *New York Times*, the *Chicago Tribune*, the *Los Angeles Times*, the *Washington Post*, or the *Boston Globe*. Throw in the *Financial Times* of London if you have the time and money. Magazines can be helpful, too. Even then, you'll be hitting only the high points, gleaning information about national politics, the overall economy, and some of the biggest companies in any of the industrialized nations. There is much less available about the second-tier and emerging markets.

But don't despair about all this. Even money managers with access to the best Wall Street research are in a constant struggle to find out more about what's happening abroad. One reason is that no other government requires as much disclosure from its publicly traded companies as does the United States. U.S. financial reporting requirements set a standard that analysts become accustomed to but cannot duplicate abroad.

Consider, too, that the quality of Wall Street research isn't always top-notch. As with other risks we have discussed, that's especially true in emerging markets. The boom in emerging-markets investing that swept the United States in the early 1990s caught many Wall Street firms unprepared. Their best analysts were involved in domestic research. What overseas expertise they had was in the rest of the industrial world, principally Europe and Japan. It was the second-rate and third-rate analysts who generally were assigned to watch over emerging markets. When the American appetite for emerging-markets stocks suddenly blossomed in 1993 and early 1994, Wall Street firms went on a mad scramble to hire analysts. All it took to command a low six-figure salary at some firms was fluency in a foreign language and the ability to read a balance sheet. Is it any wonder that most of Wall Street was solidly sandbagged by Mexico's sudden devaluation?

Having said all that, let's look on the bright side. A lack of information can create opportunities. If one investor knows something another doesn't, the person in the know can make money by trading on that information. With U.S. disclosure laws and the intense research scrutiny focused on most big U.S. companies, it's hard for one person to get an edge against competing analysts. But it isn't that difficult for a diligent analyst working abroad to uncover tidbits that competitors don't know about. For money managers, this kind of information can mean the difference between mediocre gains, or even losses, and big gains.

If your job or hobby takes you abroad, or if you are in a midlevel or higher job in an industry in which you have foreign competitors, there's a good chance you know as much if not more about certain foreign economies and companies than do most professional investors. Use that knowledge to make informed decisions about when and what foreign stocks to buy. If you are in the computer business, for example, you may have a good feel for which developing country is going to be the next winner as the industry searches out cheap and productive sources for hardware. Electronics production can give an economy a tremendous boost, and a variety of stocks are likely to benefit. Be careful, though. Knowledge that a foreign company is going to win a new contract from your company could be construed as inside information that would preclude you from buying the foreign company's shares if they are traded in the United States. Buying them abroad, however, is another matter. Insider trading laws are much stricter in the United States than in many other countries, where insider deals are common.

WHERE ARE MY SHARES?

Custody is probably a risk that you never thought about. You buy shares in the United States by calling your broker and placing an order. She calls you back and confirms that the trade was executed. If you want them, you can have the physical share certificates, but it's easier for everyone concerned if you let your broker take care of watching over your holdings, which essentially become electronic entries. Selling is just as easy. You call your broker, she calls you back to tell you the trade was done, your shares disappear from her electronic ledger, and you receive a check. It couldn't be easier.

Until you venture abroad. In most industrialized countries you don't have to worry about where your shares are. But in emerging countries, figuring out who has them and how you can get them can be a real headache. India and Russia are often cited by global custody experts as the worst examples of lax procedures. Amazing though it seems in this age of electronics, India's stock transactions are mostly paper. Shares must be physically delivered from buyer to seller. Certificates must be signed along with a transfer deed. And unlike more modern markets, which trade huge blocks of shares for institutional investors, India's Bombay market for the most part deals in blocks of stock no larger than 100 shares. It isn't difficult to imagine, then, what has happened in India as foreign money has poured into its markets. At one point custodians handling stock transactions were so overwhelmed by paper that they imposed strict trading limits on customers and began rejecting new business. Some custodians in India try to get around the paperwork burden through an elaborate system of forward selling, in which they promise to deliver securities at a later date. It isn't unheard of for records of share ownership to lag transactions by more than a year.

We aren't aware of any major disputes in which U.S. investors were unable to obtain shares they had purchased or sell them again.

But in such places as India, custody is an accident waiting to happen. Will your mutual fund be the one to which it happens? Overall, we believe the risks are small and that reputable funds and money managers who deal with established custodians will take adequate measures to ensure that investors are made whole if the accident does happen. Still, for an American investor accustomed to certainty about who owns what shares, it's all a bit unnerving.

STILL SCARED?

We hope you're convinced at this point that while investing abroad does carry risks that aren't normally encountered here in the United States, those risks are worth taking. Political risks loom large in the imagination of many novice global investors, but we think they're likely to remain imaginary—except, of course, in politically unstable countries. Currency risk is real. There are ways to mitigate it, but only at a cost. In the end, we think the long-term investor is likely to find that the fluctuations in currency values become a wash. Markets fluctuate. That's exactly why you should invest abroad. And while information might be hard for you to come by, it isn't easy for anybody else to find, either. If the minuscule risk that you'll never receive the shares you bought is keeping you from getting started, then you probably aren't cut out to be an investor after all.

PART TWO

How to Invest Abroad

We hope you're convinced now that 10% or more of your long-term investment portfolio should be allocated to markets other than the United States. There are several routes to achieve that goal, and this part of the book summarizes these methods, as well as the pros and cons of using each.

Direct investing in other countries is a good choice only for those of you who enjoy stock picking, have a successful track record here at home, and are willing to put in the necessary time. Even then you'll probably not build your entire overseas portfolio this way; you may use direct investing in combination with mutual funds and closed-end funds.

Putting aside legalisms about what exactly American depositary receipts (ADRs) are—it's explained in Chapter 5—you can safely treat them as foreign stocks traded on U.S. exchanges. The remarkable growth in the number of ADRs listed in the United States in the past few years is tribute both to American investors' increasing sophistication about foreign investing and to the desire of foreign companies to tap into the world's largest, best-regulated capital market. The happy result is that the active stock picker can assemble an exciting portfolio of foreign stocks, all easily monitored and traded from the comfort of a favorite armchair.

Some investors need more hand-holding than others. It isn't because they're dumb or scared; it's usually because they have complicated financial needs that call for dedicated expertise. You'll seldom look to a money manager for international investing expertise alone; but when you are trying to find the kind of sophisticated financial advice you need (or are willing to pay for), don't neglect the international side of your investment equation.

The rush to mutual funds in the past few years is evidence to us of the growth of a substantial core of long-term investors, sophisticated enough to recognize the value of equity investments but smart enough to realize that they have neither the time nor perhaps the inclination to set up and run their own stock portfolios. Given the risks and difficulties of dealing with foreign investments, global and international mutual funds are all the more attractive, as we explain in Chapter 3. Yet careful investors need to do a little homework before rushing into these funds. Costs vary widely, performance even more so. Indexed funds can be a useful alternative to trying to find and follow the latest hot hands in the international fund business.

Chapter 4 explains a variation on the mutual fund theme, closed-end funds. Often the only way to make a targeted investment in some countries, closed-end funds are different enough from the open-end mutual funds with which so many of us are familiar that they deserve a chapter to themselves. You'll find that funds that sell at premiums to their underlying asset values aren't necessarily bad buys, and a fund that sells at a discount might not be any bargain.

CHAPTER III

Mutual Funds

FOR most of us, who are better at our everyday jobs than we are at investing, mutual funds are the happy hunting ground. They are easy to get into and out of, and they give us access to professional managers and well-diversified portfolios. For those of us who want to invest abroad, they can make the process much easier. We can choose from broadly diversified funds that sweep the entire world or from highly specific funds that give us entrée to a single country or a single global industry. Given the complexities of all the other methods of investing abroad, it will hardly come as a surprise that the vast majority of us will go no further in our foreign investment explorations than the toll-free number of a fund company.

There are two basic types of mutual funds (and many variations on those two basic themes). In this chapter we deal exclusively with open-end mutual funds. The other kind, closed-end funds, are the subject of the next chapter. Open-end funds sell and redeem their shares continuously. They stand ready to accept your money for investment on any given day. The money is pooled with that of other investors to purchase a portfolio of securities. An open-end fund will also buy back your shares on any given day, paying you the value of those shares either from cash on hand or cash raised by selling some of the securities the fund holds. The shares are bought and sold at what is called the net asset value, which is simply the fund's assets minus its liabilities divided by the daily fluctuating number of shares outstanding.

Mutual Funds Aren't Perfect

Mutual funds are about as close as we can get to the "leave-the-driving-to-us" concept of investing. But you should know something about the drivers. For all the convenience and expertise they provide, there are some things mutual funds can't do. First, they can't eliminate the risks of investing abroad. They might hedge their fund's currency exposure, which you as an individual investor can't afford to do. But they might hedge it when they shouldn't, which ends up whittling your return; in any event, hedging costs money even when it works, and that, too, cuts into performance. Certainly, funds can't control political or economic events.

Second, there is a better-than-average chance that any particular fund manager won't make very good decisions about which countries to invest in or which stocks to buy. By and large, mutual funds underperform standard market indexes. So don't stand in awe of mutual fund managers. They aren't any smarter than the rest of us. They just have more time and more resources with which to pursue the investment game. Put them on your own turf, as journalists, cops, lawyers, teachers, or whatever, and they'd be as lost as you might feel trying to build an international investment portfolio.

The sign on the bus says: "No Talking to Driver." That sign applies to mutual fund managers, too. There is hardly ever any personal contact between you and the person to whom you are entrusting your money. If you need periodic reassurance, or someone knowledgeable with whom to discuss investment ideas or options, mutual funds aren't the way to go. About the best you can expect is a short letter each quarter from the fund manager or the transcript of a brief interview between the manager and somebody from the fund company's public relations department who asks a few puffball questions.

Mutual fund managers buy and sell stocks and bonds with no regard to your wishes or your particular tax situation. Presumably, you invest in an international mutual fund to put money to work abroad. But funds intentionally don't invest some of that money because they must have on hand an amount of cash to meet the steady flow of redemptions that occur for various reasons. Some funds maintain unusually large cash positions, which means your money isn't working as hard for you as it could. Also, if investors panic en masse because of some political or economic event and rush to cash in their shares, a fund manager may be forced to sell when markets are down sharply, whether you want to be out or not. Or, the manager may sell in anticipation of redemptions. Indeed, in the Mexican meltdown late in 1994, some managers of Latin American funds were selling stocks to raise cash even though the individual investors who bought the funds weren't selling their fund shares. Panics aside, as an individual investor you can choose when and if to take a capital gain. As part of the pack in a mutual fund, you take your gains and losses when the fund manager chooses to serve them up.

There are some specific peculiarities about global, international, and regional mutual funds that you ought to know. First, they usually are more expensive than domestic funds. That's understandable, given the difficulties in foreign investing that we already have discussed. What that means is that a little less of the money that you give the fund will actually be invested, compared to the average domestic fund. Thus, it behooves you to do some homework before writing that check to a mutual fund company.

Another point to keep in mind is that with the tremendous growth in the foreign fund industry in the past few years, many managers and researchers are young and inexperienced. A few years ago the big Wall Street securities firms and mutual funds became so desperate for "expertise" in emerging markets that they were paying six-figure salaries for what amounted to recent college graduates whose main qualification was that they spoke a foreign language. Couple that with the well-known problem of scanty information about the markets and economies of some smaller countries, and you may not always be getting the kind of professional expertise you think you're paying to get.

Finally, some markets, especially the so-called emerging markets, are very small and relatively illiquid. To invest all the money that is being thrown at them by investors eager to get into those markets, mutual fund managers may wind up buying many stocks about which they know little and that, in the long run, will turn out to be dogs.

FUND FUNDAMENTALS

We noted earlier that there are many variations on the basic open-end mutual fund. Open-end funds can be either load or no-load. The difference is crucial because it illustrates an important lesson: In the mutual fund business you don't necessarily get what you pay for. To illustrate, suppose there is a popular new show in town, and there are two entrances to the theater. If you use Entrance A, the fee is $50 to see the show. If you use Entrance B, the fee is 50 cents. You wind up in the same theater, the view is the same, the seats are just as comfortable regardless of which entrance you use. That's the difference between a load fund and a no-load fund. In mutual fund parlance, a "load" is a sales charge. Usually assessed as a percentage of the money you are investing, it is nothing more than an entry fee. And what a fee! If the load is 5.5% (the maximum allowed by the Securities and Exchange Commission is 8%) and your investment returns 10% in the first year, you've spent a whopping 55% of your gain just to get in the door.

We're pretty adamant, when questioned about the difference between load and no-load funds for domestic investments, that load funds are anathema to good investing. We argue that you can almost always see the same show without paying a fee. Study after study has shown that, on balance, there is little difference in the performance of load and no-load funds before the sales charge is taken into account. After taking the load into account, the similar no-load fund almost always does better.

But when the subject turns to international funds, we bend this rule a little. The main problem is that Americans only recently became seriously interested in investing abroad. That interest has prompted the creation of dozens of new international and global mutual funds in the past few years. Many, whether load or no-load, have no real track record and thus are more speculative for the investor coming to international funds for the first time. Of those with a lengthy track record, quite a few are load funds.

Over time this situation is going to correct itself as more no-load funds build impressive track records. But as investors research specific funds, we think many will be disappointed at the number of no-load international funds available to them that have track records of ten years or even five years. The choice may well be to take a chance on no-load funds without lengthy track records or ante up a few percentage points of your initial purchase to buy into a fund with an impressive record of long-term results.

None of this is to say that no-load funds come for free. Far from it. While no-load funds don't charge a sales fee, they do pass along management fees and expenses to shareholders. And those costs can add up very quickly, ranging as high as 3.5% annually. Your job as an investor is to get the maximum diversification and return at the minimum cost. Thus, it's worthwhile to shop around for funds that are managed efficiently.

There are dozens of other factors that can go into the ultimate selection of a fund or funds most suitable to your needs. You will have to sort them out for yourself, since only you know about such things as how much switching among funds you want to do, or what your minimum initial investment will be. Just take a look at the investing section at any bookstore and you'll find plenty of help in deciding what services—besides the investment of your money—you need.

A Smorgasbord of Funds

The menu of funds available to an international investor these days is overwhelming. From the very broadest (global funds that roam the world, including the United States, for good investments) to the most narrow (funds specializing in small Japanese stocks, for instance), the selection of investment vehicles has never been greater.

There is a downside, though, to all that variety. At some point you have to stop window-shopping and make a purchase. Or several purchases. Let's take a quick look at the major categories of funds to help narrow some of the choices confronting you.

Broadest by far are the global funds. This is truly "one-stop shopping." At their best, global funds allow an investor, with one purchase, to achieve full international diversification. The global fund manager's mandate is to search everywhere for the best investments. The trouble is, the U.S. stock market is big, it is well researched, and it is very liquid. For some managers, the temptation is to find the United States a little too appealing and wind up with more money invested here at home than abroad. If you already own a portfolio of U.S. stocks or a mutual fund that invests mainly in the United States, adding a global fund isn't going to achieve the degree of diversification you want. One subcategory of global funds is global sector funds, which invest in certain industries—construction, telecommunications, or health care, for example—anywhere in the world. The concept is appealing and will probably become increasingly so as the globalization of the world's economies continues.

Then comes the international category. These are funds that are mandated to invest outside the United States. But the subcategories are so extensive that the term international has little meaning beyond "we won't invest in the United States." You can find funds that are free to look everywhere but the United States, funds that confine themselves to specific regions of the world, funds that target individual countries, and funds that are aimed at specific industries in specific countries. There are also different styles of international investing, including the old standbys, growth and value. Emerging markets had become a particularly popular international theme prior to Mexico's meltdown late in 1994. Index funds tied to measures of various foreign markets are becoming increasingly popular lately as more investors have realized the benefit of this low-cost method of investing. And there are different international funds that invest not only in stocks but also in foreign bonds or money market instruments. By and large, the narrower the focus of a fund, the better the chance it will be a closed-end fund, which carries somewhat different baggage than open-end funds. We will explain the peculiarities of closed-end funds in the next chapter.

Finally, you can buy U.S. mutual funds that have a little international flavor to them. These include some of the best-known and largest growth and value funds. The biggest of them all, Fidelity's Magellan Fund, has held as much as 9% of its assets overseas in the recent past. U.S. bond and money market funds also often have the leeway to own some foreign securities in an effort to boost their yield.

Diversified International Mutual Funds

Includes funds with investment objectives of International and International Small Company

Rank	Fund Name	3 Years* Annualized Total Return	When Started
1	GAM:International;A	28.09	12/24/84
2	Morg Stan In:Int Eq;A	22.52	08/03/89
3	Harbor:International	21.18	12/29/87
4	Ivy:Intl Fund;A	20.20	04/21/86
5	GMO:Intl Small Co;III	19.41	10/15/91
6	Amer Aadv:Intl Eqty;Inst	19.35	08/07/91
7	Hotchkis & Wiley:Intl	19.26	10/01/90
8	Warb Pincus Inst:Int Eq	19.09	09/01/92
9	Vanguard World:Intl Gro	18.77	09/30/81
10	Warb Pincus Intl Eq;Com	18.68	05/02/89
11	BT Inv:Intl Equity Fd	18.41	08/04/92
12	SS Research:Intl Eq;C	18.18	01/17/92
13	Warb Pincus Intl Eq;Adv	18.16	04/05/91
14	Putnam Intl Growth;A	18.02	02/28/91
15	AIM Intl:Equity;A	17.93	04/07/92
16	Managers:Intl Equity	17.91	12/31/85
17	Fidelity Dvsd Intl	17.68	12/27/91
18	Glenmede:International	17.50	11/22/88
19	Schroder Cap:Intl;Inv	17.48	12/20/85
20	United Intl Growth;A	17.27	06/09/70
21	GMO:Intl Core;III	17.14	03/31/87
22	Preferred:International	17.13	06/30/92
23	SIT International Growth	16.32	11/01/91
24	Fidelity Adv Ovseas;T	16.26	04/23/90
25	Govett:Intl Equity;A	16.24	01/07/92
26	Morg Stan In:Intl Sm;A	16.21	12/15/92
27	Strong Intl Stock	16.18	03/04/92
28	Acorn International	16.04	09/23/92
29	Kent Fds:Intl Gro;Inst	15.92	12/04/92
30	Instl Intl:Foreign Equ	15.86	09/07/89
31	USAA International	15.85	07/11/88
32	Prudential World:Int;Z	15.84	11/05/92
33	Glenmede:Instl Internatl	15.78	08/03/92
34	Seligman Hend Intl;A	15.75	04/02/92
35	CG Cap Mkts:Intl Equity	15.72	11/18/91
36	T Rowe Price Int:Stock	15.70	05/09/80
37	Europacific Growth	15.67	04/17/84
38	Fidelity Overseas	15.65	12/04/84
38	Princor World;A	15.65	12/17/82
40	Piper Glbl:Pac-Euro Gro	15.64	04/20/90
41	Kent Fds:Intl Gro;Inv	15.58	11/02/92
42	IAI International Fund	15.20	04/20/87
43	Templeton Fds:For;I	15.13	10/06/82
44	Babson-Stewart Ivory	15.07	12/14/87
45	Enterprise:Intl Gro;A	15.05	11/17/87

46	Twen Century Wrld:Intl	14.98	05/09/91
47	Delaware Pld:Intl Eqty	14.94	02/04/92
48	TIFI:Foreign Equity	14.92	10/18/90
49	Oakmark International	14.79	09/30/92
50	S Bernstein:Intl Value	14.72	06/26/92
51	Phoenix Intl;A	14.68	11/02/89
52	Vanguard/Trust Eq:Intl	14.62	05/16/83
53	Victory:Intl Growth;A	14.57	05/18/90
54	Mnsty Instl:EAFE;Inst**	14.53	12/31/90
55	DFA Grp:Lrg Cap Intl	14.42	07/18/91
56	Compass:Intl Eq;Inv A	14.37	04/27/92
57	Quant:Intl Eqty;Shs	14.32	07/31/87
58	Lazard:Intl Equity	14.14	10/01/91
59	Scudder International	14.11	12/31/59
60	Alliance Intl;A	14.05	06/25/81
61	One Group:Intl Eq;Fid**	14.05	10/29/92
62	Loomis Sayles:Intl Equ	13.96	05/10/91
63	New England Intl Eq;A	13.93	05/22/92
64	Vontobel Europacific	13.92	12/28/84
65	RSI TR:Internatl Equity	13.89	04/30/84
66	Fidelity Intl Gro & Inc	13.77	12/31/86
67	Kemper Intl Fund;A	13.73	05/21/81
68	Franklin Intl:Intl Equ	13.70	09/20/91
69	Flag Inv Intl;A	13.66	11/28/86
70	Corefund:Intl Growth;Y	13.57	02/13/90
70	Delaware Intl Eq;Inst	13.57	11/09/92
72	Pilot:Intl Eq;A	13.37	01/02/68
73	Delaware Intl Eq;A	13.27	10/31/91
74	Alliance Intl;B	13.11	09/17/90
75	Morg Stan In:Active;A	12.87	01/17/92
76	Excelsior:Intl	12.80	07/21/87
77	Wright Eq:Intl Blue Chip	12.74	09/14/89
78	Scottish Widows Intl;A	12.69	10/01/90
79	IDS International;A	12.67	11/15/84
80	Wm Blair:Intl Growth Fd	12.66	10/07/92
81	Sm Barney Wld:Intl;A	12.64	03/03/86
82	WPG International	12.56	06/01/89
83	Bartlett Cap:Value Intl	12.55	10/06/89
84	Galaxy:Intl Equity;Rtl A	12.51	12/30/91
85	Nations:Intl Equ;Prm A	12.28	12/02/91
86	Pierpont:Intl Equity	12.24	05/31/90
87	UAM:TS&W Intl Equity	12.18	12/17/92
88	Fedrtd Intl:Intl Eq;A	12.01	08/17/84
89	Nations:Intl Equ;Inv A	11.97	06/03/92
90	Aetna:Intl Growth;Sel	11.74	12/30/91
91	INVESCO Intl:Intl Growth	11.68	09/22/87
92	Munder:Intl Eqty;Y	11.46	12/02/91
93	Munder:Intl Eqty;A	11.28	11/20/92
93	Munder:Intl Eqty;K	11.28	11/20/92
95	Sierra:Intl Growth;A	11.06	07/18/90
96	Nations:Intl Equ;Inv C	11.05	06/17/92
97	Merrill Consults Intl	11.02	09/14/92

98	Calvert Wrld:Intl Eq;A	11.01	06/29/92
99	Columbia Intl Stock	11.00	10/01/92
100	SEI Intl:Intl Eqty;A	10.98	12/20/89
101	Keystone International	10.90	12/31/59
102	MAS Fds:Intl Eqty;Inst	10.85	11/25/88
103	Landmrk Intl Equity;A	10.72	02/28/91
104	BBK Intl:Intl Equity	10.66	11/01/79
105	Parkstone:Intl Dsc;Inst	10.57	12/30/92
106	Goldman Eq:Intl Eq;A	10.18	12/01/92
107	BEA Intl Equity	10.11	10/01/92
108	PIMCO Adv:Intl;A	9.82	02/04/91
109	T Rowe Price Int:Disc	9.80	12/30/88
110	Stand Ayer Wood:Intl Equ	9.52	12/08/88
111	PIMCO Adv:Intl;C	9.04	08/25/86
112	GT Global Intl Grow;A	8.74	07/18/85
113	Vista:Intl Equity;A	7.15	12/31/92
114	Waddell&Reed:Intl Gr;B	3.97	09/21/92
	Average	**14.34**	

* From 12/31/92 through 12/31/95
** Passively managed index fund; all others are actively managed
Source: Lipper Analytical Services

MAKING SOME BASIC CHOICES

So, where should you begin your shopping trip? Unless you're really bored with the whole investment process, we would advise you to shy away from global funds. We think you need to have a better feel about what you are doing with your money than you will get by buying one of these "do-it-all" funds. You live in the United States, you read newspapers, you see what's going on in the economy around you, and you probably have some ideas about how and where you want to take your financial risks. All that suggests that you pay careful attention to your domestic investments, allocating money among specific types of funds or to individual stocks and bonds, according to your changing needs and the changing economic environment. A global manager simply has too broad a mandate to be an effective manager of all your money. If you really are turned off by making your own choices, we suggest that an alternative to the global manager would be one broadly diversified U.S. fund and one broad-based international fund. Your costs will almost certainly be lower and your returns probably about as good.

What about those global sector funds that are becoming more popular? For some industries that truly are global, they make some sense.

It seems to us that those sector funds that invest in commodity or commodity-like companies—oil, precious metals, or paper companies, for instance—stand to profit most from worldwide demand for such products. The trouble with many of the others is that the world economy still isn't linked together tightly enough for these funds to work well over the long term. If it were, we wouldn't need to be investing abroad to achieve diversification since all markets would tend to move in tandem. We think, for instance, that telecommunications companies—and their stocks—will respond much more to local demands, created by economic conditions and government policies in individual countries, than they will to the overall demand globally for telecommunications services. Stand by, though, particularly those of you under the age of 30. The day is coming when global sector funds will be able to realize what is for the moment only a promise.

There. We hope we have eliminated most global funds from your shopping list. Now we are in the mystifying aisles of the international fund industry. Before you start picking stuff off the shelf and putting it in your shopping cart, remember that one reason many of us buy a mutual fund is to align our investment chips with professional investment expertise. That becomes the basis for our argument that you strongly consider a broad-based international fund as your first and perhaps only choice. As soon as you choose a fund with a narrower focus—for example, a regional fund that invests in Southeast Asia—you are replacing the professional's judgment about where in the world is best to invest with your own judgment that Southeast Asia is best. There isn't anything intrinsically wrong with substituting your judgment for the money manager's, as long as you have a good reason for it. For instance, you may have decided that the economic crisis in Mexico drove down the prices of Latin American stocks so dramatically that it simply has to be a screaming buy. Fine, buy a Latin American fund. But please, don't ever decide to buy a regional fund because that region's performance was best the previous year. That's a recipe for disaster. In the end, if you don't think you know more than the manager, leave the driving to him or her.

Bond and money market funds, whether domestic or international, aren't generally what many people think they are. That became painfully evident in 1994 when interest rates rose and knocked many bond funds into the ditch. Investors look to bond and money market funds for safety. But in many cases when they buy one of these funds, they actually are making a bet on the direction of interest rates. That's because bond funds don't buy bonds and simply hold them to maturity. Instead, to try gaining a performance advantage over their rivals, bond fund managers actively trade bonds. In a falling interest-rate environment, trading is fine because it frequently generates capital gains as well as interest payments, and investors are always happy with more gains than they expected. But when rates begin rising, the value of old bonds falls. Trading them generates losses, which often more than offset the income the bonds provide.

Bond funds showed their worst side in 1994, and the worst of them all were bond funds with big stakes in emerging markets. The trouble started when the Federal Reserve began unexpectedly to raise U.S. interest rates early in 1994. The higher U.S. rates were quickly reflected in foreign markets, especially emerging markets, which attracted many investors with their much higher yields. Because some of the investors playing in emerging-markets debt were investing with borrowed money to enhance their gains, the sudden rise in rates—and declines in prices—forced them to sell their positions. That selling exaggerated the decline in bond prices and prompted further selling as more conservative investors in mutual funds decided to bail out, forcing fund managers to sell their holdings to meet redemptions. The vicious circle continued through much of the year until Mexico's financial meltdown really clobbered the confidence of the few remaining investors.

We aren't sure why anyone would want to own a bond fund, anyway, unless they are willingly and with some knowledge betting on interest-rate moves. If you want to play that game, all we can do is wish you luck. But if you want secure income, why not just buy a bond and hold it to maturity, thereby avoiding the risk—and forgoing the possible rewards—inherent in interest-rate moves. Make it a U.S. bond and avoid the currency risk, too. If it's the higher returns commensurate with increased risk that you want, buy stocks and stock funds.

IN PRAISE OF INDEX FUNDS

We are particularly fond of index funds as a vehicle for investing internationally. They solve some problems very neatly. An index fund is basically a portfolio of stocks chosen to mimic a selected index. And indexes are nothing more than unmanaged collections of stocks that serve as barometers, measuring what's happening in given markets. The best known broad-market index is probably Standard & Poor's 500-stock index, a measure of the health of the U.S. stock market. (The Dow Jones Industrial Average is better known, but it is a 30-stock index specializing in one segment of the U.S. market, quality "blue-chip" stocks.) The indexes used in international investing aren't nearly so well known. The one cited most frequently is Morgan Stanley's Europe, Austral-Asia, Far East Index, an unmanaged index of over 1,000 stocks known by its acronym as the EAFE Index. (It's pronounced EE-feh.) Morgan Stanley also maintains other indexes, including the International World Index of 1,400 stocks, the International Pacific Index, the Latin American Index, the Southeast Asia Index, and the Emerging Markets Index. We expect that you will be reading more in the future about the Dow Jones Global Indexes, which as we write cover 29 countries, including the United States, and 120 industry groups.

The beauty of index funds is twofold. First, they minimize costs. Rather than pay a fund manager and a staff of researchers to pore over company reports and economic analyses, and to jet off to faraway places with expensive hotels, all the fund company has to do is construct a portfolio out of the stocks in a chosen index. The fund is passively managed, with changes being made only to fine-tune the fund's performance to match more closely the index's results. The alternative is an actively managed fund, which even sounds more expensive.

The other reason index funds are so desirable is that they eliminate your need to work so hard and worry so much. When you choose an index fund you can be fairly well assured that your performance will be as good—or as bad—as the overall performance of the market or markets you select. You'll seldom wind up owning the best-performing fund, but you'll never own the worst-performing fund, either. There is something particularly irksome about paying a fat management fee and then finding out the fund manager can't beat a simple index (and most can't).

As with every aspect of investing, there are some drawbacks to index funds. The main one is that indexes are usually made up of the stocks of large, well-known, and highly regarded companies. Index funds, as a consequence, will own very few, if any, of the small companies that will grow rapidly over coming years, presumably providing superior stock-price appreciation along the way. Another problem is that regional indexes tend to be made up of stocks from the various countries in the region in the same proportion as the market capitalization of these countries' stock markets. The problem shows up in cases where one country happens to dominate the regional index and goes into a prolonged slide. Japan, for example, has a market weighting of 85% of some Asian regional index funds, and any prolonged decline in Japan's market is reflected in those funds no matter what the other countries are doing. By contrast, an actively managed portfolio of "Pacific Rim" stocks presumably would be able to shift assets away from Japan when it became apparent that a decline in Japan would be drawn out.

THOSE WHO HEDGE MAY GET TRIMMED

Another fundamental decision you will need to make before you pick an international mutual fund is whether you want to hedge your currency risk. You can decide that for yourself and buy either a fund that always hedges or a fund that never hedges. Or, you can buy a fund that has the discretion to hedge but doesn't have to; in this case, you are ceding the hedging decision to the manager. Some experts recommend that if your investment horizon is five years or less, hedging is the better part of valor; for longer time horizons, go naked (unhedged, that is). And there's always the solution that one financial planner recommends: Concede defeat and buy one fully hedged fund, one unhedged one, and one that hedges occasionally. That way all the bases are covered. But be forewarned: If you want to hedge, your menu is going to be very limited. About 13% of all foreign-stock funds surveyed recently said they actively hedge currency exposure. Of the remainder, 57% say they occasionally hedge, and 30% say they never hedge. You have to hunt in each fund's prospectus to find its hedging policies.

The arguments against hedging are fairly powerful. First, for long-term investors, currency moves tend to cancel themselves out. Second, a diversified international portfolio may be exposed to 25 or more different currencies, some of which will fall against the dollar while others rise. Third, hedging costs money and eats into your ultimate returns. Fourth, currency moves are unpredictable. (We mean that nobody ever has managed to forecast currency moves accurately for very long or with great consistency.) Fifth, an adverse currency move may be beneficial in the long run: When a currency weakens against the dollar (hurting your conversion of foreign returns into dollars), the move often helps the country's own economy through cheaper exports, ultimately boosting corporate earnings and stock prices. Sixth and last, most U.S. investors already have immense exposure to the dollar through ownership of their houses, bank accounts, and domestic investment portfolios. Hedging turns foreign-currency exposure into still more dollar exposure.

The arguments in favor of hedging aren't so compelling. One is that hedging can reduce volatility so that you can sleep at night. The other favors your fund manager more than it does you: Hedging can help him or her meet common benchmarks against which fund managers are measured. There is no greater crime for a fund manager (or threat to his or her compensation) than to fall short of the benchmarks.

THE WINNER IS . . .

. . . the fund you like and can live with. We know we are copping out to some extent. But it's true. There is no single best fund for all investors. So how do you go about picking the right fund or funds? The process is somewhat similar to the way you pick the right domestic funds: Look for the best long-term performance in the category of choice at the lowest cost, make sure the same manager who built the track record is still running the fund, then read the prospectus to see if the fund's investment philosophy is the same as yours.

But there are some quirks about international funds that make the process easier in some cases, more difficult in others. Take performance, our first criterion. By long-term performance most people mean five- or even ten-year performance. Ha! Given that many Americans have only become interested in investing abroad in the past few years, there are precious few international funds that have existed for five or ten years. Reviewing mutual fund performance recently, we found that of the ten best-performing Latin American funds, none were in business five years earlier. Among the ten best Pacific Region funds, only five have been around five years. And of the top ten Diversified International funds, only two are five years old. So, the search becomes much narrower if you want to exclude recent stunning performances among funds that have been around only a few years. If you want to chase the one-year returns that some new fund produced, please realize that you may be getting into a flash-in-the-pan fund after the flash.

If you decide to invest in a regional fund, make sure that its holdings are well spread among the countries of the region. If you want to own Japan, buy Japan. If you aren't particularly enamored of Japan, then don't buy an Asian fund that has 75% to 85% of its investments in Japanese companies. Consider regional funds for only two reasons: The first and best is that you want to be an investor in that region for the long haul, at least five years. Ten years would be better. The second is that the region has been beaten down recently and offers good value. Never, ever, buy a regional fund because it produced stunning results last year.

Consider more than one fund. Mutual funds often have minimum investments, but if you have enough money to meet the minimums of two or more funds it would be a good idea to buy some further diversification through an additional fund or two. A logical choice might be a large-company fund, perhaps an index fund, balanced by a small-company growth fund. You might also want to offset the inherent volatility of an emerging-markets fund with something a little more staid, say a European index fund. There also is diversification within investment style. For example, balance a broad-based fund that takes a big-stakes value approach to countries with one that plays industry themes around the world.

Know thyself. Many people get sick on roller coasters; if you are one of them, stay off. If you are unlikely to sleep well if one of your international funds drops 10%, then look for funds with low volatility. Otherwise you will wind up bailing out at the bottom, locking in your losses, and you will have all that additional ground to make up in another fund before you start profiting. Even worse, you may decide to stay away from international investing altogether. That would be a big mistake.

DOING THE DIGGING

Finding information about mutual funds isn't the problem. There is way too much of it floating around out there. *The Wall Street Journal* isn't the only publication that carries extensive quarterly reports on mutual fund performance, although its daily summaries of the best- and worst-performing funds by investment objective are unique. Then there are the personal finance magazines, whose covers invariably scream some variant of "Five Best Funds to Own Now!!" We've often wondered how long it would take a very rich subscriber to these magazines to go completely bankrupt by switching each month to the new "best investments" from the previous month's "best investments." Many of the articles in those magazines are based on research done by outside firms such as Lipper or Morningstar. You can short-circuit the magazine editors by going to the same sources and doing your own research. After your initial choices, it's a simple matter to monitor performance through the statistical pages of *The Wall Street Journal*.

Morningstar provides a wide range of resources for the mutual fund investor, beginning with its comprehensive *Morningstar Mutual Funds,* which covers 1,240 mutual funds. There also is a monthly *Mutual Fund Performance Report* (which can also be received quarterly for a lower price), a *Mutual Fund Sourcebook,* and two more focused reports, *5-Star Investor* (which deals only with the best-rated funds) and *Morningstar Mutual Fund 500,* a look at 450 top-rated open-end funds and 50 closed-end funds. For more information, call Morningstar at 800-876-5005.

For Lipper information, write Lipper Analytical Services, 67 Maple Street, Summit, NJ 07901.

CHAPTER IV

Closed-End Funds

IF you're interested in taking a more targeted approach to global investing than riding along in a broad international mutual fund, closed-end funds offer many such opportunities. Signing up with a big, open-end international mutual fund is like taking a bus; you and everyone else on it are on the same trip, and none of you has any say about precisely where you go or how you get there. Closed-end funds are like renting a van; you and a much smaller group of investors select both a particular destination and the preferred route.

Closed-end funds are similar to mutual funds in that they are pools of money gathered to pursue an investment objective. But while mutual funds create or eliminate shares at will—as investors buy into or cash out of the funds—closed-end funds are born with a finite number of shares. That's what is "closed" about them: Once the original shares are sold, no more are available to new investors. (Don't confuse "closed-end" with "closed." A closed fund is actually an open-end mutual fund that has decided not to accept any more new shareholders, usually because it can't find enough places to invest their money within the limitations of the fund's charter.) Closed-end funds are launched much like a new issue of stock. After registering with the government, the fund or its investment bank sells the shares to investors, and the fund invests the money according to the rules set forth in its prospectus. And like a new stock, the closed-end fund's shares are listed on an exchange, or on Nasdaq, or left to a network of over-the-counter dealers, who make a market in them. That's how original investors get out after the initial offering and how subsequent investors get in: The sellers and buyers trade their shares in the stock market.

While this trading is going on, the amount of capital a closed-end fund has to invest changes not a whit. At an open-end mutual fund, by contrast, the investment kitty fluctuates daily. Indeed, portfolio managers at open-end funds almost always have to stash a fair amount of cash in the till to handle share redemptions; that means they can't fully pursue their investment strategy, even if it is successful, and they always must keep an eye on the mood of their shareholders. The closed-end fund manager, meanwhile, serenely deploys all capital, has cash on hand only between investments (or as part of the overall investment strategy), and never worries whether shareholders are going to jump ship or, just as bad, come flooding in. No wonder many professional fund managers would much rather captain a closed-end fund than an open-end one.

The Closed-End Advantage

Well, we all like our fund managers to be happy, but what's in it for us? Insulation of a fund's assets from fund-investor panic, that's what. Suppose you are in two Latin American stock funds, one open-end and the other closed-end. Mexico devalues its peso, and all Latin American markets hit the skids. So far, both funds are in the same boat. But as some of the open-end fund's shareholders join in the panic and dump shares, they directly reduce the asset base. To redeem the panicking shareholders, the open-end fund manager either must have enough cash on hand or, more likely, sell stock in a hurry. The only kind of stock you can sell fast and in quantity, especially in a foreign market, are the big, liquid, high-quality stocks—the very ones the fund manager probably would rather not sell, under the circumstances. When the panic subsides, the open-end fund is left with a smaller portfolio made up disproportionately of weaker or more speculative stocks that are most vulnerable to any further home-market setbacks. Fixing this situation requires eventually buying back some of the stocks sold during the panic, thus adding to the fund's expenses. The closed-end fund's portfolio, however, is unscathed by the panic. If any of its shareholders want out, they sell in the stock market. The manager doesn't have to unload any stocks to pay off departing investors. Instead, he or she can coolly navigate the market turbulence according to what is best for the portfolio. As the panic wanes, the closed-end fund's portfolio also is smaller, but only by the amount of the market decline. Most important, the composition of the portfolio is the same as it always was, or if it is different it's because of adjustments the manager has made deliberately.

Panic also can happen on the buying side, as a fund or its targeted investment suddenly becomes immensely popular and investors line up to get a piece of the action. The open-end fund manager is in many cases hard-pressed to put to work all this new capital that comes pouring in, especially in foreign markets. In some cases, the additional capital is invested willy-nilly in whatever is out there, including inappropriate and ill-researched stocks. In other cases, the inflows are simply parked in cash-equivalent securities—sometimes just good old U.S. Treasury bills. Either way, the investors aren't getting what they think they're getting, or are paying for. At a closed-end fund, however, the buying frenzy simply boosts the share prices; the portfolio manager has no new capital to invest. Of course, if the popularity persists, the closed-end fund has the option of selling more shares, just like a company does. But in such instances, the portfolio manager knows about the new capital long in advance and can prepare to handle it.

This insulation is a very real advantage, but don't misinterpret it as meaning that closed-end funds are protected from investor sentiment—that wild card of human emotions that is such a factor in markets. It is closed-end funds' share prices that reflect investor panic and feeding frenzy, as well as the sweep of emotions in between. The main determinant of share prices is the performance of each fund's investment portfolio—just as the main factor in a stock price is the company's earnings. Then investor sentiment comes into play, tweaking the share prices either higher or lower. For closed-end funds, this means sometimes the share price is higher than the portfolio's net asset value per share, and sometimes it is lower. This "premium" and "discount," respectively, is a matter of grave concern to many closed-end fund investors, especially new ones. But in most cases it doesn't matter all that much over the long haul. Some funds almost always trade at a discount, others almost always at a premium; still others fluctuate between the two. This is the visible evidence of investor sentiment, but nobody really knows why investors feel the way they do. Over time, however, these funds tend to deliver about the same returns as their underlying portfolios. The premium-discount status should never be the primary reason for making an investment decision about closed-end funds; it ranks in importance below management fees and expenses on your checklist of considerations. Still, it is handy to have a reading of investor sentiment right there in the newspaper. *The Wall Street Journal* publishes closed-end funds' portfolio values and their share-price premium or discount once a week. By contrast, open-end mutual funds tell you once or twice a year about investor sentiment—in the form of the number of shares they have outstanding, compared to a year before—and then only long after the cutoff date.

A Bit of History

The case for closed-end funds is a good one, but you should be aware there is a skeleton in the closed-end closet. You might wonder, for instance, why older investors of your acquaintance are negative about closed-end funds. That feeling dates back to the 1920s, when closed-end funds lured investors with the promise of professional management to play the booming stock market. The trouble was, many of these funds were extremely leveraged; that is, they used their investors' money as collateral to borrow huge sums so they could make bigger bets in the stock market. When the 1929 crash came, these funds plunged deep and hard, wiping out the stakes of thousands of investors. Because of the bad taste that this experience with closed-end funds had left, the securities laws written in the 1930s favored the open-end mutual fund. That's why open-end funds multiplied so much faster in the ensuing decades. Relatively recently, as the bad memories faded, the number of closed-end funds started growing again. In 1985 there were only 47 closed-end funds in the United States. Ten years later, there were 530. Over the same decade, the number of open-end mutual funds rose to 4,800 from 1,900.

Ironically, closed-end is older than open-end as a structure for pools of investment capital. Moreover, it began as a vehicle for international investing. The closed-end form was invented by the British to invest in the empire's colonies. The first such fund was the British East India Company, formed in the 1600s. The closed-end form appeared in the United States during the 19th century railroad-building boom, but they weren't called closed-end. The name itself surfaced during the Roaring Twenties. The leverage problem of that era is not present today. But be aware that some closed-end funds use leverage as part of their strategies.

Indeed, closed-end funds are a bit riskier than comparable open-end mutual funds. Besides the option of using leverage, the structure that insulates them from shareholder panic also allows them to remain fully invested in a declining market. And some funds use this insulation to make very illiquid investments, such as buying securities not offered on open markets—for instance, stakes in private companies. You should be familiar with what risks a fund has authority to take, but also track what the fund is actually doing. If a fund suddenly goes hog-wild on risk, chances are it has lost confidence in its original investment style. It's time for a thorough reevaluation to determine whether you should continue holding its shares.

CHOOSING A DIRECTION

The structure of closed-end funds is particularly advantageous in international investing. In these sometimes illiquid, sometimes volatile markets, you want your portfolio manager to keep his or her eyes on the investment road, not to baby-sit the cash flow in and out. Moreover, closed-end funds tend to be smaller than their open-end cousins, which makes them more agile in adapting to changing investment conditions than a supertanker-sized open-end fund. A typical emerging-market closed-end fund has around $60 million in assets; they are considered unusually big at $100 million. The typical open-end emerging-market fund, by comparison, is $250 million.

About 25% of all U.S. closed-end funds are devoted to international stocks. Of these, a relatively few are "generalist" funds that allow managers to roam the globe in search of capital appreciation. Many that don't have a geographic focus are nonetheless limited in some way: for example, small stocks, emerging markets, or some other niche such as

Closed-End Funds

Diversified International	Net Assets ($ million)	Date Started
All Seasons Global	41.2	Mar-88
Alliance Global Environment	98.5	Jun-90
ASA Limited	374.0	Sep-58
Clemente Global Growth	61.4	Jul-87
Emerging Markets Infrastructure	212.1	Dec-93
Emerging Markets Telecommunications	177.4	Jun-92
Foreign Colonial Emerging-Middle East	39.3	Oct-94
G.T. Global Developing Markets	469.0	Jan-94
Gabelli Global Multimedia	93.5	Nov-94
Global Small Cap	48.1	Oct-93
Morgan Stanley Africa Investment	247.5	Feb-94
Morgan Stanley Emerging Markets	397.6	Oct-91
TCW/DW Emerging Markets Opportunities	273.6	Apr-94
Templeton Emerging Markets Appreciation	24.0	Apr-94
Templeton Emerging Markets	277.3	Feb-87
Worldwide Value	73.7	Aug-86
Regional		
Asia Pacific	283.0	May-87
Asia Tigers	251.1	Nov-93
Central European Equity	269.4	Mar-90
Europe Fund	166.7	May-90
European Warrant	101.7	Jul-90
Fidelity Advisor Emerging Asia	135.4	Mar-94
G.T. Global Eastern Europe	113.4	Mar-90
Herzfeld Caribbean Basin	9.0	May-94
Latin American Equity	147.1	Oct-91
Latin America Growth	51.1	Oct-94
Latin America Investment	152.7	Jul-90
Latin American Discovery	169.6	Jun-92
Morgan Stanley Asia-Pacific	963.7	Jul-94
Schroder Asian Growth	265.0	Dec-93
Scudder New Asia	140.3	Jun-87
Scudder New Europe	256.7	Feb-90
Single-Country Funds		
Argentina Fund	127.3	Oct-91
Austria Fund	131.1	Sep-89
Brazil Fund	426.3	Apr-89
Brazilian Equity	99.3	Apr-92
Chile Fund	363.6	Sep-89
China Fund	144.6	Jul-92
Czech Republic Fund	95.1	Sep-94

Emerging Germany	139.8	Apr-90
Emerging Mexico	104.8	Oct-90
Fidelity Advisor Korea	48.8	Oct-94
First Australia	191.4	Dec-85
First Israel	64.6	Oct-92
First Philippine	240.7	Nov-89
France Growth	191.0	May-90
Germany Fund	208.5	Jul-86
Greater China	185.1	Jul-92
Growth Fund of Spain	238.0	Feb-90
India Fund	296.7	Feb-94
India Growth	118.9	Aug-88
Indonesia Fund	40.3	Mar-90
Irish Investment	81.0	Mar-90
Italy Fund	10.6	Feb-86
Japan Equity	118.0	Aug-92
Japan OTC Equity	97.1	Mar-90
Jardine Fleming India	95.1	Mar-94
Korea Equity	64.5	Nov-93
Korea Fund	688.7	Aug-84
Korean Investment	83.0	Feb-92
Malaysia Fund	209.6	May-87
Mexico Equity Income	151.7	Aug-90
Mexico Fund	852.8	Jun-81
Morgan Stanley Africa Investment	247.5	Feb-94
Morgan Stanley India Investment	394.8	Feb-94
New Germany	543.0	Jan-90
New South Africa	72.3	Mar-94
Pakistan Investment	83.0	Dec-93
Portugal Fund	84.2	Nov-89
ROC Taiwan	352.6	May-89
Singapore Fund	116.1	Jul-90
Southern Africa	120.6	Feb-94
Spain Fund	119.8	Jun-88
Swiss Helvetia	305.1	Aug-87
Taiwan Equity	48.8	Jul-94
Taiwan Fund	364.1	Dec-86
Templeton China World	267.9	Sep-93
Templeton Russia	90.7	Jun-95
Templeton Vietnam Opportunities	110.1	Sep-94
Thai Capital	81.7	May-90
Thai Fund	320.3	Feb-88
Turkish Investment	41.1	Dec-89
United Kingdom Fund	63.8	Aug-87

Source: Morningstar, Incorporated

telecommunications. The majority of funds are geographically oriented: Spain Fund, India Fund, Asia Pacific Fund, for example.

What this means is that as a closed-end fund investor, you need to know where you are going. That's why at the beginning of this chapter we likened closed-end fund investing to renting a van. You have a particular destination in mind, and maybe even a specific route (Emerging Germany Fund, for instance). The implications of knowing in advance where you want to go are twofold, and substantial.

First, you take on the responsibility of your own international diversification. If your idea of international investing is to buy the France Fund, you indeed have diversified beyond your basic portfolio of U.S. stocks and bonds. But looking at just the non-U.S. component of your holdings, you have put all your *oeufs* in one basket. Not good. The France Fund doesn't give you even adequate European exposure, much less international. Going the single-country-fund route means you have to buy many countries to achieve the degree of international spread that will benefit your portfolio. If you are rich, you can just buy everything and be done with it. Short of that, you might start at the regional level—Europe Fund, Latin America Equity Fund, and so on—and dip into country funds when you want additional, targeted exposure. Or, you might start out in a broad-based open-end fund and use regional and country closed-end funds to add "weight" in areas you deem particularly promising. Anyway, the point here is that *you* must make those choices. To make reasoned, informed choices—rather than impulsive, uneducated ones—you will have a lot of homework to do. If keeping up with the world seems like fun to you, then the closed-end fund approach is probably a good fit. You can direct your money geographically without needing to do the additional research that would be necessary to select individual stocks.

Second, you need a fair-sized portfolio. On a random day in September 1996, we looked up the prices of ten closed-end funds that gave us reasonable international diversification; the total price was $165 for one share of each. Let's assume you are a round-lot kind of person; that's $16,500 for 100 shares of each fund. If these funds constitute 20% of your portfolio, we are talking about a total nut of $82,500. This might not be an issue for someone who just came into an inheritance or an established investor who only recently heeded the gospel of international investing. But if you have substantially less than this amount, you are better off going international via open-end mutual funds. When your total portfolio has grown sufficiently, take another look at the opportunities of closed-end funds. There undoubtedly will be even more choices by then.

As for when to move into a region or country, that's a matter of such topicality you are more likely to find useful guidance in newspapers and newsletters than in books. As we write this, much of Latin America seems teetering toward recession, while economic growth in much of Europe and Asia is decently strong with the notable exception of Japan. By the time you read this, it will be much different, we're sure. Even assuming you are making long-term investments, you don't want to move initially into a region, or especially into a country, when it has been rip-roaring long enough to push stock prices sky high. If that's the state a region is in when you first notice it, keep your powder dry until the inevitable correction comes. Then buy your shares and forget about them for three to five years. This isn't market timing—which we advise against because nobody can do it well for very long—inasmuch as the pace is so glacial. It's just common sense.

PICKING A FUND

To start with, use the same guidelines in selecting a closed-end fund as you would an open-end fund: Look at the track record of the *portfolio* for the longest possible period; it won't be very long for many funds. (Don't at this point look at the performance of the fund's shares in the market; that's a later and less significant consideration.) If there is a good track record, check to see if the manager who made it is still overseeing the fund; if not, past performance means even less than it usually does about future prospects. Finally, focus on the fund's management fees and other expenses. Every dollar the manager and fund company pockets or spends comes out of your return.

Also check the turnover of the fund, which amounts to an indication of how long the manager holds a stock on average. This is an important consideration for single-country funds, which commonly are closed-end funds, and particularly when those single countries are emerging markets. With this restricted venue, the manager's choices amount to buy or don't buy, and hold or sell. Morningstar has found that single-emerging-country funds with buy-and-hold strategies tend to do better than those trading, or "turning over," their stocks more frequently. The reason isn't that commissions were so much higher for funds trading more frequently, but rather that poor liquidity in many developing markets forces frequent traders to pay up to get shares.

Before we give a couple of examples, you should know how turnover is computed: Take the lesser of a fund's purchases or sales during a year and divide by the average monthly net assets; the resulting number is a percentage. Turnover of 100% means the manager holds a stock about one year on average—that's fairly active trading—and a number below 30% is fairly inactive.

Now for those examples. Brazil Fund had an average turnover of 8% over six years and a three-year average return of 9%; Brazilian Equity had a 73% turnover in one year, followed by a 45% turnover over the following six months, and its three-year average return was 7.3%. Korea Fund, with an average 12% turnover during nine years, produced a three-year average return of 18.8%. But Korean Investment, with an average 29% turnover during two years, had an average return of 5.2%. We must say, it's nice to see buy-and-hold rewarded so justifiably. (We admit, however, that this characteristic of low turnover equaling superior performance doesn't hold for regional closed-end funds or those single-country funds focusing on a developed market.)

Here are some points about selection that apply specifically to closed-end funds.

The first is to avoid buying closed-end funds during their initial offering. There are three reasons for this warning. One is that until the fund has raised its investment kitty from the offering, it has no track record for you to check. Let someone else own the fund until the pig is fully out of the poke. The second is that new closed-end funds usually begin trading at premiums to the net asset values of their portfolios. That's because initial pricing takes into account the costs of bringing the fund to market. Before long, however, the price usually slips to a discount to net asset value. Wait until that happens before putting a new fund on your shopping list. The third reason is that new funds usually come to market just as that region or country is going gangbusters. The fund companies, naturally, want to capitalize on investor enthusiasm for Region X or Country Y. But as you recall, high-flying is more often than not followed by low-plunging. Wait for the latter before you climb aboard.

Because closed-end funds are traded like stocks, you can buy them like stocks. As long as you are doing the research to pick your destinations and your route, buy your funds through a discount broker. If you are using a broker to gather some information for you, it is considerate to give him or her an order. Commission costs are minimized, in relative terms, by holding a fund long-term to give it the greatest chance of substantial appreciation.

DISCOUNTS AND PREMIUMS

Burton Malkiel, a Princeton University professor of economics, tells the story about two students who go out strolling with their economics professor and find a $10 bill on the street. The professor proclaims that it's an illusion. Because financial markets are so rational and efficient, he lectures, "If it really were a $10 bill, someone already would have picked it up." The students look at each other and grab the money.

Professor Malkiel uses that story in explaining about closed-end funds sometimes trading at a discount to net asset value, which is sort of like finding $10 bills lying around for the taking. Professor Malkiel, a devotee of efficient-market theory, hasn't been above picking up a few bucks that way himself.

Sometimes discounts widen to unusual extents, and you will hear investment advisors who specialize in closed-end funds pronouncing that it's a good time to buy; similarly, when these discounts narrow, or even edge over into premiums for some funds, these advisors will proclaim it's time to sell. This advice may be golden for many types of closed-end funds, such as those investing in municipal bonds, but we don't think it is for the international closed-end funds in your portfolio. If you have followed the approach we recommend, you select these funds as filling specific niches in a long-term portfolio, and you should stick to that game plan no matter which way the premium-discount wind is blowing. If the fund you want to buy happens to be at a discount to the portfolio value, then enjoy the experience of finding a $10 bill on the street. (And, of course, if you notice that a fund you want to buy is sinking to a deeper-than-usual discount, then all the more reason to act sooner rather than later.) But don't pick funds for their discount alone. You buy a fund because you would like to have it in your portfolio, even if its discount widens.

Many investors are happy enough to buy into a closed-end fund at a discount, but once in they become increasingly unhappy that the fund's share price doesn't equal the net asset value of the underlying portfolio. Some big investors become so irate that they try to take over the fund—each closed-end fund is a separate company—raising the discounted shares to par value as they liquidate the portfolio's holdings. (Alternatively, they or the fund operators sometimes opt to turn the fund into the open-end variety, wherein the net asset value immediately reflects the value of the portfolio it holds.) In our opinion, these people don't have enough real worries. As we said a few pages back, the longer you hold a closed-end fund, the less that discount—or premium, for that matter—affects your total return.

But you should keep an eye on that discount or premium nonetheless, because it will send the first signal that something may be amiss. You may be reading about the problem in the papers if it has to do with the region or country the fund invests in, so the share price simply will confirm what you already know. But it may be telling you something less public, such as that the portfolio manager quit or the fund company is considering some unpopular action. If the discount-premium status changes markedly, try to learn why. You won't always succeed, but you owe it to yourself to make the attempt. If nothing seems wrong, though, there are probably worse ways to invest than buying a closed-end fund at a deep discount.

Whatever you do, don't try to play the discount-to-premium-to-discount-again flips that some closed-end funds' shares go through. Yes, there is probably a little money to be made that way, just as there can be in short-term trading of stocks. But we assume you are interested in building your investment portfolio mainly through capital appreciation. We doubt you have read this far if you are looking for quick bucks from fast turnovers, which means that if you tried it you probably wouldn't be good at it. It's just that closed-end funds are so new to many people that some people feel obliged to try their hand at everything— just as certain new-car owners will push their vehicles to 90 miles per hour to see if they really will go that fast. Spend your time on research, instead, and repeat after us: I am a long-term investor. By the way, the funds with the most premium-discount fluctuation are those with the more volatile underlying portfolios, which are the kind you can expect in the international arena.

Once again, Lipper Analytical Services and Morningstar are the best sources of information about closed-end funds. Morningstar covers the closed-ends in its mutual funds publications. Lipper handles queries on an individual basis. The contact procedures are the same as in the preceding chapter. *The Wall Street Journal* has regular coverage of closed-end funds and their investing strategies. Sometimes, because closed-end funds trade like stocks, this coverage is in the "Heard on the Street" column.

CHAPTER V

American Depositary Receipts

A T first glance, American depositary receipts, or ADRs, seem like
the global investor's fondest fantasy come to life. Call your local
broker and buy a foreign stock that is traded on one of the major exchanges in the United States. The purchase takes place in dollars, the
dividends are paid in dollars, and you get to watch the dollar-
denominated price movement of your foreign stock right in the daily
statistical columns of *The Wall Street Journal*. All those risks that you
have to worry about when buying foreign stocks abroad just evaporate.

Well, no, not exactly. There is certainly a measure of convenience
in purchasing ADRs of foreign companies, not the least of which is that
the transaction is relatively painless. You don't have to set up a foreign
brokerage account and deal with foreign settlement, custody, and tax
headaches. You also can easily find your stock in the newspaper. But
that's about where the paved road ends. All the risks that attach to any
other foreign stock—political, economic, currency, and market risk—
are all as wrapped up in that ADR as they would be in a foreign stock
bought abroad. That isn't to say you should avoid ADRs. In fact, we're

big fans of ADRs for some situations, especially since so many have been listed in the past few years. But you have to understand them to be able to use them intelligently.

THE ANATOMY OF AN ADR

The first thing you must understand is that American depositary receipts and their close cousins, global depositary receipts, aren't stocks. Rather, they are negotiable certificates or electronic entries certifying that the holder owns shares of a foreign company, which are on deposit in the company's home country. (Incidentally, the industry is rapidly moving toward simply calling these things depositary receipts, forgoing the American or global designation.) A look at how an ADR is created will give you a better idea of what it is and what it isn't.

Here's the process as seen from the viewpoint of the U.S. investor, who wants to own, say, shares of JollyGood Corporation, a fictitious British manufacturer. You place your order with your local broker, who in turn contacts a British broker and asks him or her to purchase 1,000 shares of JollyGood. Once the shares are purchased, the British broker deposits them with the local branch of a big U.S. bank, such as Citicorp, J. P. Morgan, or Bank of New York; all three of these are major players in the ADR business. The U.S. bank then issues a certificate—this is the ADR—to your local broker, who holds it either in your name or the firm's street name. The actual shares evincing ownership in JollyGood Corporation never leave the United Kingdom. If you just couldn't stand not to have your hands on those shares, it probably could be arranged for them to be shipped to you, but the costs would sharply raise the break-even hurdle for your investment.

When the time comes to sell out of your JollyGood holdings, all you need do is tell your local broker. He or she will put your ADR on the market, and you'll get the best price being quoted at the moment. The entire transaction, from your point of view, takes place in good old U.S. dollars. Until then, if JollyGood pays a dividend, the bank branch in the United Kingdom will collect it and remit it to you in U.S. dollars. You'll also receive investor literature from JollyGood Corporation, including regular financial reports that meet U.S. Generally Accepted Accounting Practices.

It strikes some investors as odd that one ADR in many cases represents either more or less than one share of the foreign stock—one ADR for ten shares, for example, or one for one-tenth share. The reason for this variance is to keep the ADR prices at levels that are appealing to U.S. individual investors. Few investors can afford to buy enough of a $1,000-a-share stock to feel they have a real stake in a company. For that reason, the ADR for this stock probably would represent 1/20th of a share and be priced at about $50 in the U.S. market. Conversely, a foreign stock whose price in U.S. currency would be 20 cents might result in an ADR for 100 shares priced at about $20.

Now let's look at it from JollyGood Corporation's point of view. What's in it for the company? By making its shares more widely available, the stock will probably be more liquid. All things being equal, investors both here and in the United Kingdom like liquidity (which is the ability of investors to buy or sell shares readily at the prevailing market price; though not precisely the same thing, trading volume is the closest widely available statistical indicator of liquidity). Having the stock traded in the United States could also help JollyGood's marketing program to establish itself in this country as a major competitor in the widget business. And if it wants to raise more capital in the future, it can tap the U.S. market, one of the best places in the world to find new money. So far, it looks like a win-win situation for you and Jolly-Good.

The crucial thing to remember is that you own a foreign stock, and it behaves like a foreign stock. If you were to compare JollyGood's stock price as quoted on the London Stock Exchange with the New York Stock Exchange (NYSE) quote you see each day in *The Wall Street Journal,* you would notice that they don't move in tandem. Don't worry, neither your broker nor the depositary bank is trying to cheat you. Instead, the price of your JollyGood ADR is reflecting not only Jolly-Good's price moves in London but also the changing value of the British pound as measured against the U.S. dollar. In the worst situation, you could own an ADR in a foreign company whose stock price, quoted on the local market in the local currency, rises while the value of your ADR, quoted on the NYSE in dollars, falls. Of course, we could turn that situation around and you could watch your ADR's value rise while the share price at home falls. Or, in the best of all worlds, your ADR's value benefits from both a rising stock price at home and a rise in the local currency against the dollar. If the relationship between the local currency and the dollar remains steady, then an ADR's price

ADRs by Country of Origin

(As of Oct. 1, 1996; not all are readily available to individual investors)

Country	No.	Country	No.
Argentina	25	Lebanon	1
Australia	162	Liberia	1
Austria	13	Luxembourg	9
Belgium	4	Malaysia	18
Bermuda	2	Mexico	87
Bolivia	3	Netherlands	35
Botswana	1	Norway	23
Brazil	53	New Zealand	8
Chile	22	Pakistan	6
China	22	Peru	10
Colombia	13	Philippines	16
Czech Republic	3	Papua New Guinea	3
Denmark	6	Portugal	6
Ecuador	4	Poland	2
Egypt	1	Russia	25
El Salvador	1	South Africa	118
Finland	12	Singapore	17
France	41	Slovakia	3
Germany	40	Spain	14
Ghana	1	Sri Lanka	2
Greece	4	Sweden	26
Hong Kong	107	Switzerland	16
Hungary	14	Taiwan	32
India	93	Thailand	8
Indonesia	9	Trinidad	1
Ireland	29	Turkey	8
Israel	12	United Kingdom	234
Italy	36	Uruguay	1
Jamaica	4	Venezuela	16
Japan	149	Virgin Islands	2
Korea	26	Zambia	1
		Zimbabwe	1

Source: The Bank of New York

can be expected to move in tandem with the share price in the home country.

Now that you know how an ADR works, we'll go a little further and discuss *sponsored* ADRs and *unsponsored* ADRs. If an ADR is sponsored it means that the original issuing company has explicitly decided to court U.S. investors. It has entered into an arrangement with a U.S. bank, which agrees to act as the depositary. Firms that sponsor their

ADRs are obligated to supply English-language versions of their corporate shareholder documents. What's more, as a buyer of a sponsored ADR, you, the U.S. investor, have full voting rights, with a few exceptions.

Unsponsored ADRs, on the other hand, are created when a broker or bank detects sufficient U.S. investor interest in a foreign stock to make it worthwhile to set up a deposit program. The broker or bank purchases the underlying shares on its own, deposits them in the home country, then tries to sell ADRs in the United States. The foreign company itself isn't directly involved.

There are several key differences to keep in mind. One is that holders of unsponsored ADRs seldom have any voting rights. Another is that only sponsored ADRs can be traded on the major U.S. stock exchanges, although only about half are traded on the Big Board, American Stock Exchange, or Nasdaq markets. Unsponsored ADRs—with the exception of some South African and Japanese unsponsored ADRs that were grandfathered before October 1983—are traded along with all the other non-exchange-traded sponsored ADRs on the non-Nasdaq over-the-counter market or in the "pink sheets" (so named because prices are available only by subscription to a publication originally printed on thin sheets of pink paper). Be forewarned that it is going to be difficult at best to get good, up-to-date information on ADRs traded off the major exchanges.

USING ADRs EFFECTIVELY

Any investor who knows something about a particular foreign company—perhaps as the result of a business relationship—and who thinks that company is a sound investment should probably own the company's ADRs. But for the most part we recommend that only veteran stock pickers make ADRs a significant part of their portfolios. You're taking on a sizable responsibility when you begin to build any portfolio out of individual stocks. When you add foreign stocks, you are compounding the problems of stock picking simply because it is more difficult—sometimes very difficult—to learn enough about what is happening in a company's home market that might affect the stock value. But the beauty of ADRs for the skilled stock picker is that he or she can invest with surgical precision, owning only the best companies in any given country. Investors who buy international, regional, or country funds typically own a hodgepodge of companies—some good, some dogs—because the fund managers have to spread around the money they are investing to avoid taking too large a stake in any one company.

If you are going to invest in ADRs, the strategies and tactics are very similar to those used to research and build a portfolio of domestic stocks. Investors with a value orientation will look for stocks with low price-to-earnings ratios but good prospects. Growth investors will want to find companies that are providing new products or services that are in high demand.

But keep your overall portfolio in mind. Generally, you aren't buying these foreign stocks to pick up still more great values on the cheap, as many value investors try to do, or to grab some hot little growth stocks that are doubling in price every six months, as some aggressive growth investors try to do. Instead, remember that you are buying foreign stocks to gain diversification outside of the U.S. market. It is far more important to the long-term investor to put money to work in a variety of markets than to pick super-performing individual stocks. And be forewarned that as an individual investor it will be almost impossible for you to use ADRs to duplicate the kind of diversification equivalent to the most popular international benchmarks, such as Morgan Stanley International's EAFE Index. Some pension fund managers have constructed portfolios of 300 or so ADRs, representing about 60% of the capitalization of the EAFE Index, which track that index within 1% or so over five years. But you certainly don't want to own 300 ADRs of different foreign companies.

Once you begin constructing your ADR portfolio, you may find your knowledge or interest is leading you to research and select ADRs of companies in one region of the world, say Southeast Asia, or, still worse, one country, such as Great Britain. If that's the case, you need to consciously steer some of your foreign money to a broadly based international mutual fund, or perhaps to a regional mutual fund that concentrates its efforts where you aren't focusing your own.

ADRs also open the door to certain global strategies that can't be duplicated at home. Global sector investing has become increasingly popular in the past few years. Several mutual funds have been created to pursue such themes as global infrastructure (the building of high-ways, dams, and other basic needs for any modernizing nation), global health care (an aging population around the world will need more of it, goes the argument), and global telecommunications (sort of a specific infrastructure play). You can use ADRs to invest in these themes or others that suggest themselves to you. For example, the stocks of banks, insurance companies, and other financial concerns in any country often rise and fall in tandem with local interest rates. And since other nations' economic and interest-rate cycles are different from our own, an astute investor could follow the "wave" of rising and falling rates around the world for years. Buy financial stocks in the United States when rates begin falling, sell them when rates bottom, and buy financial stocks in Europe as rates begin falling there.

Another way to play sectors is to watch commodities prices, which tend to rise and fall globally rather than locally. If oil prices are increasing, for example, compare U.S. producing companies to oil concerns in other countries. Because many foreign markets are less efficient than our own, there is a good chance that the prices of some foreign oil stocks won't reflect the rising price of oil as fast as the U.S. oil company shares do. This discrepancy creates a bargain "window" for buying the foreign oil stocks. And there are some commodity-like products, such as paper, that respond to global demand, but without the close synchronization of prices that mark the true, raw-material commodities. Industries like that are likely to produce even bigger discrepancies in stock prices between U.S. companies and their competitors abroad. Taking advantage of those disparities can provide lucrative returns as rising demand eventually lifts all the companies' share prices.

RESEARCHING ADRs

Obviously, anyone seriously interested in using ADRs as the basis of an international portfolio is going to be doing some heavy research. Here are some tools that may be valuable.

The foundation of your research will be *The Complete Depositary Receipt Directory*, published in August each year by the Bank of New York. It lists ADRs alphabetically, by industry and by country of origin. The listings identify the exchange, how many shares each ADR represents, and whether the issue is sponsored or unsponsored. The cost for the directory is $50, and it can be ordered from the Bank of New York, ADR Division, 101 Barclay Street, 22nd Floor, West Building, New York, NY 10286. Further information can be obtained from the Bank of New York at 212-815-2175.

CHAPTER VI

Taking the Direct Approach

T HIS is it, the frontal assault. Buying stocks directly in foreign markets is like eating spaghetti without a napkin, driving without a seat
belt, high-wire walking without a net. You do this only because you have
to, or you are very good at it, or you are a compulsive risk taker.

As you can tell, we aren't wild about your jumping headlong into
this method of international investing. That's not because we think buying and selling foreign stocks directly is intrinsically wrong. There is
nothing the matter with the approach; it's just not a good idea for newcomers. It isn't even recommended for intermediate investors who still
have a distance to climb on the learning curve. You are much better
off mastering the investment basics at home.

And yet, like Little Leaguers on their first awestruck visit to a
major league baseball stadium, it is easy to catch The Dream. Here is
where you can hit your portfolio-exploding home run. Blink for scene
change: Strong, tough, cool-headed, you ride the bucking bronco to a
lavishly rewarded championship. Blink. It is your skill, your years of
preparation, your well-deserved luck that enables you to blast out of

the rough, over the sand trap, onto the green, and into the cup. Oh, God, it feels great! Those poor slobs in the bleachers—investors who play vicariously through their fund managers—can never fully sense this achievement.

If you are an accountant and normally dream in numbers, you can even quantify the advantage of direct investment. Let's say your supernova stock triples in price this year. If it's part of an equally weighted portfolio of ten stocks, and the other nine fell asleep for the year, your portfolio jumps 20%. But if it is 1 stock out of 100 in a mutual fund under the same circumstances (unlikely, we know, but this is a mathematically correct dream, remember?), your fund holding ekes out a 2% gain. Inescapable conclusion: Fly direct!

Is that coffee we smell? Dawn's cold light reveals The Dream for the mirage that it is. For one thing, you don't have to go overseas to find stocks that triple; they do that in the United States, too, though not nearly as often as we would like. For another, emotional release is undoubtedly healthy but should not be the reason why you invest; if fulfillment or excitement comes your way in the process of building and tending your portfolio, by all means enjoy it, but don't twist your financial life out of shape for a fleeting thrill. Finally, the next time you identify a stock that's certain to triple, please call us collect.

Basics for the Beginner

Here are some commonsense ground rules to run through before you act on the notion to buy foreign stocks directly:

1. Learn how to pick U.S. stocks first. It is especially important to develop your investment "style." That is, are you better at finding beaten-down stocks, buying them on the cheap, and profiting as they rebound? If so, you are a value-style investor. Or, do you look for stocks of companies that steadily grow their earnings, buy them on temporary setbacks, and then hang on for a sweet ride as they plow steadfastly upward? This approach makes you a growth investor. Neither style is 100% reliable; indeed, both have extended dry spells. Many individual investors mix the two styles into a personal hybrid. Anyway, the important point is that you have identified your style and have learned it and practiced it successfully *at home* before trying to apply it overseas. If you are into golf analogies, doesn't it make sense to mas-

ter the East Overshoe Municipal course before hacking your way around St. Andrews?

2. Go slow. Buy no stock before you have investigated it yourself to the best of your ability. Do not buy solely on a broker's recommendation or an analyst's report. Grub around for your own information, and feel comfortable with the stock's fit into your investment style. Above all, don't pressure yourself with the idea that to get foreign stocks into your portfolio you have to pick every one of them yourself. Instead, buy some international mutual funds to establish a broad base of foreign stocks. Do your stock picking at your own speed, supplementing or complementing the funds. If you don't know quite where to start looking for individual stocks, you could do worse than review those your mutual funds have bought. Or, get a recent copy of *The Dow Jones Guide to the Global Stock Market,* which contains capsule descriptions and data on 2,700 companies in the Dow Jones Global Indexes.

3. Start your foreign adventure in a part of the world with which you are at least somewhat familiar. Perhaps you know a little about a country or region because you or your firm does business there, or because you have traveled it extensively. Nothing beats firsthand knowledge, even if you gained most of it through the window of a tourist bus. Remember that in investing overseas, you are always fighting an information handicap. Anything you can do to lower that handicap is to your advantage. As you gain confidence and want to expand your investment picks into other parts of the world, visit those places. (No, such trips are *not* tax deductible; don't even think about it.) Talk to the locals, see what's on the shelves in the stores, get a sense of how people there live and think. You will acquire an invaluable context for absorbing economic statistics and news developments, and for assessing potential stock picks.

4. Think long-term. Even if you are something of a "trader" at home—darting into stocks to capture short-but-sweet runups or quickly bailing out when prospects fail to materialize promptly—your overseas picks should be made for the long haul. There are two principal reasons: First, foreign markets are volatile and many foreign economies are fragile; it simply might take a while for a company (and its stock) to achieve its full potential. Second, every time you go into and out of a stock, the pit bull named foreign exchange has a chance

to bite you in the portfolio. It won't happen every time, and as we discussed in Chapter 2, there are times currency translation can work to your benefit. Still, the more often you present yourself at the garden gate to get in or get out, the more likely you are to be chomped. So, how long is long-term? Five years, we think. During the first year, watch the stock's performance to see if it is telling you that it isn't likely to deliver what you had in mind. Assuming it demonstrates no such thing, allow three years to let a stock show its stuff. At the four-year mark, if not before, review each stock to see if it is still on track with the scenario you envisioned when you bought it. If all looks well, hang on. If not, investigate as though you were considering it for the first time, then decide whether to get out, buy more, or stand pat. We think it's fine to hold a foreign stock (many U.S. stocks, too, come to think of it) for more than five years. But it isn't all right to go that long without making a thorough checkup.

THE THERE OVER THERE

Individual investors are not welcomed with open arms everywhere in the world. India, for example, doesn't allow foreign individuals to invest at all. If you want to play in Bombay, you have to do so through one of the funds the government has seen fit to approve. In other countries, the restrictions are so tough that you might as well be banned altogether. For instance, South Korea limits the amount of stock foreigners can hold in any South Korean company to 18%, though that ceiling is rising. In other countries, the foreign-ownership limits are somewhat higher (49% in Indonesia) or are applied only to certain stocks or industries rather than across the board; holdings in financial companies, such as banks, are limited in several countries.

We don't imagine that you are going to put down this book and immediately set out to buy 5% of some South Korean company. But these restrictions and limitations do affect you. The direct effect is obvious. In South Korea, for example, funds and other institutional investors have sopped up most of the 18% allotment, so as an individual intent on buying a Korean stock you may be forced to scrounge for shares that have been unloaded by another foreigner in some over-the-counter market. Rest assured that your broker will feel entitled to charge you plenty for tracking those babies down. If others like you are seeking these shares, be prepared to pay more than the home-market price for them.

The indirect effect of these limitations is to force you into headache-inducing decisions that you might not have made—or had to make—on a wide-open playing field. Let's suppose you have decided you want to play Asia directly. Well, you can't play India that way, but it's too big to ignore. Your choice is to buy the India Fund—a closed-end fund specializing in that country—or an Asian or emerging-market fund with some investments elsewhere besides India. If you choose the latter course, you never know whether you are holding too many or too few stocks in the other Asian countries because you don't know what the fund manager is doing from moment to moment. If, intentionally or not, you are "overweight" in a single country and something unfortunate happens—such as Mexico's peso devaluation—you get whacked hard; some of the worst-hurt mutual funds in late 1994 and early 1995 were those overweighted in Mexican securities. Such losses are even more irritating when you recall that you started out in quest of greater diversification. So, the India Fund seems like the way to go. But what do you do if that fund is overpriced at the time you want to start this Asian play? Choice No. 1: Grit your teeth and overpay, thereby giving that portion of your portfolio an extra heavy overhead to overcome on the way to profitability. Choice No. 2: Don't buy the India Fund until its price goes back to normal levels, but meanwhile have an Asian portfolio with a gaping hole in it—and risk the chance it is precisely when you aren't in it that India's market will go through the roof.

None of these problems are insurmountable, just awfully nitty-gritty for our taste. For other investment challenges, read on.

THE COSTS OF INVESTING

If you found a box at your supermarket labeled "More Fat! Less Vitamins!" you would surely wonder what the manufacturer was thinking of. Well, get a load of foreign stock markets: Higher Costs! Lower Liquidity! These are the facts of life that all international investors have to contend with. But fund managers can deal with them far more effectively than you can as an individual. One reason is that the fund managers have bigger portfolios to spread costs over. Another reason is that most foreign stock markets favor the professional and institutional investors and make little effort to accommodate individuals with ordinary amounts of money. In this regard, most foreign markets today are like the United States was 15 or 20 years ago.

Investment costs, as you know, are the cover charge for getting into the game. The higher they are, the more your picks have to advance to break even and then to make money. There are two types of costs: Those you can see—most of them probably will be itemized on your brokerage statement—and those you can't. The good news is that the costs you can see have been coming down. Brokerage commissions overseas are generally much lower than they used to be, thanks first to the dropping of fixed-commission structures in most countries during the 1980s, and second to increased competition among brokerage firms and stock exchanges, which is continuing. Nowadays, the highest commission rates—along with the least competition among brokers—tend to be found in just barely emerging markets such as China.

Second, most countries have lowered or even discontinued the taxes they slap on stock transactions by foreigners. These levies were imposed back when these governments had only a hazy notion of what investing is all about, and they saw foreign investors as a source of quick, easy cash; if these jokers want to play in our markets so badly, let 'em pay for it. Now, most countries understand that the money these foreigners bring in can be used by their own companies to grow and prosper, and the revenue potential is much greater from taxing corporate profits than stock transactions.

The cost of investing isn't just fees and taxes, however. Liquidity cost also can eat into investment profits, though you won't find it on your brokerage statement or quoted in the newspaper. Liquidity is simply being able to get into or out of a market without paying a significant pricing penalty. Suppose the market price of a Spanish stock has been 1,025 pesetas a share all morning. Then you come with your order to buy 1,000 shares, and you have to pay 1,100 pesetas to consummate it. Maybe you could disregard 25 pesetas of the 75-pesetas difference as a normal reaction for a stock that is trying to go up; after all, isn't that why you're buying it? The remaining 50 pesetas of higher price, however, is due to insufficient liquidity, and it raises the cost of your stock nearly 5%. Poor liquidity hurts just as much when you are selling. The market is at 1,500 pesetas, where you decide to bail out. Your sell order, however, is executed at 1,425. Again, shrugging off 25 pesetas as a tolerable, that's-life move against you, the remaining 50 pesetas of liquidity cost means your profit on the stock was trimmed by more than 3%.

Liquidity is not an unknown hazard in the United States, particularly with smaller stocks traded on the Nasdaq Stock Market. But it's worse in almost every foreign country. How much worse is hard to pinpoint because liquidity isn't conveniently measured. Laszlo Birinyi, who heads his own stock analysis firm, looked at it several ways in a 1993 study. The first was the "spread" between prices bid by prospective buyers and asked by prospective sellers. These are the parameters within which trades should theoretically occur, so the wider the spread the higher the liquidity cost, and vice versa. The results of this measurement are shown in the table titled "Measuring the 'Spread'."

Mr. Birinyi's second reading was of "pricing continuity," which basically is tracking price changes from one actual trade to another. Simply averaging them has the effect of counting a 100-share lot as heavily as a 1,000-share transaction, so Mr. Birinyi weighted the changes by size of trade. This method produced the results shown in the "Measuring Pricing Continuity" chart. A third approach—which isn't easily

Measuring the 'Spread'

Country	Index	Number of Issues	Bid-Asked Spread (in %) Mean	Median
U.S.	DJIA	30	0.36	0.32
U.S.	Nasdaq 100	100	1.82	1.54
U.K.	FTSE-100	100	1.44	1.22
France	CAC-40	40	0.36	0.3
Germany	DAX	30	0.54	0.35
Belgium	BEL20	20	0.5	0.39
Denmark	Copenhagen	19	2.23	0.81
Italy	selected large stocks	11	0.6	0.33
Norway	OBX	21	1.56	1.1
Spain	IBEX	35	0.53	0.44
Sweden	OMX	30	1.08	0.89
Switzerland	SMI	18	0.43	0.31
Australia	20 Leaders	19	0.35	0.31
Hong Kong	Hang Seng	33	0.77	0.72
New Zealand	NZSE-40	39	1.31	0.99
Malaysia	selected large stocks	19	0.74	0.77
Singapore	ST	30	0.9	0.83

Source: Birinyi Associates, Inc.

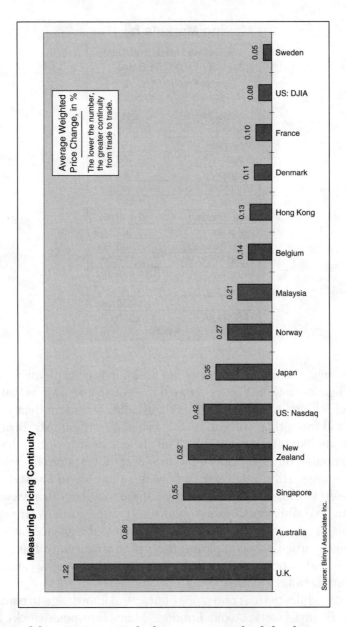

Measuring Pricing Continuity

Average Weighted Price Change, in %

The lower the number, the greater continuity from trade to trade.

Sweden	0.05
US: DJIA	0.08
France	0.10
Denmark	0.11
Hong Kong	0.13
Belgium	0.14
Malaysia	0.21
Norway	0.27
Japan	0.35
US: Nasdaq	0.42
New Zealand	0.52
Singapore	0.55
Australia	0.86
U.K.	1.22

Source: Birinyi Associates Inc.

duplicated by any investor lacking an arsenal of databases—was to measure how many dollars it took to push a stock index up and down 1%. Read all about it in the "Moving Markets by 1%" table.

The point of all this isn't to certify liquidity to the third place past

Moving Markets by 1%	
U.S. Dollars Needed, at 1993 Currency Exchange Rates	
[The less money it takes, the less liquid the market.]	
Country	US$
Norway	458,740
Malaysia	461,180
Sweden	465,969
Singapore	793,665
Denmark	990,595
Australia	1,487,773
New Zealand	2,116,487
Belgium	2,461,859
U.S.: Nasdaq	6,303,156
Hong Kong	6,786,232
France	17,879,184
Japan	18,741,517
U.K.	61,438,156
U.S.: DJIA	113,310,000
Source: Birinyi Associates Inc.	

the decimal; this stuff changes all the time, anyway, so please regard it as a rough indication. The lesson we'd like you to take away is that buying and selling foreign stocks directly usually costs more than you realize, and more than you can readily calculate without Mr. Birinyi or somebody like him at your side. This means, dear investor, that you don't know—you *can't* know—the true cost of your directly held foreign holdings. It's another reason why, if you decide to invest directly in foreign stocks, you should strictly adhere to a long-term view. You want to give your stocks every opportunity to perform as strongly as possible. At the same time, you want to maintain vigilance over their progress, particularly comparing their performances to their home markets and to other issues you have identified as worthy candidates for your portfolio.

Meanwhile, there is one piece of practical knowledge to come out of Mr. Birinyi's work: Avoid London. Many European stocks trade both in their home markets—Paris, Frankfurt, Madrid, or wherever—and in London, which humbly esteems itself as the center of the financial universe. Many non-British issues, in fact, trade more heavily in London than at home, thanks largely to institutional investors. In

The London Premium

French Stocks Company	Average Bid-Ask Spread (%) In London	Average Bid-Ask Spread (%) In Paris
BSN	2.27	0.23
LVMH	2.66	0.22
Carrefour	2.54	0.30
Eurotunnel	4.75	0.60
Rhone-Poulenc	9.40	0.36
Club Med	5.60	0.17

Italian Stocks Company	Average Bid-Ask Spread (%) In London	Average Bid-Ask Spread (%) In Milan
IFI	1.28	0.07
Olivetti	1.01	0.15
Benetton	4.00	0.41
Mediobanca	3.53	0.21
STET	1.85	0.32
Pirelli	2.79	0.29

Source: Birinyi Associates Inc.

Trading in Two Cities

How a French Stock Traded in Paris and London on July 26, 1993

Trade Time	London Trade	Last Sale In Paris	London Differential (In Percent)
9:06	237	238.5	-0.63
9:16	236.5	236.4	0.04
9:37	238.5	238	0.21
10:15	242	238.5	1.47
2:15	242	238	1.68
4:00	238	238.6	-0.25
4:01	237	238.6	-0.67
5:00	242	238.6	1.42

Source: Birinyi Associates Inc.

pursuing the elusive liquidity question, Mr. Birinyi discovered some unflattering truths about the London market: One is that bid-ask spreads for these stocks are typically much wider in London than in the home market. Two, these stocks often traded in London at prices outside the home market's spread, even when the home market was open. See the tables on p. 95. Taken together, these observations mean not only that it costs more to trade in London but also that many allegedly professional investors don't seem to care (since they keep doing it). You, however, should care. If you are buying or selling a European stock, ask your broker to make the trade in the stock's home market rather than in London. It will save you money, unless your broker charges more for that particular home market. In that case, shop for another broker.

HELP FROM YOUR BROKER

Speaking of brokers, you should determine before getting started how much assistance you can expect from yours in trading foreign stocks. Normally, we encourage people to do their own research on stocks because we feel strongly that nobody should buy a stock without knowing something about it. In the United States, this position leads naturally to the use of discount brokers; if you already have done the research, you don't need to pay for advice but only for execution of trades. For foreign stocks, however, you will appreciate all the help you can get. Full-service brokers—and big ones, at that, with foreign offices—are in the best position to supply you with information about nearly every country and about many companies. Remember, you shouldn't buy any stock—U.S. or foreign—just because a broker or analyst recommends it. But as you begin trying to understand a stock, material from your broker can fill in much of the basic information you need, as well as suggest sources you can check on your own.

Any broker, including discount and deep-discount firms, can execute your ADR trades. So, consider these much the same as U.S. stocks: Research them yourself and have your orders executed as cheaply as possible.

The next level up on the hassle ladder are brokerage firms that make markets in selected foreign stocks. That means these firms probably have inventories of most of these stocks and can fill any reasonably sized order with little trouble. It also means the firm may make extra money on the bid-ask spread, in addition to the commission it charges. Most investors aren't troubled by that so much—some broker somewhere would be making this money, no matter what—as by the suspicion that if a stock's price is moving up, the firm will buy for its own account first, at the lower price, and then fill your order at a higher price. It happens, but its importance is minimal if you are making a long-term investment. More significant is that when it comes time to sell, you are able to go back to the brokerage firm you bought the stock from—or another one making a market in the same stock—and expect the shares to be taken off your hands at the going price. If you ever get hemming and hawing from your broker in this situation, take your business elsewhere. Also, keep track of which brokerage you bought such-and-such shares through, so that you know where to go to sell. Beware when your broker says the firm doesn't make a market in the stock you want to buy but does in another one "just like it." Stocks aren't any more "just like" each other than companies are. They may be in the same business, but they have different managements, strategies, and so on, and their stocks have their own distinct behaviors, as well. The "just like it" stock may be fine, but remember: You don't buy anything without researching it first. The foreign stocks in which a U.S. brokerage firm makes markets change over time, so this becomes another detail you have to keep track of. If you obtained information or research on the stock from the firm, it most likely plans to make a market in these shares for the foreseeable future.

By the way, it is to these market-making firms that some discount brokers turn to execute foreign-stock orders from their clients. As we write this, the discounters are just beginning to expand their capability of handling foreign stocks themselves. Until then, you pay the discounter's fee plus whatever the market maker charges the discounter. You get a similar double-fee treatment when your full-service broker doesn't make a market in a foreign stock but another U.S. firm does. The only mitigating fact is that the market-making firm will charge your broker less than it would charge you. Ask your broker if the firm, in addition to charging its own commission, just passes along the market maker's fee or marks it up.

The upper level of transaction hassle is reached when you want to buy a stock no U.S. firm makes a market in. You don't have to open an account with a foreign broker, though some U.S. investors do that. We don't recommend it unless you have a working relationship in the country in question, perhaps as the result of regular business visits. In setting up this account, you can stress the local contacts you have so that the broker doesn't regard you as someone he or she will never see again. Be sure you understand the regulations on tax withholding, capital gains, and dividend taxes, and any restrictions on your ability to take your profit out of the country. These regulations vary from nation to nation and in some instances become quite bizarre. Frankly, we think the hassle of a foreign brokerage account is worth it only if you plan to trade a fair number of stocks in that country.

Otherwise you can stick with your domestic broker. In the case of a stock your brokerage firm doesn't make a market in, your broker must "go agency," which is jargon for finding a foreign broker to handle the trade. Most big firms have preestablished relationships with brokers in the important world markets, so they don't start from scratch each time this kind of order comes in. But agency relationships become few and far between when you get to such obscure markets as Sri Lanka or Turkey.

Bring plenty of money when you ask your broker for agency service. Not only are the fees higher but the minimum order sizes are also larger. You can buy $500 of shares in Glaxo, the big British pharmaceutical company, but you will need from two to five times as much to put in your order for Pakistan Telecom. All right, you sigh, how much bigger must the orders be? Nobody knows, at least not in advance. Your broker decides each situation separately, depending on the country involved, the nature of the firm's agency relationship, and what's going on in the world at the moment. If you are a frequent customer, you might be able to negotiate a better deal on fees and order size than your broker first presents to you. But don't forget that the point of all this is to invest, not to exercise your haggling skills.

Finally, don't expect U.S.-style service when your broker has to go agency. It will take a little time to relay your order to wherever "there" is, and a little more time to resolve any questions. Then, the home-market broker has to attempt making the trade. U.S. brokers already make markets in the biggest, most frequently traded foreign securities, so if you are going agency you are involved with either an obscure country or a little-known stock, and maybe both. Some of these stocks trade "by appointment," which means the home-market broker has to scare up a seller, if you are buying, or a buyer, if you are selling. This process can take hours, days, or even weeks. When the home-market broker locates an opposite party, both sides show up at the exchange at the predetermined time and do the trade. Don't be surprised if the price is substantially different from the preceding trade, whenever it occurred. This is what volatility looks like, close up.

THE TWO FACES OF VOLATILITY

If there is one word that scares some people so terribly that they almost never venture their portfolios outside the United States, it is volatility. If you question these people closely, you discover that they aren't *really* afraid of volatility, which in the case of stock markets is the magnitude of price changes over time. Finland was home to one of the world's most volatile stock markets in 1993; it went up 73%. Do you think people are afraid of that kind of volatility? Not on your life. They may talk about volatility, but what they are really afraid of is the unpleasant surprise of downside volatility. These days, that means Mexico. Many people feel they were led down the garden path on Mexican investments by all the "experts." Never mind that the path was crowded with fund managers and other professionals, as well as themselves. When the rug is pulled out from under them, these people flee for the exit as fast as they can. And it takes a very long time before the memory fades enough for them to dip their toes back into a foreign market—any foreign market—again.

These people aren't investors. They're savers. They want the safety net of federally insured certificates of deposit: guaranteed returns, no loss of capital. They love to quote Will Rogers, who in the midst of the Depression cracked, "I'm not interested in the return on my principal so much as the return *of* my principal." True investors, on the other hand, know that not only is there no Depression now—on the contrary, the world seems embarked on a prolonged period of economic growth—but also the size of the potential reward is directly related to the degree of risk. The yardstick for risk is volatility—both up and down. Here we introduce a table that looks quite boring at first glance but which has some revealing things to tell us about volatility. It is a table of standard deviations from the mean of Dow Jones Global Indexes for 29 countries. Standard deviation is a statistical measure of volatility commonly used in market studies. It is more complicated than its definition, which is how widely the values in a series are dispersed from the average value (the mean). Without getting into the mathematics of it, all you need to know to understand this table is that the higher the number, the more volatile the market; an unchanging market has a standard deviation of zero.

The first thing we'd like you to notice is that the United States isn't

Jumpin' Around

Volatility (standard deviation) of the Dow Jones Global Indexes

Country	1992 Local Currency	1992 In U.S. Dollars	1993 Local Currency	1993 In U.S. Dollars	1994 Local Currency	1994 In U.S. Dollars	1995 Local Currency	1995 In U.S. Dollars	All Four Years Local Currency	All Four Years In U.S. Dollars
Australia	5.23	7.77	10.17	7.97	5.73	3.70	6.75	7.00	13.09	13.67
Austria	11.88	8.74	11.22	8.98	6.42	3.47	3.99	4.99	10.74	9.54
Belgium	5.01	3.73	8.31	5.02	5.86	2.97	5.58	7.51	11.07	13.88
Canada	3.74	5.91	6.25	4.21	3.23	3.95	5.24	5.66	11.12	6.68
Denmark	10.38	8.42	8.75	5.60	7.07	3.52	3.43	4.62	10.53	11.06
Finland	15.34	13.85	29.80	20.91	10.67	19.07	31.95	33.12	67.46	66.09
France	6.00	4.41	8.57	5.76	8.34	3.80	3.80	5.71	9.45	7.80
Germany	7.75	5.75	10.99	8.70	4.39	4.38	5.18	5.89	12.69	15.30
Hong Kong	11.95	12.13	31.18	31.39	20.61	20.78	15.55	15.63	40.37	40.60
Indonesia	10.21	9.95	36.53	33.66	20.19	20.30	13.53	11.57	39.76	33.93
Ireland	5.30	7.98	10.72	8.87	5.53	5.50	12.88	9.78	27.56	21.09
Italy	11.10	9.55	12.97	9.25	13.00	11.27	9.02	7.17	25.78	14.69
Japan	7.71	7.79	8.16	13.91	3.14	5.92	5.78	4.15	8.74	16.39
Malaysia	7.67	9.03	33.76	36.46	16.34	18.20	11.21	15.08	47.45	50.49
Mexico	11.07	11.19	17.97	17.69	13.08	18.12	20.80	10.14	29.44	35.03
Netherlands	3.22	3.42	10.96	8.11	4.94	3.77	7.24	8.68	17.24	20.44
New Zealand	4.43	4.86	16.09	18.56	6.39	6.36	4.98	8.56	21.47	32.97
Norway	11.15	9.57	21.52	7.73	32.14	4.34	42.14	5.72	37.05	16.79
Philippines	18.40	21.08	54.70	45.85	23.89	28.16	20.07	21.81	78.37	76.30
Singapore	6.12	5.66	18.11	19.70	8.11	11.13	6.32	8.57	27.78	36.06
South Africa	7.30	8.51	10.38	6.67	12.84	8.81	8.48	7.42	33.41	18.49
South Korea	10.03	10.47	9.58	8.68	14.71	14.78	6.75	6.99	30.03	29.22
Spain	9.01	10.13	12.58	4.99	8.47	3.36	7.70	7.86	16.86	8.40
Sweden	9.82	8.39	17.66	9.29	5.57	4.76	15.05	16.10	35.00	23.73
Switzerland	3.65	6.04	14.36	14.09	9.44	3.63	14.48	20.37	26.03	37.04
Taiwan	11.43	11.85	11.91	11.47	13.17	13.50	15.96	17.94	28.27	27.15
Thailand	9.14	8.37	34.43	32.01	18.06	17.07	13.77	13.04	47.37	45.00
United Kingdom	5.31	5.43	6.78	5.44	6.09	3.82	7.38	5.56	14.71	9.36
United States	2.20	2.20	2.38	2.38	2.27	2.27	11.01	11.01	13.14	13.14

always the least volatile market. That's not surprising, considering how robust the U.S. market has become, plus the fact that during this period the U.S. economy was starting to grow. (The U.S. segment of the Dow Jones Global Indexes has more than 700 stocks, including some Nasdaq and American Stock Exchange issues, as well as those from the New York Stock Exchange.) Countries with consistently low volatility are Canada, France, Japan (in local currency), and the United Kingdom—all among the largest stock markets of the world. The list of countries with consistently higher volatility is almost twice as long, and it is comprised almost entirely of small markets: Finland, Hong Kong, Indonesia, Italy, Mexico, Taiwan, and Thailand.

Next, you should observe how volatility in most of the countries varies sharply from year to year. The major exception is the United States, where volatility runs at roughly the same rate each year (except for 1995, when stock prices surged). This is also true of the other countries with consistently low volatility. Of course, if one of the years in the table happened to be 1987, you would see some big changes in U.S. volatility. But except for such occurrences, U.S. volatility is remarkably steady year in and year out, though on a slight increasing trend. People get used to it; most of the time, it's predictable. In many foreign countries, however, the volatility is unpredictable. Look at Singapore, for example. In 1992, that market was only three times more volatile than the U.S. market; in 1993, Singaporean volatility was nine times that of the United States, and in 1994 it was back down to four or five times. This sort of thing happens even in Switzerland, for crying out loud. Sudden changes in volatility are what make investors nervous. But for the long-term investor, such changes matter only if they occur when you happen to be getting in or getting out. Even then, volatility works against you only part of the time, when prices move adversely to your game plan. You aren't going to complain about volatility if sharply moving stock prices allow you to buy in more cheaply or sell out more handsomely.

Notice, too, that translations of local currencies into U.S. dollars sometimes magnify volatility and sometimes diminish it. This data ba-

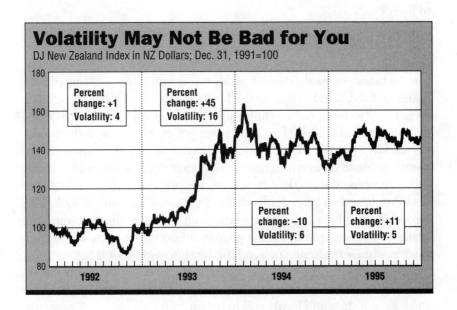

Volatility May Not Be Bad for You

DJ New Zealand Index in NZ Dollars; Dec. 31, 1991=100

Percent change: +1
Volatility: 4

Percent change: +45
Volatility: 16

Percent change: –10
Volatility: 6

Percent change: +11
Volatility: 5

sically underscores our advice in Chapter 2: Don't lose any sleep over currency risk; in the long run, currency movements will help your investments about as often as they hurt.

Volatility doesn't tell you a thing about whether a market is going up or down. In New Zealand, for instance, the stock market was 60% less volatile in 1994 than in 1993. Which year would you rather have been in New Zealand stocks?

For something that so many people claim disturbs them, volatility statistics aren't of much practical use, except as a rough indicator of liquidity. The more consistently volatile a market is, the less liquidity it probably has. (But not always; in some cases too much liquidity—usually waves of cash pouring into a country—can cause volatility, though this sort of situation seldom lasts more than a year or so.) Knowing relative liquidity before you get in should prepare you for the magnitude of price penalty you likely will have to pay. If that eases your mind even a little, we are pleased.

Sharing with Uncle

Let's see, what else is there? Ah, yes, taxes. How quickly we would like to forget.

The basic rule about taxes for foreign investors is that you pay twice: once in the foreign country where you collect your dividends and your capital gains, and then again here at home. But you also get credit for foreign taxes you paid. The net result is that you pay at whichever rate is higher, the United States' or the foreign country's. In some instances it's smarter to forgo the credit for foreign taxes and take them as a deduction instead. The difference between a credit and a deduction is . . . oh, forget it. We advise you to focus your attention on your investments, present and future, and to hire an accountant to take care of these numbing details. For your part, vow never to make investment decisions based on tax considerations. Pick a stock because it looks like a good one for long-term appreciation, not because there is some tax wrinkle in it someplace. As for picking an accountant, be sure he or she has some experience in handling foreign investments.

Don't dismiss the growing joy of state taxes. With the trend in Washington to flush more of the expensive problems down to the state level, expect state and local taxes to become an increasingly larger part of your overall tax bill. States can treat foreign-source income any old way they want. And since they are going to want more and more tax revenue, you would do well not to expect favored treatment of your successful return of foreign bounty back home. Already, the State of New York, bless its heart, allows neither credits nor deductions for foreign taxes paid. You unnerstand, Mac? You pay over there and you pay here, too. Got it?

CHAPTER VII

Bonds

IF you are one of the millions of American investors who own U.S. government or domestic corporate bonds, either directly or through one of the hundreds of bond mutual funds, we hope you paid close attention to what happened to you during the Great Bond Bear Market of 1994. That memory will be very important as you think about whether and how to invest in foreign bonds.

Unless you were very smart, or you owned bonds simply for the interest income, you doubtless lost some money on your domestic bond investments in 1994. That's because, with the exception of investors who buy and hold a bond until maturity, everyone else investing in bonds is really gambling on the direction of interest rates. The average investor buys a bond fund hoping to get not only the yield from the bonds in the fund's portfolio but also some capital gain. The only way the fund can get a capital gain from the bonds in its portfolio is if interest rates fall. There, that's gambling on interest rates. Now if you *want* to gamble on interest rates, that's fine. The trouble is, many naive investors in 1994 didn't realize they were gambling. Imagine their shock when at the end of 1994 they had less money in their bond funds than they had at the beginning of 1994. Not surprisingly, the amount of money invested in bond funds fell precipitously during the year as the losses became increasingly apparent. Even money market funds were not immune to losses. In their constant quest to outperform one another and lure more money into their funds, some money market fund managers took outsized risks by buying "derivatives"—financial instruments that can be used either to hedge a risk or add to a risk in search of extra reward.

By and large, we counsel against investments in domestic bond funds simply because we realize that many investors don't know the downside risk of funds. The remainder who do know it, and who proceed to buy a fund as a bet on interest rates, probably could do just as well for themselves by buying the bonds directly, choosing if and when to sell at a profit (or a loss if the bet doesn't work out) rather than letting a fund manager make the decision.

We recommend investors use bonds not as a speculative tool but as a safe haven for a portion of their portfolio. In other words, make your bets on stocks. They can be researched (far more easily than bonds), they each have a character all their own, and the potential gains are much larger. Use the reliable stream of income from bonds for the safe part of your portfolio.

FOREIGN BONDS

If, as we recommend, you use bonds for the safe side of your portfolio, you will have a hard time making much use of foreign bonds. That's because in the case of many foreign bonds, you can't eliminate one of the most potent risks: currency. If you buy and hold a U.S. Treasury bond to maturity, you face virtually zero risks. About the only thing that can go wrong is that during the period in which you're holding it, inflation rises sharply, reducing the value of the income stream you receive from that bond. But with a foreign bond—even the aptly named British government "gilts" and the supersafe German government "bunds"—you run the very real risk of the dollar rising in value against the currency in which the bonds are denominated during the time you hold that bond. This adverse currency move would put a possibly big dent in the amount of income you receive, to the extent of wiping it out. To be sure, if the dollar falls in value, it would provide a healthy boost to the bond's income stream. But remember, this is supposed to be the safe part of your portfolio. You shouldn't have to worry about the risks or the rewards of unpredictable currency moves.

Having provided that warning, we can't deny that virtually every other government's bonds will, from time to time, sport higher yields than equivalent-maturity U.S. Treasury bonds. The reasons, of course, are twofold. One is that hardly any other government is regarded as more durable than the U.S. government. In other words, the assumption is Uncle Sam will pay off his obligations 30 years from now. Who knows if there will be a Russian Republic even three years from now to pay off those high-yielding bonds? The second reason is that inflation varies from one country to another, forcing up interest rates where it is rising, allowing them to fall where it is under control. Recognizing that the allure of higher interest rates is strong, we know that some investors will simply insist on owning foreign bonds.

Is This Really the Best Use of Your Time?

The problem, of course, is finding these desirable bonds, then tracking them. Few foreign bond prices are reported by U.S. financial publications, so doing your due diligence research won't be easy. Certainly you'd be better off limiting yourself to the purchase of government-issued bonds. Trying to research corporate bonds in the United States is difficult enough, and it is virtually impossible for corporate bonds from any but the largest and best-known companies in Japan, Great Britain, Germany, and France.

Once you have decided that buying a particular foreign government bond is what you want to do, brace yourself: It will be difficult and expensive. First, you must find a broker that carries the bonds you want and that will deal with you. Several brokerage firms, including Charles Schwab & Company, don't even offer foreign bonds to individual investors. Those that do have widely varying initial investment requirements, ranging from $10,000 to $25,000 or more, depending on the type of bond. An alternative to brokers is to open an account at a foreign bank, such as Deutsche Bank AG in Germany, or in a U.S. branch of a foreign bank, and have the bank buy the bonds for you. That's easier said than done unless you travel abroad frequently or live in a major metropolitan financial center such as New York, Chicago, or Los Angeles. Even then, foreign banks usually don't want to deal with sums of less than $200,000 or even $1 million.

When you finally find someone to place the order for you, you will find that buying foreign bonds is considerably more expensive than buying U.S. bonds. First you have the currency translation costs. By the time you convert your dollars into another currency, then convert your interest income back into dollars, you will have taken a large bite out of your potential returns. (Currency exchange rates printed in *The Wall Street Journal* are for amounts of $1 million or more; the rates you pay when you buy a foreign currency, or receive when you buy back dollars, will be "retail" exchange rates, which are considerably to your disadvantage.) And don't think you can sell a foreign bond nearly as easily as you can trade U.S. bonds. Foreign-bond markets, by and large, are not nearly as liquid as the U.S. market, at least in part because foreign investors treat bonds as hold-to-maturity income producers, not something to be traded such as stocks or other speculative instruments.

As they always do, taxes figure into your international bond transactions. Be sure to check whether the country that issued the bonds withholds taxes on interest paid to foreigners and, if so, how and if you can get back that money. Needless to say, that, too, becomes extremely complex.

FOREIGN BOND FUNDS

It's of little wonder, then, that mutual funds are far and away the most popular choice for Americans who want to own foreign bonds. International funds can, for a low minimum investment, give you access to well-diversified portfolios of international bonds of varying duration, from short-term money market–like funds to longer-term plays. (The United States is unusual in selling 30-year government bonds; most governments limit their long-term issues to 10-year maturities.)

Among the most popular international funds prior to Mexico's financial meltdown late in 1994 were those called short-term world multimarket income funds. These funds basically chase short-term yields around the world. Most use some form of currency hedging, although such protection is seldom complete.

CHAPTER VIII

Money Managers; or, Do You Really Need Your Hand Held?

THE fact you're reading this book suggests that you might not need a money manager to help you set up a foreign investment portfolio. Money managers are paid mostly to tell you what to do with your money. You already have paid us to tell you that. The difference is, they cost a lot more.

But before the National Association of Money Managers (we made up that name) attacks us for impugning their integrity or ability, we are quick to add that there are legitimate times when anyone might want or need someone to help them solve certain financial problems. We freely admit that a book like this one can't replace advice based on personal interviews with you and a review of your financial circumstances. Money managers can be useful in a wide variety of situations, from simply helping you get your finances under control—getting rid of excessive credit card debt, for example—to doing the financial and legal work that will help you pass along a sizable estate to your heirs with a minimum tax bite.

Regardless of the financial situation in which you find yourself, there is someone out there willing to help you, for a price. You just have to recognize that the price might be high.

Before you decide you need professional financial help, think carefully about your assets, your financial goals, and exactly what kind of help you think you need. We have a good friend who recently decided that his finances were out of control. He wasn't sure he was adequately planning for his kids' looming college expenses or for his own not-so-looming retirement. We advised him to visit a fee-only financial planner. They're the ones that you pay by the hour to devise a financial plan. They don't make any money by selling you financial products, such as life insurance or annuities. Our friend and his wife visited the planner one evening after work for a free initial interview, at which the planner told them that before he could formulate a plan for them, they would have to organize and bring him certain financial data, including all of the family's income and expenses for the past year. They could either bring him a shoe box full of canceled checks and deposit tickets that he would charge them $125 an hour to sort out, or they could do it themselves and bring him the results. Even though our friend wasn't exactly the thrifty type, he figured he would save a bundle by doing the work himself.

That was his last visit to the financial planner. Sorting through his checking and savings accounts for a year opened his eyes to all sorts of problems and opportunities. Restaurant meals in New York were costing a fortune. Cutting back there could save him well over $4,000 a year. Other relatively painless measures saved the family another $7,000. Before it was over, he had drawn up cash flow charts, opened three mutual fund accounts, and invested some $30,000 that had been sitting in low-return checking and savings accounts. He was well on his way to planning an inflation-beating retirement portfolio that would supplement his company's profit-sharing plan. The lesson is that if you're organized and thoughtful about money, the chances are you won't need a financial planner, or at least you can minimize the money you spend on planning.

Nevertheless, we are assuming for this chapter that you want some level of help with your financial planning. We think that help should include advice on how much of your money to invest abroad, where, and how. We will start simply, with a little hourly advice, and progress up to the really big leagues, the large private hedge funds that take immense risks to make immense profits and charge you mightily for the privilege of playing in their game. Be aware that financial planning is in many ways an art, not a science, and the industry is full of fools and charlatans. There are plenty of good people out there who can be useful, but it will require some effort on your part to find the right ones and avoid the bad ones.

PAY ONLY FOR WHAT YOU GET: FEE-ONLY PLANNERS

For the relatively simple financial plan, we prefer fee-only planners who are paid, usually hourly, to draw up a financial plan that you can then follow for years. You can always go back to your planner for a little fine-tuning when circumstances change, but by and large it's your responsibility to follow the plan that he or she devises for you. Since international investing will seldom be the driving need for seeking out a financial planner, don't expect your planner to provide much sophisticated advice about using ADRs or hedge funds to play various foreign markets.

Do expect your planner to suggest that some portion of your long-term investment portfolio be outside the United States. And he or she almost certainly will suggest that you make those foreign investments through mutual funds. As a fee-only planner, this person should have no interest in selling you a load fund that would pay him or her a commission. In the world of international mutual funds, however, load funds tend to have been around longer and have better-established performance records, so your planner might wind up recommending such a fund for good reasons. If your planner is really conscientious about saving you money, he or she will suggest a few no-load international index funds. To start your search for a fee-only financial planner, contact the National Association of Personal Financial Advisors in Buffalo Grove, Illinois, at 800-366-2732. The association will send you a list of fee-only planners in your region.

The other kinds of financial planner that might meet your needs, but that we're wary of, are the fee-and-commission and commission-only financial planners. The fee-and-commission planners will charge you to set up a financial plan, but they make most of their money by selling you the products necessary to implement their plan. The commission-only planners make *all* their money selling you products. To our minds, there isn't much difference between these two. Since they make their livings on commissions, don't expect either of these planners to recommend no-load mutual funds or index funds. Also, they are unlikely to know much about such topics as ADRs or direct investment in foreign countries. In short, for the international part of your portfolio, you will get much the same advice from fee-only advisors as you will from commissioned planners. So, decide on which type you want to consult based on other factors.

FULL-TIME MONEY MANAGEMENT

Let's assume you need more than the one-shot financial planning we just discussed. You need someone who can look over your money full-time, making decisions about when and where to invest and when to sell. You want someone available on a continuing basis to discuss your finances, do your taxes, prepare your will, and otherwise oversee the financial aspects of your life while you get on with whatever else it is you are doing, whether running a business or sailing around the world. Get out your checkbook. It will cost you plenty.

Unless you have $100,000 of investable assets, you probably shouldn't even be thinking about a full-time money manager. Few of the good ones will bother with any accounts of less than that amount, and the really elite firms (which isn't to say they are especially good, just elite) will want you to deposit $5 million with them before they deign to advise you. The most common arrangement is for the firm to charge you a percentage of the assets under management, with extra fees for such ancillary services as tax preparation or estate planning. Some firms with stated minimum accounts will take on clients with less money to invest, but that money usually winds up commingled with other funds in what amounts to a mutual fund with awfully high expenses. Be sure the firm of your choice won't treat you like that.

Money managers aren't stupid. They realize that in the past few years more and more American investors want to put some money to work abroad. So, it would be hard to find a money management firm that doesn't *claim* to have overseas expertise. Finding out if they really do have that expertise is your job, and it won't be easy.

We assume you are looking for a money manager for reasons other than simply seeking advice on international investing. That means you first must find a firm that meets whatever other needs you have. Once that is done, find out just what the firm does and doesn't know about foreign investing. The best way is through personal interviews with the firm's principals and a review of their long-term performance. Ask to speak with whomever at the firm is responsible for international research. At some of the larger money management firms, especially those that also handle pension fund money for small companies and institutions, there will be a dedicated individual who handles international research. At smaller firms—the kind you're most likely to wind up with if you have less than $1 million to invest—there may not even be a research director, per se. Obviously, the more time someone devotes to studying such issues as currency valuations, political developments, and individual foreign company balance sheets and profit reports, the better equipped he or she will be to make decisions about how to invest your money.

Some of the small firms that don't have international specialists will claim that they use research done by some of the world's biggest investment houses, including the likes of J. P. Morgan, Goldman Sachs, and Merrill Lynch, to make investment decisions. Big deal. Those investment firms send international research reports to just about anyone who does business with them. While the reports can be useful, they don't replace the basic research that the bigger money management firms and the international mutual funds do for themselves (and many of the mutual funds will be considerably cheaper for you).

One way to get a feel for the international capabilities of a money management firm is to review its performance over the past five to ten years. Don't settle for some hypothetical results. You want to see actual portfolios. If the firm can't show you a five-year-old portfolio that sports at least 10% to 20% of its assets in international stocks, don't trust the firm's foreign investment expertise.

Also, be sure that the money manager's style jibes with your own investment objectives and philosophy. The best firms have a pronounced bias toward a style, such as value or growth investing. That style should be reflected in their international selections. Value investors, for instance, typically buy beaten-down stocks that are cheap. They should be able to explain what it is about each of the foreign stocks they hold that makes it a "value" play. Similarly, a growth manager should be able to show you a portfolio that contains a number of recognizable names of foreign stocks based in Europe. There are plenty of companies in the United States, Europe, and Japan that are certifiably "growth" companies; you don't have to be invested entirely in emerging markets to obtain good performance from rapidly growing companies. Indeed, you should beware of firms that have portfolios loaded with stocks in whatever the hot market *du jour* happens to be. Chances are, such a showing is evidence that you're dealing with a market timer who is simply part of the money manager pack chasing big returns without any style or discipline for guidance.

HEDGE FUNDS AND LIMITED PARTNERSHIPS

George Soros. Michael Steinhardt.

These are the living legends of international finance. If you think you would give almost anything to be able to invest with them, you wouldn't be far off. You would have to pay them between 1% and 2% of your money just to get in the door. Then you'd turn over a staggering 20% to 25% of any profits each year to the managers. But that assumes you could even get in the door. Even client-desperate, fledgling hedge funds require minimums of $50,000, and the biggest and best known won't take investors with less than a $25 million ante.

Hedge funds and other limited partnerships have a certain glamour about them, the result of the strong personalities that run them and the sometimes phenomenal gains they have made. But they aren't for all of us, or even for very many of us. Set up as private partnerships to escape the scrutiny of the Securities and Exchange Commission (SEC), these funds can have only 99 investors. And those 99 must be able to demonstrate that they are financially sophisticated and that they have enough resources to sustain the loss of most of their investment. The funds are becoming stricter about qualifying new investors, given the massive litigation in recent years surrounding misleading sales tactics by some promoters of limited partnerships.

Even if you could get into some of these funds, we question whether you should want to. Historically, hedge funds are rooted in an investment technique called hedging, in which a manager buys some stocks on the presumption their prices will rise, while selling short other stocks on the presumption those prices will fall. In practical terms, though, hedge funds forgo advertising and limit the number of investors who can participate in exchange for freedom to do pretty much as they please. In the 1990s, many have gone far beyond any notion of

hedged investing. Instead, they make their spectacular returns by placing very few, but very large, bets on such things as the relative value of
the yen versus the dollar, the performance of emerging stock markets,
or the direction of worldwide interest rates. Those bets also are often
highly leveraged—that is, the fund manager borrows money to increase the size of the bet. When things go right, the results are astounding. The Strome Susskind Fund, managed by Mark Strome, is
estimated to have turned in a 134% gain in 1994. But that was the same
year that Mr. Steinhardt lost an estimated 33% of his funds' value, and
a fund managed by David Asken utterly collapsed.

The trouble with hedge funds—besides the entry requirements—
is that they are in many cases the antithesis of diversification. With their
leveraged bets, they depend too heavily on the managers' skill at predicting correctly where a given market is headed or how a financial in-
strument will behave. The massive rewards for getting it right
undoubtedly attract real talent to the funds. But the typical investor,
who has to be worried about what happens to sums like $50,000, has
no business playing these speculative games. The SEC rules on limited partnerships were designed for a purpose—to keep the unwary investor out of hedge funds—and we think those rules are just fine.

PART THREE

Where to Invest

By now we hope you have decided to invest some of your portfolio abroad. You should also have some idea about how you want to do it: the convenience of mutual funds, picking individual stocks via ADRs or on your trips to other countries, or the services of a money manager who knows something about foreign investing. Now we're going to suggest *where* you might want to invest. In the chapters that follow, we look at three dozen countries that you might consider as locales for your foreign investments. We combine countries (Canada and Mexico, for example, or the Asian Tigers) mostly for convenience, but occasionally for the purposes of illustration, as well. The first chapter in this section, for instance, shows that while Canada is an easy place for an American to invest, the Canadian market tends to mimic the U.S. market too closely to achieve the real diversification of a foreign investment. At the same time, Mexico, which has been so much in the news, provides the diversification we're all looking for, but at the price of seemingly high risk.

In most chapters we include charts that compare the performance of the market under discussion to the U.S. market. The purpose of that chart is twofold. First, it will show you graphically how well correlated the two markets are. Remember that, all other things being equal, you're trying to escape the U.S. market cycle. The chart will also show you to some extent whether the foreign market under discussion is undergoing a long-term decline or increase. We're no fans of technical analysis, which purports to use charts of past performance to forecast the future performance of stocks or entire markets. But we think it's useful to know where in its own cycle a market may be, since (again, all other things being equal) it's better to buy a market when it's down than when it's up. The trouble with making investment decisions based on charts like this is that you never know how much higher a rising market can climb nor how much lower a falling market can fall. In that sense, caveat emptor!

After a discussion highlighting the salient points of a country's culture and recent history that will be useful to interested investors, we list some stocks to watch as potential investments. By and large, these will be large-capitalization stocks, because they are the most liquid and more is known about them. For those countries that are part of the Dow Jones Global Indexes, most of the stocks we list will be components of that country's Dow Jones index. We are in no way recommending any of these stocks for purchase. Conditions change quickly in any market, and what may be a good investment today may be a certified dog by the time you read this. Treat these lists only as a tool to familiarize yourself with the markets in question. You can do your own study of the companies to determine their worth as investments, or you can use our lists to check up on what your mutual fund manager is buying.

CHAPTER IX

Canada and Mexico

WE have harped about diversification as one of the main reasons American investors should consider venturing abroad. Recall from Chapter 1 our discussion of the arcane "coefficient of correlation"—the degree to which one country's market moves conform to another country's market moves. In this first chapter of our travelogue of world investment sites, Canada and Mexico show us what diversity is—and isn't—all about.

CANADA, THE FAMILIAR NEIGHBOR

There's a lot about Canada that is attractive to Americans. Montreal is a beautiful city with considerable charm (which wears off quickly in brutal Canadian winters). Toronto is clean, Vancouver is strikingly pretty, the Rockies offer some great skiing, and Nova Scotia is a waterman's paradise (in summer). It's easy to travel back and forth, and

Canada vs. U.S.
Dec. 31, 1991=100

Legend:
— U.S.
— Canada (Local currency)
— Canada (In U.S. dollars)

Y-axis: 80, 100, 120, 140, 160, 180
X-axis: 1992, 1993, 1994, 1995, 1996

Source: Dow Jones Global Indexes

most of Canada speaks the same language we do. Even the Quebecois are not as snooty about speaking français as the French.

But for U.S. investors our neighbor to the north is, to put it politely, boring. Consider that only two U.S.-based mutual funds specialize in Canada. Canadian investing is all about natural resources with a veneer of finance thrown over it. Both natural resources and finance are cyclical industries. And guess whose cycle they tend to follow? As much as Canada likes to assert its independence, the fact is that Canada's market is closely tied to the ups and downs of the U.S. economic and market cycles. One need realize only that 75% of Canada's exports go directly across the border to the United States. The chart comparing the U.S. stock market to the Canadian market tells the story. As a potential foreign investment haven, Canada has one big strike against it at the outset.

There's another strike, too, in the form of political risk. Canada's parliamentary government is modeled on the British system and has operated smoothly for decades. But all during that period the feud between the English-speaking and the French-speaking parts of the country has been simmering, occasionally threatening to break out into an open split between Quebec and the rest of Canada. The last vote on independence for Quebec failed, but it was close enough to suggest that the next one might pass. What the effect of such a split would be depends very much on the form it would take; complete and real independence for Quebec seems unlikely, but something looser than the current links between the two factions seems almost certain. In any event, it is the uncertainty created by this dispute—combined with the close correlation of the U.S. and Canadian markets—that makes Canada an unappealing choice for substantial foreign investments.

Canada also poses a currency risk to U.S. investors. Many economists contend that Canadians have lived too high on the hog for too long. (However, it's nice to hear that criticism applied to somebody other than the United States for a change. Thanks, Canada!) The country's "current account"—the total of its trade in goods and services plus financial flows—is among the worst in the world, while Canada's debt measured against its gross domestic product ranks as one of the highest. Part of the problem has been Canada's uncommonly generous social welfare programs, which, because the government won't tax sufficiently to pay those bills, has resulted in high budget deficits. The government is working on those problems, and by 1997 was showing some remarkable progress in shrinking the budget deficit, largely through tight controls on spending. Meanwhile, the Bank of Canada is gaining respect among international investors for its tough stand on inflation control. The upside of Canada's currency situation is its reliance on natural resources; most of the production of Canada's resources companies is sold in U.S. dollars, while the costs of producing are in much cheaper Canadian dollars. And, of course, if the Canadian dollar rises against the U.S. dollar, U.S.-based holders of Canadian stocks will profit.

But even Canada's huge natural resource base doesn't make it especially attractive to investors. If you're looking for a natural resource play, try Australia. Commodities make up 57% of Australia's exports compared with 34% for Canada. And Australia's export base, focused as it is on the entire Asian continent, is much broader than Canada's U.S.-oriented export base.

It Isn't All Bad

Yet for all Canada's problems, a U.S.-based investor shouldn't completely ignore it. After all, Canada's market capitalization is about 2.5% of the total world capitalization, so a small investment in Canada wouldn't be out of line. One reason for considering Canada as an investment location is the ease with which U.S. investors can do the homework and make the investments on their own. There are some 140 Canadian companies listed both on the Toronto Stock Exchange and U.S. exchanges. In fact, eight Canadian companies are part of the Standard & Poor's 500-stock index. The largest, such as Alcan Aluminium, Noranda, Inco, and Seagram, are well covered by *The Wall Street Journal* and other U.S. financial publications.

Canada might also appeal to the market timers among international investors. First, Canada's economy and markets tend to lag the U.S. cycle to a slight degree. In 1997, for example, as the U.S. growth rate decelerated slightly, the Canadian economy stepped up to a vigorous 4% annualized growth rate. More important, the expansion was fueled by more than exports to the U.S.; thanks to short-term interest rates falling to their lowest levels in 35 years, spending by domestic businesses and consumers became a major contributor to growth. Since more of Canada's overall gross domestic product and more of its stock market capitalization is tied to cyclical industries, the breadth of cyclical moves tends to be larger than it is in the United States. That means Canada tends to do worse than the United States in an economic downturn but better in an upturn. The savvy investor who has the time and inclination to track such things, and the nerve to make the play, can time Canadian investments to catch the beginning of an upturn that may carry him or her beyond a similar move in the U.S. markets. We aren't enthusiastic about such speculative investing techniques, but some people have the discipline—and the time—to use them effectively.

Beware of Vancouver

Judging by news reports, the full name of the Vancouver Stock Exchange should be Scandal-Plagued Vancouver Stock Exchange. Billing itself as an exchange for entrepreneurs and emerging companies, the Vancouver Exchange has a long and sordid history of scam and artifice that should keep all but the most gullible, get-rich-quick investors far away. While at this writing the British Columbia government is considering changes in regulation of the Vancouver Exchange, we aren't hopeful that the sweeping changes necessary to fix all that ails the exchange will be enacted; certainly the people who run it now are working hard to undermine any chance that the exchange will instill anything resembling the transparency and investor protections that any modern stock exchange should have.

Stocks to Watch

The most-liquid, most-followed stocks in Canada tend to be the big natural resource companies. Inco supplies 25% of the world's nickel. Noranda produces copper, oil, and gas and has forestry operations. Imperial Oil Company is Canada's largest oil and gas concern. American Barrack Resources owns the largest gold reserves in North America, and Placer Dome owns precious metals mines not only in North America but also in Australia, Chile, and Papua New Guinea. Cameco Corporation is one of the world's largest producers of uranium. Among processors that turn Canadian raw materials into semifinished products are Alcan Aluminium, one of the world's largest aluminum producers; Stelco, a steel producer; and Abitibi-Price, a major producer of pulp and paper products.

Canada's financial sector is much more concentrated than the U.S. financial industry, with six major banks dominating the scene: Canadian Imperial, Toronto-Dominion, Bank of Nova Scotia, Bank of Montreal, National Bank of Canada, and Royal Bank of Canada.

Other major companies give a bit more diversified flavor to this picture of Canada as a vast mining pit surrounded by a few big banks. Bombardier is an interesting amalgam of defense, transportation, and recreational equipment. Besides subway cars and amphibious aircraft, it produces popular lines of snowmobiles and jet skis. Molson Companies owns half of Molson Breweries, the source of some fine Canadian beers and (we hope there's no connection here) it also has a big interest in cleaners and disinfectants for water systems. You no doubt also are familiar with the Seagram label on such tasty products as Mumm Champagne, Chivas Regal Scotch, and Tropicana fruit juices. And you probably have used some of Moore Corporation's business forms and adhesive labels at home or in your office. Northern Telecom produces digital telecommunications systems, including the world's largest international switch, used by British Telecom's Automatic Call Distribution Network.

Mexico, the Exotic Neighbor

Mexico is everything to the U.S. investor that Canada is not. As one of the premier emerging markets, it has huge potential for growth. Its economic and market cycles have only the loosest relationship to the U.S. market cycle. Indeed, the volatility of Mexico's market moves can be frightening to the uninitiated investor. Unfortunately, the meltdown that hit Mexico late in 1994 when the peso was devalued doubtless is responsible for hundreds of thousands of American investors congratulating themselves on staying away from international investing. And it probably drove thousands more investors who had ventured abroad back to the seeming shelter of the U.S. market. But there are sound reasons to think that in the long run Mexico should be part of any investor's portfolio.

For our purposes, the investment history of Mexico begins with the election in 1982 of Miguel de la Madrid Hurtado to the presidency. Unlike his predecessors, who were professional politicians, President de la Madrid brought to the office a background as a professional administrator. Together he and his budget minister, Carlos Salinas de Gortari (who succeeded him as president in 1988), brought about much-needed economic reforms. Among the problems they had to solve were huge defaulted debts, high unemployment, rampant inflation, and a deep-seated protectionism. The de la Madrid administration opened the doors to increased trade, allowed foreign companies to own their Mexican subsidiaries outright, and began privatizing a large part of Mexico's government-owned industries.

President Salinas continued and expanded on those policy initiatives in the late 1980s and early 1990s. He also engineered a policy that tied the peso closely to the dollar, fixing its value in a band that would allow very gradual depreciation but that was sufficient to reassure foreign investors that there was little likelihood of a major devaluation. When he left office in 1994, Mexico was verging on recovery from an economic slowdown, the inflation rate was in single digits, public debt was modest, and a program of privatizing Mexico's state-owned companies was well entrenched.

But as with any strict economic regimen, there were unintended side effects. To a large extent the economic policies fostered by the de la Madrid and Salinas administrations were welcomed by investors but

Mexico vs. U.S.
Dec. 31, 1991=100

Legend:
— U.S.
— Mexico (In U.S. dollars)
— Mexico (Local currency)

Source: Dow Jones Global Indexes

resented by Mexico's poor. And given that nearly half of Mexico's 90 million people live in poverty, that resentment could not be ignored. The Chiapas revolt in southern Mexico early in 1994 sent the first warning signal to many foreigners that problems were developing under the successful veneer of Mexico's economic experiment.

Ironically, though, it was Mexico's costly industrialization—which eventually will generate jobs for some of the poor—and the country's peso-stabilization policy, so reassuring to foreign investors, that finally laid bare the weak foundation of the Mexican miracle. Early in 1994 both the Salinas government and the U.S. government were well aware that Mexico was headed toward some kind of crisis. Yet both governments put on a false front, reassuring Mexicans and foreign investors alike that the outlook for economic growth was bright. Only after Mr. Salinas left office, succeeded by Ernesto Zedillo Ponce de León, did the mounting problems spin out of control. Within a few weeks of taking office, the Zedillo administration attempted a modest devaluation of the peso. But even that cautious step was enough to trigger a massive flight from the suddenly shaky currency, leaving the government no choice but to cut the peso loose from the dollar. While the Mexican market ended 1994 with a 12% loss, in local currency terms, the peso's plunge handed American investors in Mexico a stunning 42.5% loss for the year, the worst of any foreign market. Perhaps worse, the

Mexican meltdown left many U.S. investors suddenly acutely aware of the risks of foreign markets, particularly emerging markets, and forgetful of the long-term rewards.

What Now?

There is nothing worse for a country than to lose the confidence of investors, whether the investors are the country's own citizens or foreigners. Regretfully, that is precisely what the Mexican government did at the end of 1994. The country now must regain that confidence, and it won't be easy.

The social problems afflicting Mexico are severe, and the lack of a stable currency will make it difficult for the government to make much headway against the country's economic problems. But, as a result of the Chiapas rebellion and other events of 1994, the problems are well known now. Foreign investors will be watching the government's approach to the social problems carefully for that fine balance between wasteful government spending and intelligent programs that create jobs and provide rising living standards for the broad base of Mexico's population.

President Zedillo's strategy of inflicting short-term pain for long-term gains has brought interest rates and inflation down, and Mexican stocks have regained some of the ground lost earlier. In June 1997, President Zedillo presented an ambitious three-year economic program in an attempt to assure Mexicans that the economic pain they have endured for the past two years will pay off in stronger, sustainable growth. The cornerstone of the three-year plan is a rise in private savings to 17.7% of gross domestic product in the year 2000 from 16.1%, which will in turn fuel an upsurge in investment and reduce the country's reliance on foreign capital. Mexico is hoping to accomplish this partly by privatizing its pension system. The result, according to the plan, was to be robust growth of 4.5% in 1997, 4.8% in 1998; and 5.2% and 5.6% in 1999 and 2000, respectively. Mexico's GDP rose 5.1% in 1996, after falling 6.2% in 1995 following the peso devaluation.

The speech was important for President Zedillo because some members of his own party have begun to doubt the effectiveness of free-market policies that have included the sale of more than $20 billion in state enterprises, and opened large sections of the economy to foreign competition. President Zedillo's team has basically re-invented Mexico's economic model with a focus on export-led growth, higher savings rates, and careful management of finances. The model has resulted in robust growth in certain export industries, but the domestic economy and the salaries of people who work in it have taken much longer to recover.

With political pressure growing for Mr. Zedillo to ease off of his tough economic tactics, there are questions about the Mexican government's resolve to carry through with long-term reforms. Mexican politics are likely to become even more fractious in the years ahead as the ruling party loses its stranglehold on the electorate. That could create more market volatility. Just how the turmoil in Mexico will affect the workings of the North American Free Trade Agreement remains uncertain. But over the long run the reduction of trade barriers is bound to be good for the Mexican economy.

Mexican Stock Selection

If you have only one Mexican stock in your portfolio, make it Telefonos de Mexico. This nationwide utility is widely viewed as a proxy for the entire Mexican market. As goes Telefonos, so goes the Bolsa. In the market rout that followed the devaluation of the peso late in 1994, Telefonos's ADRs lost a total of about $40 a share, only about 15% of which was the stock's price. The rest was the loss caused by the peso's plunge. To give you an idea of what kind of long-term growth Telefonos has the potential to enjoy, consider that in 1993 Mexico had 8.7 telephone lines per 100 inhabitants, a stunning 32% increase from 1992, but far from the level of most fully industrialized nations. Competition will increase in coming years as deregulation takes hold, but Telefonos is strong enough to withstand that. Grupo Carso, a holding company with interests in a variety of industries, holds a controlling interest in Telefonos.

Although they would fare poorly in an economic downturn, infrastructure companies should benefit over the long haul as Mexico industrializes. Cemex is Mexico's largest and the world's fourth-largest cement maker. Its operations extend outside of Mexico to encompass the Caribbean, and its customers tend to be developing countries that will be investing sizable amounts in infrastructure in coming years. In the aftermath of the 1994 peso devaluation, Cemex's ADRs lost more than 50% of their value, reflecting not only the plunge in the stock's price and the devaluation of the peso but also the fact that Cemex had huge debts denominated in dollars.

Another cement play is Apasco, Mexico's second-largest cement maker. Empresas ICA-Soc. Controladora is a diversified concern with interests in heavy, urban, and industrial construction, including highway construction. Grupo Sidek, another holding company, has an interest in steel and aluminum processing plants, while also managing hotels, marinas, and shopping centers. Vitro makes glass containers, automotive and architectural glass, and glass kitchenware.

Consumer stocks are represented by such companies as Cifra, Mexico's largest retailer; Controladora Comercial Mexicana, which operates a large network of clothing and general merchandise stores; Grupo Embotellador de Mexico, which produces and markets bottled soft drinks (it is the world's largest independent bottler of Pepsi products outside the United States) and makes bottles, caps, and packaging; Fomento Economico Mexicano, a producer of soft drinks and beer; Grupo Gigante, an operator of stores, restaurants, and real estate; Grupo Industrial Maseca, Mexico's largest corn-flour producer; and Grupo Televisa, the world's largest producer and broadcaster and Spanish-language television, which holds 90% of Mexico's television audience.

A sharp drop in the value of a nation's currency tends to bolster the fortunes of the country's exporters. Tubos de Acero de Mexico, Internacional de Ceramica, and Transportacion Maritima Mexicana all posted sharp gains in their ADR prices after the peso devaluation. Tubos de Acero produces seamless steel pipe used in the oil industry and exports about 65% of its total sales. Internacional de Ceramica is one of the world's largest producers of ceramic tile and runs plants and retailing outlets in the United States. Transportacion Maritima Mexicana ships most of Mexico's international trade and receives virtually all of its revenues in U.S. dollars.

CHAPTER X

Europe's Big Three

AMERICANS remain largely Euro-oriented, you should pardon the word play. They are much less that way than they used to be, certainly, but still significantly so. U.S. investors first thinking of diversifying internationally will tend to place Europe among their top three choices. There are plenty of reasons for this, including ethnic and ancestral ties, cultural similarities, and more. But in investing, the familiar is not necessarily your friend, and the well-trod path seldom surprises.

This tour includes visits to Europe's three largest markets, the United Kingdom, Germany, and France. Though they often move in sympathy with each other, these markets are as different as the three languages. For the U.S. investor, they represent a step or two toward international diversification, but by no means do they, in themselves, constitute the final destination.

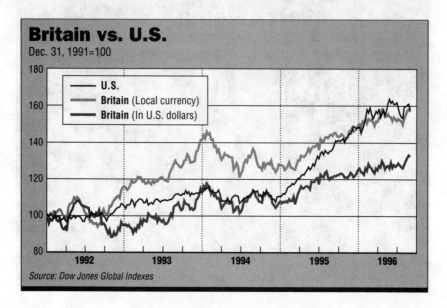

Britain vs. U.S.
Dec. 31, 1991=100

Legend:
- U.S.
- Britain (Local currency)
- Britain (In U.S. dollars)

Source: Dow Jones Global Indexes

UNITED KINGDOM

The London Stock Exchange is home to the third-largest stock market in the world, based on capitalization, following New York and Tokyo. It is bigger than Britain itself. The total market value of stocks listed on the exchange was, in mid-1996, nearly 40% more than the British gross domestic product. That's possible because many large British companies are thoroughly multinational, with much if not most of their revenues and earnings coming from outside the United Kingdom. This worldliness began more than three centuries ago, when English kings and queens granted companies exclusive rights to trade in various parts of the world in exchange for money to fight wars.

Though third in size globally, London is more than twice as large as any other European stock market, and it is first in trading foreign stocks. Thanks to the market's liquidity, and to its convenience for English-speaking money managers the world over, more foreign stocks change hands in London than in any other single market on the globe. Indeed, on some days the activity of, say, certain Belgian or French stocks is greater in London than in their home markets. In 1993, trading of foreign stocks on the exchange accounted for more than half of the total volume. The exchange's involvement with foreign companies goes back more than two centuries. Its strategy of focusing on world trade and of helping to finance foreign companies was to increase demand for British goods. It succeeded very well, but at the expense of the home team; even today, some British entrepreneurs complain the exchange seems to prefer helping foreign companies rather than them.

The London Stock Exchange is one of the oldest in the world, with roots reaching back to the 1600s. Trading began in 1773 in the exchange building on Threadneedle Street, in the heart of London's financial district, a one-square-mile area by the Thames River known as the City. Today, only administrative staff work there. London doesn't have a trading floor anymore. All trades are handled electronically over the Stock Exchange Automated Quotation System, or SEAQ (SEE-ak) for short; SEAQ International handles the foreign stocks.

For our purposes, the London market dates to October 27, 1986, when the "Big Bang" of deregulation exploded. Among many other things, fixed commissions were dropped in favor of negotiated and competitive ones, and foreign entities were permitted to buy British brokerage firms. The takeover spree was breathtaking, but many firms went out of business just a year or so later, following the stock market crash that began in New York and quickly spread around the world.

The Privatization Push

Big Bang did not occur out of self-enlightenment. Margaret Thatcher, then the prime minister, prodded the exchange and the investment community into action by repeatedly threatening to bring antitrust charges. Beginning in 1979, when Britain was considered the sick man of Europe, Mrs. Thatcher for 11 years led a Conservative government that slashed income taxes, sharply curtailed the power of labor unions, and privatized unprofitable, state-owned industries. She sparked an era of wholesale restructuring throughout the rest of the economy as well, which has become over the past decade increasingly vigorous with declining unemployment and decelerating inflation. Not the least of her achievements was selling off large, state-owned businesses to private investors—such as British Airways and British Telecommunications—which enabled these companies to metamorphose from bureaucratic fiefdoms into global competitors.

But having led the privatization bandwagon since the early 1980s, the British government is running out of things to sell. When it finally does, the British market will lose some of the exciting allure it has held these past 14 years for foreign investors. Plans to privatize the post office were hurriedly shelved in late 1994 after a storm of public protest. Privatization of the nuclear industry has proven to be deeply unpopular. The biggest privatization project still in the works is the railway system, so long known for inefficiency and poor service that British Rail jokes are as common on the U.K. comedy circuit as gags about mothers-in-law. Let's take a brief look at the process of privatizing the railways, both to illustrate how privatization works and to introduce you to an element of uncertainty that hasn't been present in the United Kingdom for a long time.

In mid-1996, the government sold stock in Railtrack, the £2 billion ($3.02 billion) company that owns the tracks, signals, and stations of the country's train network, as part of a larger rail privatization process that started back in 1993 to inject private capital into Britain's railways. The network was sold off piecemeal, and it was designed to run as an internal market: Railtrack leases use of the track to the train operators. They in turn lease their rolling stock from separate leasing companies. All three contract out services such as maintenance, catering, and security to other companies, with the notion that the demands of each different unit will ensure that the others provide a decent and efficient service. Though the jury is still out on whether privatization has improved the rail system—a bad accident in September 1997 renewed the debate—most lines are reporting an increase in passengers and fewer delays. Not all of the rail system was privatized, by the way; political concerns make it essential that trains continue to run in sparsely populated areas that can't justify the cost of service.

The British have enough privatization experience to do these deals right. The Railtrack stock was offered to individual investors at a cheaper price than was required of institutional investors. Individuals had to buy at least 200 shares, but if they registered with any of the official "share shops"—registered brokers, some banks, and building societies—there were extra benefits. Investors could choose between getting a further discount on their first 800 shares or getting one extra share for every 15 bought, up to a maximum of 80 bonus shares. Moreover, the government set aside £69 million for dividend payments for the first year. Railtrack is expected to behave and be treated very much like the other U.K. utilities, such as water and electricity concerns, that have been privatized. Those companies tend to boost earnings by cutting costs, which also spawns high stock market yields. Analysts estimate that newly privatized companies tend to be able to cut costs about 30% through efficiency savings, notably staff reductions. In 1995, one-quarter of the £2 billion in costs incurred by Railtrack was spent on administration and staffing.

But now political risk is rising on the British economic and business scene for the first time in nearly two decades. The Conservative Party of Mrs. Thatcher and of John Major, who succeeded her as prime minister, was toppled from power in May 1997 by the Labor Party in a landslide victory. So far, Labor hasn't veered sharply to the left in British politics or made sweeping changes in policies. Under leader Tony Blair, who was 43 years old when he became prime minister, Labor has moved away from its socialist roots, embracing the free market and promising to pursue a tight fiscal policy. In its first budget, the new Labor government avoided imposing major tax increases on individuals, and it even surprised business by modestly reducing taxes on company profits. Although the budget included a widely expected "windfall profits" tax on utilities and other privatized companies, and some minor tax increases for individuals, it reassured many who feared the party might return to its old tax-and-spend ways. The budget was the first real test of Mr. Blair's determination to stick to his moderate, probusiness policies. Perhaps the best news for business was that the tax on corporation profits would be cut to 31% from 33%, giving Britain one of the lowest rates in any major industrial country.

Market Problems

The combination of Big Bang and easy-to-use computerized stock trading briefly elevated London to the pinnacle of world exchanges in the late 1980s. We remember the chairman of the London Stock Exchange making a grand tour of New York and Washington, where his advice and counsel were solemnly solicited and respectfully noted. This was about the same time that Japan temporarily eclipsed the United States as the nation with the stock market of highest value. But nothing lasts forever. Before long, other countries were big-banging their own markets into more hospitable treatment of investors and installing even better computerized trading systems. Now there is a major push by home-market exchanges to win back the trading of their own stocks from London. In 1994, for example, market makers of Australian shares pulled out of SEAQ, although some Australian stocks are still traded in London. The home markets are making some headway, but money manager inertia still works in London's favor.

That may change, too, unless London polices itself effectively. Early in 1995, a two-centuries-old banking and securities firm, Barings, collapsed after a young trader in its Singapore office lost more than $1 billion playing futures and options on Japanese stocks. The Bank of England decided not to bail out the foundering firm, which subsequently was sold for £1 to a Dutch concern that agreed to pick up Barings' liabilities. The event stung British pride and unleashed a barrage of calls for reexamination of the Big Bang regulatory legacy. "Minimal regulation in London is not a source of competitive strength if it generates such doubts about the integrity of the City that British-based financial institutions are seen as unreliable business partners," fumed a columnist for *The Guardian*.

Regulators are considering a variety of changes that would both increase surveillance and loosen brokers' grips on fees and charges for services. The exchange is working on a new computer-trading system that redresses the balance away from market-making dealers and toward investors. In June 1995 it opened a new market for small, young companies. And it remains quick to cater to the enthusiasms of the international investing crowd, which is a sizable and vocal part of the exchange membership; in 1994, SEAQ International created sectors for Mexican and Indian stocks.

A Global View

Interestingly, the London market is sometimes too sensitive to international developments for the good of its British listings. In 1994 and 1995, for example, Britain's economy was growing strongly, producing steadily rising profits—and the likely prospect of more to come—with very little inflation. But the market fell nearly 10% in 1994 and was very sluggish in the first part of 1995. Why? It was reacting to rising interest rates in the United States; investors feared that the chill of higher U.S. rates might bring on economic pneumonia in Europe. Even after U.S. stocks began rallying in late 1994 and early 1995, British stocks were slow to shake off the wet blanket.

So, here is Lesson No. 1: The London market doesn't always reward superior performance of British companies to the extent it should. Its preoccupation with a global viewpoint seems to be at least one of the reasons.

Lesson No. 2 is that British stocks don't offer the best diversification for a U.S. investor. Though a common language separates the two countries, and notwithstanding a rising European consciousness, the British economy and the British currency are inexorably linked to those of the United States, its former colony. This relationship isn't as tight as the one between the United States and Canada, but it's close enough to take into consideration when planning your international portfolio. The saving diversification grace is that historically, according to economists, the British economy lags the United States by about 12 to 18 months. But that timetable was accelerated in the most recent market cycle. The British economic cycle started in early 1992 and got really rolling in 1993—about the same as the United States. Although the United Kingdom derived much of its growth from exporting goods to the Continent, the U.K. economic cycle of the past four years has correlated more with the United States than with the rest of Europe. While the United Kingdom hasn't had as much growth as the United States, it was more than Europe managed. British gross domestic product grew 2.5% in 1995 and was estimated to expand 2.3% in 1996. By contrast, the British economy contracted an average 0.1% annually in the three years through 1993.

One reason for Britain's economic empathy with the United States is that each country is a major trading partner of the other. It's not just importing and exporting stuff, either. Companies in both countries have made major direct investments in each other. For instance, a British holding company called Bardon derives more than 40% of its revenue from crushed rock, gravel, and similar materials from two U.S. subsidiaries. Grand Metropolitan acquired Pillsbury several years ago, and with it came Häagen-Dazs ice cream, Burger King restaurants, and Green Giant vegetables. Hanson, a diversified industrial company, generates 50% of its sales in the United States versus 44% in the United Kingdom. Buying stock in such companies may be warranted for any number of reasons, but international diversification of your portfolio isn't high on the list. A U.S. investor could accomplish about the same kind of secondhand international diversification with shares of Caterpillar, Coca-Cola, or McDonald's—without any currency risk.

It is true that many British companies offer investors some exposure to other parts of the world that aren't so easy to buy into directly. B. A. T Industries, for example, sells a lot of cigarettes in places other than the United States and the United Kingdom; one of its brands has a 45% share of the Hungarian market. Blue Circle Industries makes cement in Africa. Barclays operates retail banks in Africa and the Caribbean. BICC's wholly owned subsidiary, Balfour Beatty, builds roads, bridges, and such in 45 countries, generating nearly half the parent company's total revenue. Lonrho, a mining concern with interests in several very different industries, runs the largest motor vehicle distributor in Africa and also is Africa's largest commercial food producer. Sun Alliance, a full-line insurance company, has operations in the Middle East, as well as in other parts of the world. In most such cases, though, the companies are so big that the business done in exotic locales constitutes relatively little of the whole.

Some well-known companies are only half British. Shell Transport & Trading operates through its joint venture with Royal Dutch Petroleum of the Netherlands; together they are known as Royal Dutch/Shell Group. Reed International merged its operating businesses—information services, newspapers, books, and magazines—with Elsevier, a Dutch company; jointly, they are Reed Elsevier. Unilever, the big household-products concern, is also half British and half Dutch. Eurotunnel, which is struggling to make a business out of hauling cars and people under the English Channel between England and France, is half British and half French. HSBC Holdings is the result of a 1992 merger of Hong Kong and British banking companies. These stocks trade both in London and in the other "home" markets, Amsterdam, Paris, or Hong Kong. It doesn't matter from an operations standpoint which stock you buy, but as always with different markets, there are sometimes different prices. These discrepancies are fleeting—traders known as arbitrageurs move quickly to take advantage of them, buying in the cheaper market and selling in the more expensive, which brings the prices back into equilibrium—and won't save you or cost you much unless you are dealing in an enormous number of shares.

Because of the close links to the United States, most of the British stocks that U.S. investors are interested in are available as American depositary receipts. There are, in fact, more ADRs from the United Kingdom than from any other country. Among the favorites are Glaxo Holdings (pharmaceuticals), British Petroleum, Hanson, and BT (British Telecommunications). If you are going the ADR route in your portfolio, be careful not to overdose on British stocks. It's easy to do, partly because you may have heard of many of these companies and partly because they are readily available.

Germany vs. U.S.
Dec. 31, 1991=100

— U.S.
— Germany (In U.S. dollars)
— Germany (Local currency)

Source: Dow Jones Global Indexes

GERMANY

Here's a trivia question for you: How many stock exchanges does Germany have? Answer: Eight. Try another one: In which European country are investors extremely wary of stocks and favor bonds instead? Answer: Germany. There you have it, folks. In the nation many have dubbed the economic engine of Europe, ordinary investors dabble only a little in stocks but they do it on an excess of exchanges. Well, mainly they do it in Frankfurt, which has nearly three-fourths of all the trading in the country; Dusseldorf is a distant second with about 10%.

The point, nonetheless, is that Germans aren't much help in boosting German stocks. Pity, because among the reasons to venture abroad is to profit from local investor enthusiasm. In the case of Germany, foreign investors have been taking up the slack; a third to a half of German equity trading comes from London, New York, Tokyo, or elsewhere. But foreign capital is fickle, and it is controlled by people who, not being Germans, are apt to have non-German considerations more in mind when they make investment decisions. That helps explain why the German market sank 5% in 1994 while its economy grew 2.8%; it was the same obsession with interest rates that affected the U.S. and British markets.

Germany and its stock market are at a crossroads as we write this, which makes investing there somewhat riskier than it used to be, but much more interesting. In terms of investment opportunity, some view the glass as half full, others insist it is half empty.

Take, for example, the matter of rebuilding what before 1989 was East Germany. The glass-half-full perspective is that this effort will provide jobs for many Germans and years of profitable business for many companies. The half-empty crowd thinks it will hurt the economy by fostering inflation and raising either taxes or government deficits, or both. Half-full likes the rampant restructuring of German corporations because it will help these companies compete in export markets, even with a strong currency, the deutsche mark. Half-empty says restructuring means moving production jobs to cheaper locations outside of Germany and ballooning the unemployment rolls at home so much that mass emigration may be the only solution to an increasingly burdensome welfare problem.

The facts at this stage don't obviously support either thesis. Consumers are reacting to the higher taxes they are paying to help finance the reunification of western and eastern Germany by spending less on consumer goods. Consumers have had to dip into savings, which is as traumatic for thrifty Germans as it would be for Americans to swear off credit cards. The retail recession, which dragged on for three years into 1996, should have brought Europe's largest economy to its knees, because consumers account for 55% of economic activity. But the German economy is growing instead, thanks to soaring exports and massive investment by government and business.

However, the unemployment rate stands at 11.2%, despite the recovery, and more Germans are out of work than at any time since World War II. Layoffs in eastern Germany are part of the unemployment problem. More than one million people have fled the former East Germany since the border opened in 1989. That works out to one of every 16 East Germans. Indeed, more people have left eastern Germany in the seven years since reunification than in the seven years prior to the construction of the Berlin Wall in 1961, when the Communist government put it up to stem the outflow of people. The migration is not only turning some eastern cities into ghost towns, but also is putting pressure on western Germany's housing stock, bringing down western wages for low-income jobs, and adding to overall tensions between the two halves of the country.

To us, this scene looks far more promising for investment than someplace where everything is coming up roses and everybody knows it. We acknowledge the risks, but we remind you that's where the rewards are. The German currency is strong as we write this, but something will come along to knock it down—a bit higher inflation than was forecast, perhaps, or more government red ink than had been promised. A less robust mark will help Germany keep its important export markets without shrinking corporate profit margins. More important, we are bullish on Germany because of the Germans. These people built a war-flattened nation into an economic powerhouse (as did the Japanese). This country's central bank, the Bundesbank, has so much prudence that it hurts. Right on Germany's doorstep is a new frontier of former Communist countries that dearly need its assistance well into the 21st century. There are and will be problems, but we think Germany has the right stuff to deal with them.

Banks and Accounting

Lest you think we have turned starry-eyed, we hasten to point out some unflattering facts about investing in Germany that you ought to be aware of. We will start with another condition Germany shares with Japan: the substantial stakes that the big banks hold in many companies, including the biggest and most prestigious. Deutsche Bank, whose $370 billion in assets make it the biggest bank in Europe not owned by a government, owns about one-fourth of automaker Daimler-Benz, for example. This arrangement makes the banks both major creditors and shareholders of the same companies; in some cases, bank officers serve on companies' boards and even as chairmen. Cozy, huh? What's more, under German law, a company's creditors—mainly the banks— have priority over everybody else, including shareholders.

This situation will be changed in the years ahead, but it will be slow and, for some, painful. Germany needs huge new infusions of capital, and investors want to see what happens to their money after they inject it. That will mean prying open the clubby ties between corporate Germany and its financial institutions to the sunshine of public scrutiny. The process is under way; Deutsche Bank announced in mid-1996 that it planned to reduce its holdings in Daimler-Benz and other companies, but it wasn't specific about how much of its stakes it would sell and when it might do so. There will be far more kicking and screaming, but stay aware of the headway this opening-up process makes, because it's important: A German business professor says the performance of bank-controlled companies is far worse than of those without heavy bank influence.

Somewhat faster progress is being made on another front—accounting. The German variety is opaque. You can't tell by looking at the published statements what shape a company is in. That's why it's always a surprise when one of them does a belly flop. But now, because they need to woo international investors, several leading German corporations are adopting international accounting standards that will reveal far more about their financial performance. This shift away from inscrutable accounting amounts to a minor cultural revolution in Germany, where the concept of shareholder value was all but unknown until recently. Though some big German corporations hope the accounting change will help them get full listings on the New York Stock Exchange, the international standards they are adopting don't pass muster with the U.S. Securities and Exchange Commission. International accounting standards were devised by a London-based committee of leading accountants beginning in 1987 in an attempt to bring consistency to rules that change from country to country. The standards are far more forthcoming about corporate performance than the German rules, because they lay open such issues as the size of reserves and pension-fund commitments and require companies to give detailed breakdowns by major business sector. They fall short of U.S. standards, however, by allowing looser treatment of goodwill and leaving open such issues as how to account for oil and gas reserves.

As we write, Daimler-Benz AG is the only German company that has overcome the obstacles to a New York listing. But two more were scheduled to follow. Veba AG and Hoechst AG were to be listed on the New York Stock Exchange in October 1997. Veba, with $44 billion in sales, is the world's largest utility-based conglomerate. It is best known as an electric utility but is also active in chemicals, logistics, oil, real estate, and telecommunications. Hoechst is the world's largest chemical company, with a sizable pharmaceutical business to boot.

Daimler-Benz solved its U.S. listing requirements by issuing two separate sets of accounts, one German-style and the other U.S.-style. Cumbersome but worthwhile, from the company's viewpoint. About 8% of Daimler stockholders are now in the United States, double the number before the listing in 1993, and the company hopes that proportion will increase to as much as 20% in the future. Among those adopting—or those who are expected to adopt—international accounting standards are the pharmaceuticals company Schering, and two chemicals companies, Bayer and BASF. Others introducing more information into their balance sheets include Germany's largest diversified technology concern, Siemens, and several utilities in addition to Veba AG. These changes are being driven both by investors and by the companies themselves. U.S. fund managers in particular have been investing heavily in German stocks, demanding answers to the sort of sharp questions that their German counterparts never asked. Schering says about 52% of its stock is held by non-Germans; U.S. investors are at 10%, up from around 6% in 1991. U.S. holdings of BASF stock have jumped from less than 1% in 1988 to about 4% in early 1995. The companies themselves have major interests in lifting the veil of secrecy. As well as making it easier to tap the huge pool of international capital, most are at pains to become better known as they expand internationally. Bayer, for example, recently reacquired the rights to its trademark name in the United States after 70 years—it had been expropriated after World War I—and renamed all its U.S. operations. Some of the companies are moving to sell their stock to U.S. investors via American depositary receipts. By sponsoring ADRs, a U.S. bank or other institution takes on such responsibilities as shareholder communications.

Aversion to Equities

We will wind up our look at the warts of German investing back where we started this section, with the Germans' own uneasiness about equities, which they regard as too risky, and their preference for bonds, which pay a steady income and are backed by corporate assets. Taxes play a role, too, because marginal income-tax rates for individual investors range as high as 70%. Because of this situation, many such investors funnel their money into airplane leasing, shipping and other, often exotic, projects to take advantage of special tax treatment. The unfortunate result is that the stock market is terribly stunted, for an economy as big as Germany's, and it can't help direct capital to vigorous young companies.

Deutsche Bank research says direct investment in stocks by Germans plummeted from 24% of savings in 1960 to 11.3% in 1970 and 5.4% in 1993. Several consequences flow from this situation. One is that German corporate finance is tremendously debt heavy. The aver-

age debt-to-equity ratio is as high as 4 to 1, compared with about 1.3
to 1 in the United States. In the recession that ended in 1993, many
companies were pushed to the wall for lack of capital. Other downturns
are sure to come, so look for this condition as you consider German
stocks.

Another consequence is that German investors won't soak up their
fair share of the rising number of initial stock offerings. It is largely up
to foreign investors to take these offerings or leave them, and those that
are left will be a drag on the entire German market. The big lolla-
palooza offering was in November 1996, when the German government sold more than 600 million shares of Deutsche Telekom for 17.5
billion marks ($11.6 billion). The offering—the largest initial public of-
fering in Europe's history—went exceedingly well. An advertising blitz
persuaded 1.9 million Germans to buy shares, many for the first time
in their lives.

Should you buy into some of these offerings? We don't recommend
it. For one thing, the state-owned companies such as Deutsche
Telekom haven't proved themselves yet as independent concerns. We
suspect it will take them a while to get their sea legs, so our advice is
to follow them for a year or so before making a commitment. For another, many German companies come to market at unsustainably high
prices—which you don't necessarily recognize in advance as being too
high because of the uninformative accounting. The track record of the
few initial public offerings (IPOs) sold during the early 1990s has not
been inspiring. Of 46 small companies that sold IPOs in the early
1990s, fewer than one-third had stock prices in early 1995 that equaled
or surpassed their initial offering prices. By contrast, well over half the
IPOs in the U.S. market and on the London Stock Exchange were
above their offering prices at that same time. One that did well was
Plettac, a maker of construction scaffolding, which sold initially at 380
marks a share in June 1993 and 21 months later was trading at 790
marks, a 108% gain. Significantly, the company used most of the 60 million marks from its IPO to finance new acquisitions or open new foreign markets. In many other cases, proceeds from initial offerings
simply line the pockets of the companies' private shareholders.

Another reason new offerings often slump is that there isn't any
follow-through marketing to investors by the banks that bring these
stocks to market, as is common in both the United Kingdom and United
States. The equity culture is developing a foothold in Germany, but it
still awaits its time of flourishing.

FRANCE

It's a nice place to visit, but investing there requires some patience. France has always had a *vive-la-différence* tradition of going its own way on matters, and only now is it beginning to question the price of this prickly independence. Expect some bumpy years ahead in the French economy and stock market as the country struggles to come to terms with, first, the fiscal and monetary requirements for European Union and, second, the realities of global competition. Investors with payoff timetables in mind ought to invest cautiously in France, because there undoubtedly will be delays in the accommodation process. Those who are willing to sign on for the long haul will become practiced in that most applicable French gesture: a shrug, followed by a glass of wine.

Economic Problems

France enjoyed 30 glorious years after World War II of full employment and steady growth. Since 1980, however, the French economy has grown only 2.5% annually, the lowest of the top seven industrialized nations. There are many reasons, but one of them is the high degree of central government control over, or influence on, the economy. This authoritarian approach simply does not work efficiently anymore. Political authorities determine the distribution of more than half the national wealth; 55% of gross national product is in public spending. The labor market is too rigid, thanks to the unions' attempt to retain all the high-cost benefits they acquired in the boom years and the government's seeming inability to keep its nose out of labor negotiations. The result is structural unemployment syndrome; companies are reluctant to hire workers who can't be dismissed easily. France's overall unemployment rates, as we write in mid-1996, is roughly 12%.

The good news is that the technocrats who really make most of the important decisions in France are coming to realize they have no choice but to cut public-sector spending significantly. France must reduce its budget deficit drastically in 1997 to qualify for European economic and monetary union in 1999. France's overall deficit, which includes the red ink from the welfare system, can be no higher than 3% of gross domestic product, compared with 5% in 1995 and a hoped-for 4% in

1996. Thus, the government has little leeway in attempting both budget-deficit reduction and tax cuts.

The bad news is that such feats are impossible without the politically risky move of jettisoning some of the 1.7 million government jobs. The threatened, and highly unionized, government workers could repeat the strikes that paralyzed the nation in November and December of 1995. The government wants to avoid such confrontations, which ensures that change will be gradual and negotiated.

Conservative president Jacques Chirac, elected in 1995, was characteristically Gallic in stirring worldwide wrath by resuming nuclear testing in the Pacific. At home, his political strategy turned out to be equally explosive. Mr. Chirac dissolved the national assembly in April and held elections 10 months ahead of time, in June 1997, in the hopes of giving his Conservative government a free hand in carrying out economic reforms. He was bidding for a vote of confidence before inflicting unpopular spending cuts. Instead, the French electorate delivered a stunning victory to the Socialists, punishing Mr. Chirac for failing to deliver on his promises to cut France's record 12.8% unemployment. The result is that Mr. Chirac is forced to share power with Socialist leader Lionel Jospin, the very man he defeated in presidential elections barely two years earlier. The Socialists, contending that French growth is held back by insufficient demand, have pledged to revive the economy by creating 700,000 jobs for the young, half of them in the public sector, cut the workweek to 35 hours from 39 without lowering pay, and push for wage increases. But at the same time, they have pledged not to raise public spending and taxes.

Another reason France's deficit is so big is that it keeps having to bail out state-owned firms that get into trouble. One, in late winter 1995, was Credit Lyonnais, Europe's biggest bank and the world's largest non-Japanese bank. It had posted three successive years of large losses, culminating in a 1994 loss of 12 billion francs ($2.4 billion). The bank, which wiseacres began calling Debit Lyonnais or Crazy Lyonnais, was forced to turn to the state for its second bailout in a year. This time the government ordered the 132-year-old bank to spin off about $27 billion of poorly performing assets into a new company that is guaranteed by the state. Potential losses on these assets could total the equivalent of another $10 billion. To thwart criticism about unfair competition and to save French taxpayers from footing the final bill— although they certainly will be footing it in the meantime, to the tune of an estimated 100 billion francs ($17.5 billion)—Credit Lyonnais will have to reimburse the state for these losses by ceding a share of its profits for at least 5 years and possibly as long as 20 years. Also, the bank will shrink its $400-billion balance sheet by a further $20 billion over 5 years through job cuts and asset sales that will include most of its non-European retail-banking operations.

Credit Lyonnais got into this fix by too-rapid expansion and a seeming inability to say no to anybody who wanted to borrow money, no matter how cockamamie the purpose. During the boisterous 1980s, Credit Lyonnais's advertising slogan was: "The power to say yes," and the bank said *oui* to just about any acquisition or lending opportunity that came along. But Credit Lyonnais's problems weren't simply a matter of atrocious management. They also stemmed from an unhealthy relationship between France's top executives and government, plus an absence of controls. "The crisis at Credit Lyonnais," said a group of top civil servants and businesspeople in a report, quoted in *The Wall Street Journal*, is the crisis "of a closed-circuit power system, sure of itself to the point of excluding all possibility of error by one of its members and that found itself totally lost when the accumulation of errors became obvious."

If you are one of those "vulture" investors who likes to buy stocks when they are down for the count, you could take a flier on the recovery potential of Credit Lyonnais. That's because you can buy nonvoting investment certificates in the bank and in other French state-owned firms. There aren't many places in the world where government-owned companies rent investors a seat in the visitor's gallery; here's your chance.

Problems with Privatization

Actually, we like the way France privatizes companies. There is usually something in these offerings for investors, which isn't always the case. Take the big automaker Renault, for example, which was nationalized following World War II as punishment for its collaboration with occupying German forces. The government's first sale to investors was a 29% stake in November 1994, reducing its holding to 50%. (Banks, other major French companies, and Volvo AB of Sweden own the rest.) The government allocated portions of the stake to different kinds of investors so that big bucks wouldn't take it all. Institutional investors in France and overseas were eager, oversubscribing their allotted share 15.5 times. About 75,000 Renault employees bought shares, and the portion allotted to them was oversubscribed 1.5 times. The government also set aside a portion of Renault's capital for "core" shareholders, mainly industrial partners who agreed, among other things, to retain their stakes for a certain period of time and to buy at least a 1% stake.

The second sale, in July 1996, was a 6% stake to 12 institutional investors. The buyers were barred from selling the shares for four months, and after that had to offer them first to the "core" holders. The sale officially made Renault a private-investor controlled company.

With the rise of the Socialists to power, France's next big privatization push is open to question. Based on the leftist campaign promises, it was assumed for a couple of months that privatizations would come to a screeching halt. But in September 1997, the Socialist government let it be known that it was developing plans to sell off minority stakes in state-owned France Telecom SA and Air France. Apparently, Mr. Jospin was trying to show that he is a pragmatist who isn't tied down by dogma. Though the France Telecom sell-off would be smaller than the sale of up to 49% envisaged by the former conservative government, it marks an evolution by the Socialists toward a greater acceptance of market economics. At the same time, their unwillingness to cede more than a minority stake in Air France clearly underscores the limits of their conversion to economic realism, and the political constraints under which Mr. Jospin is operating. With his government dependent on the support of the Communist Party and the Green Party,

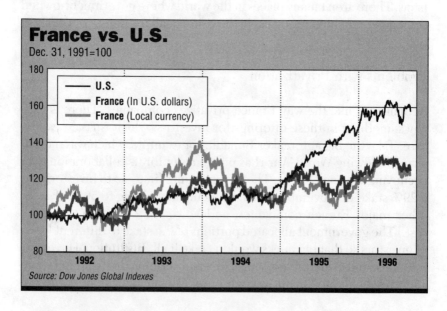

France vs. U.S.
Dec. 31, 1991=100

U.S.
France (In U.S. dollars)
France (Local currency)

Source: Dow Jones Global Indexes

Mr. Jospin was unwilling to open up a split in his coalition by picking a fight with his Communist transportation minister.

But this something-for-everybody approach was not without repercussions. The chairman of Air France, who was widely credited with salvaging the airline from financial ruin, resigned in protest of the government's decision not to follow through on the former conservative government's promise to privatize Air France fully. Meanwhile, three phone company unions started calling for strikes to stop partial privatization of France Telecom.

It is a labor dispute that already has played out elsewhere in Europe, as national phone companies have been moved into the private sector. The price to buy labor's consent has varied widely—from nil in Britain, where the government simply rammed through the 1984 privatization of British Telecommunications PLC, to plenty in Germany, where Deutsche Telekom AG's unions were granted lavish concessions to accept the company's stock market debut in the autumn of 1996. In each case, if the phone companies pay too high a price for labor peace—in wages, pension, and job-security provisions—they find their future profits sapped and their stock market value depressed.

Taking Stock

While France doesn't seem to us quite as promising as Germany is, its stock market is much more hospitable to investors. There is genuine enthusiasm for stocks. In June 1996, for instance, some 850,000 individual investors sought more than three times the number of shares in insurance company Assurances Generales de France than the government offered, so the quantity was raised to 18.7 million shares for individuals from 17 million, at 128 francs ($24.79) each.

In the private sector, initial public offerings were the rage in 1996, with investors seemingly unable to get enough shares. The *Nouveau Marche*, or New Market, is also attracting interest. It was created in March 1996 for small, growth-oriented companies, and it is intended to be a European version of the Nasdaq Stock Market in the United States. It also is France's answer to a similar move in London less than a year earlier.

There is reason for foreign investors, unfamiliar with France's corporate culture, to be cautious, however. For example, informal ties with the state and certain laws may affect company operations in ways American investors may not realize. Foreign investors tend to overlook the often arcane corporate statutes, or the influence of a family or the state on an otherwise widely held company.

Moreover, certain practices that are seen as normal in France are less than desirable for Americans. For instance, many French companies grant double-voting rights, which can strengthen a company's defenses against a hostile takeover by giving long-term shareholders a stronger voice than anyone who has recently acquired a stake. Critics of double-voting rights say they are unfair to recent shareholders, that they make a company's shares less liquid on the market, and that they help insulate management from any shareholder pressure for change. Despite these misgivings, France's largest corporations, including Rhone-Poulenc and Elf Aquitaine, show no signs of scrapping them.

Even so, you should be aware of some good French companies worthy of your investment consideration. L'Air Liquide makes industrial gases and has interests in welding, engineering, construction, and medical products. Half its sales come from Europe, making it a suitable cyclical play on the region, and it is expanding its operations in much of the world. Alcatel Alsthom is a big telecommunications equipment and transportation services company, which has had some tough times lately, including a misuse-of-funds scandal involving its chairman. But this outfit is plugged in around the world, and if you think telecommunications is going places, this company will be on the trip. Groupe Danone is a food and beverage maker that is buying up some nice brand names here and there around the world; Evian mineral water is one of its products. Havas is a diversified media and communications firm that is moving aggressively into the information-highway/multimedia milieu with acquisitions and joint ventures. L'Oréal is the world's largest producer of cosmetics, perfumes, and hair-care products, and it has a bevy of well-known brand names; more than two-thirds of its sales are in exports. LVMH Moët Hennessy Louis Vuitton makes booze and assorted luxury products, and oh! what brands: Moët & Chandon and Dom Perignon champagnes, Hennessy cognac, Givenchy perfume and cosmetics, and Louis Vuitton luggage. Rhône-Poulenc is a giant chemicals and pharmaceutical company that has had some setbacks lately but also has a long-term record of success.

There are more, but the point is made: Even if a country or its market isn't in peak condition, there usually are some meritorious stocks. If stock picking isn't your thing, go with a regional fund that is good at plucking nuggets; a country fund can do no better than the country.

CHAPTER XI

The Rising Sun's Encore

IF you wonder what the juggernaut Asian Tiger countries might look like when they reach middle age, gaze now upon Japan. For the modern Japanese economy—the second largest in the world, as is Japan's stock market—began rising 50 years ago like a phoenix out of the ashes of World War II. In the amount of time it took us to develop midriffs, the hardworking and self-denying Japanese created an economic marvel. Its businesses have taught the world's know-it-alls—including but not limited to the U.S. auto industry—valuable lessons about product quality, efficient manufacturing, and listening, really listening, to customers. After five decades of robust expansion, its economy is in such relatively good shape that the Japanese currency, the yen, was able to gain strength against the U.S. dollar even in periods of devastation, such as that caused by the earthquake in Kobe in early 1995. In its schools, the children actually learn, and they lead the world in aptitude and achievement tests. Its stock market soared 300% in the 20 years prior to its peak in 1989.

There was a price to be paid for this explosive growth, and for a long time the Japanese paid it willingly because a vigorous economy was the answer to so many of their country's postwar problems. Individuality was stifled in favor of the collective effort, which in the business world eventually came to mean little encouragement for entrepreneurialism. State control of the planned economy helped prevent growth from getting out of hand, but it wove so thick a web of red tape that both people and institutions came to find themselves hardly able to maneuver in response to changing conditions. Self-reliance enabled Japan to recreate itself largely on its own terms, only to discover with astonishment that many people now interpret this once-prized characteristic as being standoffish and arrogant.

Today, Japan is in something of a midlife crisis. Its people want to begin enjoying the quality of life that their labor should provide them, though they are not eager to relinquish the guarantee of lifetime employment that the government required of corporations as a tradeoff for a multitude of favors. Its corporations want to disentangle themselves from inflexible workforces and from the clinging clusters of cross-ownership that were mutually supportive in the past, but which in the 1990s do not measure up as worthwhile uses of capital. Its central planners want to get a new economic model up and running be-

Japan vs. U.S.
Dec. 31, 1991=100

U.S.
Japan (In U.S. dollars)
Japan (Local currency)

Source: Dow Jones Global Indexes

fore the old one clanks and wheezes its last. These changes will not come easily. Indeed, coupled with concurrent social and cultural changes—such as elevating the status of women and allowing dissidents to fulminate freely—Japan can look forward to being afflicted with years of gut-wrenching upheaval. Let's look at a couple of situations, fairly current as we write this, to gauge how extensive and how fundamental are the changes facing Japan.

THE KOBE EARTHQUAKE

On January 17, 1995, an earthquake measuring 7.2 on the Richter scale struck the Japanese cities of Kobe and Osaka. More than 5,100 people were killed. The death toll was as high as it was, wrote Eamonn Fingleton, author of *Blindside: Why Japan Is Still on Track to Overtake the U.S. by the Year 2000* (Houghton Mifflin, 1995), because of policies adopted during the fast-growth years to restrict consumer demand in favor of building up Japan, Inc.:

> Tight controls on land development form an important part of Japan's industrial policy. And thanks in large measure to these controls (and specifically to a virtual total ban on high-rise apartment buildings outside a few city-center neighborhoods), countless Japanese citizens still live in traditional wooden houses that are egregiously vulnerable to earthquakes. When the ground shook on Jan. 17, the roofs of many such houses in Kobe caved in, trapping residents. Fire did the rest.
>
> The fate of these houses contrasted markedly with that of Kobe's few modern high-rise apartment buildings, which held up very well. So why, in a country famous for an acute shortage of land, does the Japanese government discourage the development of safe high-rise structures?
>
> The policy is often mistakenly attributed to bureaucratic gridlock or dysfunctional politics. But in fact there is nothing irrational or unintended here: The truth is that the high-rise restrictions are enforced by Japan's top economic bureaucrats as a way of limiting the amount of living space available to the Japanese people and thus of suppressing consumption. In economic terms, low consumption is another way of saying high savings, and high savings in turn go a

long way to explain Japan's persistent balance-of-payments surpluses.

The most obvious savings effect is that Japanese citizens have to
accumulate large down payments before they can take out mortgages.
They must tightly curtail their spending on luxuries in order to repay
these mortgages. Families who spend as much as half of their income
servicing mortgage debts have little discretionary spending power to
buy California wine or French cheese. Japan's cramped housing also
physically limits the potential market for American and European
furniture and appliances, which are usually too large for Japanese
homes.

The big winner from the government's land policy is corporate
Japan. Japan's major house-building companies are typically . . .
owned by the big banks, insurance companies and manufacturers.
These companies profit massively from a land market skewed in their
favor and their gains are applied in expanding Japan's industrial capacity.

The official response to the earthquake was either measured or woe-
fully inadequate, depending on one's enthusiasm for euphemism. "The
country that awed Wall Street could barely deliver one rice ball a day
to homeless quake victims freezing on the streets," wrote Yoichi Clark
Shimatsu, editor of the Tokyo-based *Japan Times Weekly*. "Perhaps a
thousand people or more died unnecessarily because of bureaucratic
footdragging." *The Far Eastern Economic Review* editorialized that it
took two days

for 13,000 troops from Japan's Self-Defense Forces to be deployed
to disaster areas as bureaucrats and politicians bickered over the
precise wording of the official request for assistance. American
doctors and nurses who rushed to Kobe to treat survivors were
stopped for several days because they didn't have Japanese medical licenses. A Swiss rescue team of dog handlers that might have
arrived within hours was delayed for days awaiting official permission. Even the Mob came out of the quake looking better than
the bureaucracy: The Kobe-based Yamaguchi-gumi gang won
praise for giving out food, water and other emergency supplies to
distressed residents.

The editorial concluded, ". . . we sense in the political aftershocks now rattling the nation a Japanese public moving to take back their country."

These commentaries are significant, even discounting the writers' politics. Ten to 15 years ago, Japan, Inc. was so celebrated for its stunning successes that the Japanese people themselves were caught up in the euphoria. Now, several hard knocks later, they are beginning to question some underpinnings of their postwar society. Japan is unlikely to spawn a radical, Cambodia-style revolution in which everything is dismantled and rebuilt from scratch (although that isn't to say somebody won't try, as the poisonous gassing of the Tokyo subway on March 10, 1995, demonstrated). But the Kobe earthquake seemed to strengthen the feeling among a growing number of Japanese people that big business no longer needs society, government, and the economy to be stacked so heavily in its favor. To the extent they redress the balance, the big Japanese firms will be less coddled and more vulnerable to global competitive forces—two long-term trends that prudent investors will want to keep in mind.

In strict investment terms, the Japanese stock market behaved predictably immediately after the earthquake. Shares of Osaka-based construction companies soared: Fudo Construction Company rocketed nearly 20%, and Daisue Construction Company jumped almost as much. But shares of non–life insurance companies fell: Tokio Marine & Fire Insurance Company and Sumitomo Marine & Fire Insurance Company each sank 3.5%, while Mitsui Marine & Fire Insurance Company lost 5%.

Later, economic studies indicated an initial slowdown in Japan's economic growth because of the earthquake, as consumer spending dropped and as companies lost production and sales because of ruined factories and severed distribution routes. Beginning in fiscal 1996 (which, for most of Japan, began on April 1, 1995), economists predicted five quarters of higher growth than otherwise would have occurred as government rebuilding money flowed in. The government-spending plan instituted in August 1995 was valued by analysts at 73 trillion yen ($682.8 billion). The cash injection benefited such industries as construction, housing, steel, glass, and lumber. Japan's huge trading companies, which move tremendous amounts of raw materials through their global networks, also saw additional business. Overall, however, economists said the growth fostered by rebuilding Kobe was undercut significantly by the strong yen, which weakened exports.

THE STRONG YEN

In the financial year that ended March 31, 1995, the yen rose 19% against the dollar. At first glance, it seemed easily explained. The United States had the world's biggest trade deficit, Japan the biggest surplus. The United States had one of the lowest savings rates among the world's major industrial countries, Japan one of the highest. On top of that, the mammoth U.S. budget deficit helps ensure an addictive dependency on a steady stream of foreign investment. Japan in the past has supplied much of that capital "fix," but just as American assets—stocks, bonds, plants, equipment—became dirt cheap in yen terms, the Japanese stopped buying. They had good reasons: They needed the money at home to buoy a wobbly banking system, support corporate restructuring, and rebuild after the Kobe earthquake. Besides, they had taken a shellacking on the U.S. assets they already owned: Merrill Lynch & Company estimated in April 1995 that Japanese institutions and individuals had lost $715 billion on their U.S. Treasury securities alone since the early 1980s.

But nothing is simple in Japan, the land of endless connections. One reason why the Japanese yen was so strong in 1994–95—and why the Japanese stock market fell to its lowest point in almost three years— was that Japan's biggest investors sat resolutely on the sidelines. These investors are the Japanese life insurance companies, which manage almost one-fourth of the financial assets owned by individual Japanese people. In the late 1980s, these firms promised their customers a higher yield on their life insurance savings than on yen-denominated bonds. To deliver, they invested their customers' money heavily into Japanese stocks and foreign bonds, which yielded more than the yen bonds. From 1985 to 1989, the insurers' holdings of foreign securities, nearly all bonds, rose to 15% of their portfolios from 9%, and their holdings of Japanese stocks rose to 20% from 15%. The insurance companies were cushioned from the risk of these investments by the booming stock market of that time, which provided them with unrealized profits that could absorb unexpected losses.

The stock market bubble burst in 1990. Stocks were cheap suddenly, but the insurance companies didn't buy many because their precious cushion of unrealized profits was in tatters. They really wanted to sell, in fact, but because they collectively owned 10% of the Tokyo stock market, any heavy selling on their part would reduce the value of the holdings they kept. For five years, the insurers played a cautious strategy of selling shares when others, usually foreigners, were willing to buy, and sitting tight when the foreigners retreated. Without any support from Japan's biggest investors, the Tokyo market wilted. The insurance companies also lost their taste for investing abroad because they correctly perceived that a strengthening yen would erode the value of foreign bonds. In the first half of the 1990s they unloaded about 50% of their foreign securities portfolios. They brought this capital back home, buying Japanese bonds instead. Keeping more and more portfolio capital within Japan helped the yen grow even stronger.

But following the end of the fiscal year on March 31, 1996, insurance companies and other Japanese institutional investors joined the foreigners in buying Japanese stocks. Most big insurers had finished rebalancing their portfolios away from stocks and toward bonds to meet new solvency guidelines the government set up in 1995. By the middle of 1996, the Japanese stock market had gained 7% from the end of 1995. The yen also started to fall back from the very strong position it had reached in the spring of 1995, eventually falling 40% against the dollar into 1977.

Even so, the yen's period of strength knocked many Japanese companies off their feet. Mazda Motor Corp., which sells 60% of its cars and trucks outside of Japan, saw its sales slip for four straight years and its losses mount dramatically. The strong yen meant that sales made overseas were less profitable unless prices were raised, which hurt competitiveness. Mazda reacted by cutting production in Japan and slashing exports, but it wasn't enough. By the spring of 1996, Ford Motor Company of the United States, which had held a 25% stake in Mazda since 1979, announced it would invest $481 million to resuscitate the auto company. Its stock holding was boosted to 33.4%—enough for a controlling interest—and for good measure it installed its own man as president. This move proved the most shocking of all to the Japanese: Henry D. G. Wallace, born in Scotland and raised in England, is a green-eyed *gaijin,* the first foreign president in memory of a big Japanese company. Was this to be the shape of things to come as Japanese companies faced real free-market forces?

Maybe, but meanwhile Mr. Wallace has his hands full. The new president of Japan's No. 5 automaker can't read or write Japanese, nor can most Japanese even pronounce his name; the closest they come is *Uorisu*. Though he has mastered several traits essential to managing in Japan—a calm demeanor inside the office, an ability to schmooze on the golf course, and a knack for karaoke—Mr. Wallace will need both luck and fortitude to administer the bitter medicine that Mazda needs to survive, much less flourish. "I think we're making progress," Mr. Wallace told *The Wall Street Journal* in May 1996, but added: "We still have a long way to go to get to a level where I would feel comfortable." On his agenda are lowering Mazda's high cost of manufacturing, bolstering the balance sheet, and sharply reducing the number of car models and sales channels. He also intends to reduce Mazda's vulnerability to foreign-exchange fluctuations by putting more overseas capacity in place, increasing overseas sourcing of components, and strengthening its presence in the Japanese market. A large part of Mazda's future, Mr. Wallace said, will involve "leveraging synergies" with Ford Motor.

Mazda always has been considered the weakest of the Japanese automakers. Nissan Motor Company, by contrast, is giant, ranking behind only Toyota as Japan's largest. But it, too, feels the pressure of the yen's strength. Five years ago, its prospects were among the worst in Japan's auto industry. As the economic boom of the late 1980s came grinding to a halt, Nissan found itself with far too much capacity. By 1993, it recorded its first losses in its history, and it began selling off assets. It even closed a factory in Japan, an unprecedented move that came to symbolize the glut in Japan's auto industry.

The losses continued for four years. Finally, Nissan turned the corner during the year ending March 31, 1997, and recorded a profit on its global operations.

Long the dandy of the Japanese automakers, with its headquarters in Tokyo's high-rent Ginza section and its numerous sports car models, Nissan's rapid expansion in the 1980s made its costs far higher than those of its more-nimble rivals—No. 1 Toyota, Honda Motor Company, and Mitsubishi Motors Corporation. To help it through these trying times, Nissan has drawn on its hefty portfolio of assets—a stash of real estate and securities that so far has placated the bankers. But the cash-flow problem remains big, and the road to financial recovery is long. In spring 1996, Nissan, too, named a new president, but no foreigner. Yoshikazu Hanawa, not an engineer like most of Nissan's presidents, is an economist who worked his way up through the personnel department before helping start Nissan's Smyrna, Tennessee, plant in 1982. In his three years in Smyrna he became fluent in English. He has his work cut out for him, both in strengthening Nissan's overseas plants and in combating aggressive Toyota for market share in Japan. Perhaps his greatest challenge is overcoming ennui within Nissan itself. The outgoing president, Yoshifumi Tsuji, expressed concern at the ceremony announcing Mr. Hanawa's appointment that "there was no sense of crisis inside the company" despite its large losses.

Nissan did manage to sidestep Japan's taboo on layoffs and cut 20% of its domestic staff through attrition and voluntary retirement. Mr. Hanawa suggests the worst of those cuts is over. "There comes a time when you have to focus on growing again," he said.

GODZILLA BANK

As if this weren't enough, Japan's banks aren't in great shape, either. The banks are struggling under a mountain of bad loans that are a hangover from the heady 1980s, when lenders were dishing out low-interest loans for investments in land and other assets at severely inflated prices. Real estate prices collapsed in the early 1990s and now are at a level of about one-third of their peak in 1991. The government estimates the bad loans total 37.4 trillion yen, or $356 billion, but private analysts think the amount could be twice that. No one knows for sure because Japanese finances remain terra incognita. With disclosure rules so murky, it's unclear how many bad loans are festering at the nation's smaller lenders: its regional banks, credit unions, and agricultural cooperatives. Then there's the government itself. It runs several financial institutions with bad loans that analysts can't even begin to tabulate. This banking crisis, which has run four years as we write this in mid-1996, could take another five years to resolve. Japanese taxpayers have at least temporarily blocked plans to use public money to clean up the banks. Beefing up disclosure might help ensure the system doesn't go haywire again. But Japan won't come clean overnight. The Finance Ministry hesitates at the thought of having little lenders reveal more about their condition because depositors might panic and move their money elsewhere, leaving a string of failures in their wake.

Seems like another headache for the poor Japanese, doesn't it? But here is where Japan shows it deserves its place in the big leagues of business and finance. From out of this banking morass comes the biggest merger of its kind: Mitsubishi Bank and Bank of Tokyo combined on April 1, 1996, to become the largest private bank the world has ever seen. While Bank of Tokyo-Mitsubishi is huge—its total assets are about $688 billion and its shares account for more than 3% of the value of the Tokyo Stock Exchange—it is emerging from Japan's banking crisis as a leader in more than just size.

Thanks partly to its listing on the New York Stock Exchange—where it becomes subject to U.S. disclosure requirements, which are much tougher than Japan's—the bank reveals far more about its operations than other Japanese banks. This disclosure shows that Tokyo-Mitsubishi is closer to settling its problem loans than its rivals. And analysts say it is moving ahead of the pack in disposing of repossessed collateral. To compete with this titan, Japan's other banks must overhaul themselves extensively. That, in addition to the resulting competition itself, could eventually revitalize Japan's ailing banking industry by spurring the cleanup of the festering bad-loan problem. Indeed, Bank of Tokyo-Mitsubishi might participate directly in future workouts of distressed banks and credit unions. The new bank could buy the good assets of distressed banks while regulators oversee the disposal of bad assets.

Both banks in the merger were founded about a century ago and were the money behind Japan's swift ascent to the ranks of an economic superpower. Mitsubishi formed the financial core of Japan's premier *keiretsu,* or corporate group, whose interests range from oil (Mitsubishi Oil) to automaking (Mitsubishi Motors) to shipbuilding (Mitsubishi Heavy Industries). As such, Mitsubishi Bank helped bankroll the building of industrial Japan. In 1887, the group purchased from the Emperor Meiji a tract of swampland around his palace that today is Tokyo's Marunouchi business district. One of Mitsubishi Bank's fastest-growing businesses is its derivatives unit, an area long shunned because of the Japanese dread of volatile financial products. The unit's manager, Akira Watanabe, brought in hired-gun foreign experts to tutor his staff. He earned the nickname "the Crocodile" because of his go-for-the-jugular way of doing business. "Tradition is kind of boring," he said in a *Wall Street Journal* interview.

While Mitsubishi built Japan's iron, Bank of Tokyo financed the nation's export drive. It has a unique past: Before World War II, it held a monopoly on foreign-exchange transactions in Japan, and the word around Tokyo is that it also managed the emperor's money; officials won't comment on that. The bank transformed this heritage into the Japanese banking industry's one truly international operation. It has a vast network of overseas offices, and it has had far more success than other Japanese banks in winning foreign clients. Before the merger, it employed more Americans than Japanese.

With the merger, Mitsubishi stands to win more business from its stable of corporate clients, including the members of its vast business family, because it will be able to draw on Bank of Tokyo's overseas expertise. Bank of Tokyo should see its thin network of domestic branches increase more than tenfold, to a combined 382 from 37, helping it peddle more of its niche services. The merged bank concedes that it will take time to streamline operations made redundant by the merger. Tokyo-Mitsubishi has a plan to cut staff by 2,000, to a total of 18,000. But that will take three years to implement because Japan's cultural ban on layoffs means the bank can cut only through attrition. However, because it is ahead of other banks in solving its bad-loan problems, it can focus on more profitable lending. The Bank of Tokyo-Mitsubishi's goal, according to analysts, is to raise its return on equity to 8% before March 1998, eventually raising that to 10%, up from 1.79% in mid-1996.

By the way, the merged bank owns two banks in California, both based in San Francisco. Bank of Tokyo's Union Bank subsidiary is the state's fourth largest, with assets of $16.8 billion, nearly 7,000 employees, and more than 200 California branches; it is trying to woo Pacific Rim customers, including 1,200 Japanese companies operating in California. Mitsubishi's Bank of California unit, the state's sixth biggest, with $7.7 billion in assets and 2,800 people, is strong in corporate lending and trade financing.

THE INVESTMENT SCENE

So, what sort of investment picture have we painted for Japan? The foreground certainly has plenty of dark problems with unknown outcomes. But don't fail to appreciate that glow just over the horizon. We like Japan for much the same reasons we like Germany: Countries that can run the 50-year sprint from standstill to economic colossus are good bets, in our opinion, particularly when their stock markets are experiencing a setback. The Japanese market will be red hot again some day in the next 5 to 10 years, and it will be as smart to be in it then as it was in the mid-1980s. You want a second opinion? Merrill Lynch projects a 40% to 50% gain in stock prices during the next five years, fueled by a 150% surge in corporate earnings. Over the long haul we can't expect the growth rates of yesteryear, but we value the capability Japan has shown of surmounting problems far greater than those it faces now. True, the world is different than it was in 1945, more competitive and so forth. But all of those differences can be traced in significant measure to achievements that were made in Japan.

To be sure, the sledding will not be smooth. In the second quarter of 1997, for example, Japan's economy unexpectedly contracted at a startling annual rate of 11.2%, effectively wiping out all the growth Japan had achieved over the preceding three quarters. A sharp fall in consumer spending was the chief culprit behind the weakness. Domestic consumption, which accounts for roughly 60% of Japan's economy, dropped 5.7% from the previous quarter, largely because of a rise in the nationwide consumption tax to 5% from 3% in April and the repeal of an income tax rebate in June. These tax increases were designed to help cut the government's huge budget deficit, but angry consumers snapped their wallets shut and sent consumption slumping. While economists still expected growth of 1.5% to 2% for the entire fiscal year, the setback made it clear that the good old days had not returned. The last time Japan was recovering from a recession, in the mid-1980s, it averaged annual growth of about 5%.

While the government's intention to deregulate finance and other sectors promises eventually to open new markets, it may also damp growth in the shorter term by creating tougher competition for existing companies and exacerbate unemployment. In part because of such uncertainty, investors are reevaluating the whole financial system. They are debating the way shares should be bought, traded and issued, the rights a shareholder should have, and how the whole process should be overseen. As Japan reconsiders all of these things, it's moving gradually toward a more mature financial system.

These aren't the sorts of transitions that can be accomplished in a year or two—some economists suggest it may take decades—and certainly without somebody feeling some pain. Yet many people argue that the worst is now over. Indeed, there seem to be some silver linings glimmering through, here and there, from among Japan's clouds of troubles.

Consider, for instance, the social and economic problem of big Japanese companies restructuring themselves by either laying off workers outright or not hiring many young ones. Japan's biggest companies have so sharply cut white-collar hiring that recent college graduates talk grimly of this era as the "Employment Ice Age." But it looks more like a great thaw to employers in the vast second tier of Japanese commerce, and it may be just what the nation's economy needs for the long haul

As plum jobs disappear at the bigger companies of Japan, new graduates are flowing into smaller companies that previously had a hard time tapping the nation's college-educated talent. The shift is happening quickly: 60% of 1995 college graduates joined companies with fewer than 1,000 employees, up from 35% just five years before. Small and midsize firms make up two-thirds of Japan's economy, but their productivity rates are only half those of Japan's big companies. So, the flow of new talent could create huge productivity gains and bolster Japan's competitiveness. As more graduates give up on the "Japanese Dream"—a prestigious lifetime job at a big company—they are forming a more mobile workforce that shows signs of producing the kind of entrepreneurial spirit Japan badly needs. "There is nothing bad about the Employment Ice Age," says Satoru Koyama, an industrial policy planner at Japan's Ministry of International Trade and Industry. "It turns on the faucet of good talent for small companies, and that is only good for the economy." Many smaller companies and regional firms say the new blood is helping them innovate, market, and expand in ways they couldn't have dreamed of before.

Or, consider the big fraud cases that have rocked the Japanese boardrooms. In 1995, a bond trader at Daiwa Bank Ltd. lost $1.1 billion on illicit trades; one of the consequences was that Daiwa lost its U.S. banking license. But another repercussion of the case promises a more pertinent benefit for investors: The Japanese government imposed new rules that beginning in 1997 require banks to disclose more about their trading activities. In 1996 came the case of a Tokyo-based Sumitomo Corporation trader, Yasuo Hamanaka, who is alleged to have racked up losses of $1.8 billion in unauthorized copper trades. At Sumitomo's annual meeting, senior executives bowed in unison to apologize to shareholders for the huge losses, and managers explained Mr. Hamanaka's trades were so "clever and intricate" that the company couldn't keep up with him. In truth, Japanese companies have long stood by their hoary old system of risk management, which basically calls for employees to be trusted not to do bad things. But some managers are now doing more, including implementing computerized accounting systems that ideally make fraud more difficult to commit and, when it happens anyway, easier to detect. Others are instituting new procedures, such as daily reporting of trading positions to the accounting department, instead of weekly. As big as this step is, several more lie ahead: Nonfinancial companies, such as manufacturers and service concerns, have barely begun.

Moreover, the market itself will be increasingly hospitable to foreign investors. Companies themselves are fostering some of this change as they raise more funds from financial markets and less from Japan's troubled banks. Another way this will happen is through better market regulation. Since the 1991 scandal of Japan's four biggest brokerage firms being caught compensating big clients for investment losses, the nation's stock markets say they've been cleaning up their act. Make no mistake, Japan's stock market remains far more opaque than Wall Street. Japanese financial accounts are often difficult to decipher. Many listed companies refuse to meet big mutual fund managers. And Japanese stocks, trading on average at 50 times projected earnings, still seem absurdly expensive. But the revelation that Japan's four biggest brokers regularly compensated some clients for their stock market losses enraged most Japanese, who got hammered as the Tokyo market lost more than half its value between the end of 1989 and 1992. It also illustrated how poorly Japan's markets were regulated. No one knew exactly what was against the rules because Finance Ministry officials used a confusing tangle of informal memos to "draft" the rules. And only prosecutors could enforce securities law, even though practically none of them were trained for it.

In 1992, Japan wrote clear securities laws and regulations and set up its first full-time stock market regulator, the Securities and Exchange Surveillance Commission (SESC). Unlike earlier Japanese market regulators, it can raid offices, confiscate evidence, and request that prosecutors indict a suspected offender. By the spring of 1996, it had asked for six indictments, including allegations of market manipulation, insider trading, and "circulating rumors." When SESC auditors perused computer records at Chiyoda Securities Company during a regular visit in 1994, they exposed the kind of scheme that brokers used to get away with. The midsize broker was channeling money from some winning "accounts"—actually its own—into the accounts of favored clients whose own investments had lost money. Investigators spent months scouring computer printouts of Chiyoda's trades, pinpointing compensations totaling $636,701. Chiyoda was ordered to halt trading stocks for its own account for two months, and the Japan Securities Dealers' Association fined the company 10 million yen, or $93,370.

But the turn to fundamental analysis may be the most important step in keeping Japan's markets clean. The use of "real valuation" tools will make it more difficult for Japan's pension and life insurance companies to buy stocks largely to cement business ties or to send a stock soaring or plunging on the short-term advice of brokers.

Actually, Japanese cross-holdings of affiliated companies are declining, another good sign for foreign investors. In the past, the majority of almost every large company's shares were owned by other members of its *keiretsu*—a group of affiliated firms including the company's bankers, insurers, suppliers, and distributors. Members of the *keiretsu* were permanent shareholders for the most part, which meant a Japanese company could focus more on building market share than on making the biggest profit it could. Since stock prices began tumbling in 1990, however, this system of cross-holdings has been unraveling. According to the Daiwa Research Institute, the average cross-holdings of Japanese companies have fallen from a majority to about 40% of total outstanding shares, and they will likely fall to 30% over the next few years.

The obvious ramification of this trend is that Japanese companies will have to pay more attention to improving returns on all their assets if they hope to retain and expand the interest of foreign shareholders. Cash, for example. Many Japanese companies have mounds of it, despite the low returns available on Japanese short-term instruments. Instead, the companies could pay down their high-interest debt, incurred several years ago, or could buy back their own shares in the Tokyo stock market. Such buybacks were prohibited until 1995, but now Japanese shareholders can authorize companies to undertake them. Stock buybacks would make a Japanese company more attractive to foreign investors by, first, decreasing the total number of outstanding shares and thus raising the per-share earnings, and, second, by lowering the price-to-earnings (P/E) ratio to more appealing levels. Suppose Fuji Photo Film earns 161 yen ($1.50) a share, which gives it a P/E ratio of, say, 20. If the company used half its net cash hoard of 491 billion yen to repurchase its own shares, its earnings would rise 16% to 187 yen a share and its P/E ratio would fall by a similar magnitude to 17.

Japan's stock market is so big and diverse that telling you here about a handful of stocks will barely scratch the surface. In fact, we'll skip the ones most of you have heard about, such as the big auto companies, Nintendo, and Sony, and give you a smattering of lesser-known issues. If you are a stock picker, be sure to check the latest listings of American depositary receipts, because stocks of many Japanese companies are available as ADRs. If you are into funds, see if your portfolio manager picks up any of these: Ajinomoto is a food-product maker with some global brand names (Knorr is one) and a major restructuring under its belt. For a play on Japan's economy, All Nippon Airways owns about half the domestic Japanese air-passenger market, and it is branching into hotels. An early play on a rebound of the economic cycle is Amada, a leading machine-tool company; for those who miss the early rush for shares, there is usually a fallback before a second buying wave lifts prices again. If you itch to bet on the recovery of Japan's banking industry, a candidate to consider is Asahi Bank, which is Japan's ninth largest and the first to open a securities firm after deregulation; it loans mainly to medium-size and small companies. Or, you might try conservatively managed Hachijuni Bank, which serves the region where the 1998 winter Olympics will be held and which has an unusually healthy balance sheet with relatively few bad loans. If you like semiconductors globally, you will like recently restructured Hitachi, but the company's consumer electronics division faces strong competition from other Japanese firms and from abroad. Ito-Yokado sells food in supermarkets (it is Japan's second-largest chain), convenience stores (it owns most of 7-Eleven worldwide), and restaurants (Denny's Japan is one chain), and it has industry-leading profit margins. If you foresee Japan becoming increasingly suburbanized, the third-largest supermarket chain, Jusco, is building stores in smaller places where the competition is nil. Kao is the Japanese version of Procter & Gamble, and it is every bit as competitive; its best-known U.S. brand is Jergens. Makita is the largest Japanese maker of portable electric tools, but it sells most of them overseas so its earnings are heavily influenced by the yen's value. Olympus Optical controls about 80% of the world market for endoscopes (instruments for examining the interior of a bodily canal or hollow organ) and is unstinting on its research and development of high-tech products. There are hundreds more, which gives you a sense of how rich with possibilities the Japanese market is.

THE JAPANESE WAY

Before we move on, we want you to know about the economic influence Japan exerts throughout the world and particularly in Asia. Here is the message Japan is spreading: Free-market theory has failed in many areas, such as Russia, Eastern Europe, and sub-Saharan Africa, because it is too shortsighted and too market-oriented. Not enough attention was paid to these countries' own economic and social structures. These are the words of Katsuhisa Yamada, the head of Japan's Institute of Developing Economies, a state agency that runs a school in Japanese industrial policy for aspiring Asian bureaucrats. Many of these Asians are uneasy about trying to apply traditional free-market advice from the World Bank and the International Monetary Fund. Japan's own experience suggests a different way, Mr. Yamada told *The South China Morning Post.* "Japan started from a planned economy post war, to become gradually liberalized over the years. I would say we are now 80% of the way to being a free-market economy. In developing countries it should be more like 50%. We are not saying that developing countries should imitate Japan. But they do need to study an alternative to neoclassical economic theory."

Another advocate of an Asian alternative to Western free markets is Eisuke Sakakibara, the forthright president of the Institute of Fiscal and Monetary Policy, which also trains foreign officials. Mr. Sakakibara says the most important difference between the Asian and neoclassical market economies is the balance between companies using direct and indirect funding. Businesses in pure free-market economies raise most of their funds directly, from the equity or bond markets. In Japan, he observes, banks provide most of the funds. It is easier for the government to influence lending than direct financing, where markets allocate cash irrespective of government policy. Another virtue of a strong savings-based banking system, rather than capital markets, is that it supports social and cultural traditions through local banks lending to local businesses, he argues. "We have lost lots of our Japaneseness, but compared to Western countries we have maintained some of our traditions," Mr. Sakakibara observes.

These men emphasize that the idea isn't to impose Japanese economic ideas, but rather to leave pupils to draw their own conclusions from the main points in Japan's postwar economic development. One example is using ubiquitous post offices to attract citizens' savings at low rates, providing the government with cheap funds to channel through specialized banks into priority industries. Underlying such strategies is the tradition of what one of these evangelizing bureaucrats calls "people-ism"—the idea that companies are for the benefit of employees and customers, with shareholders last.

CHAPTER XII

The Asian Tigers (and Cubs)

FOUR Asian countries have burned up the economic-growth track so decisively in the past two decades that they are known as the Tigers. Hong Kong, Korea, Singapore, and Taiwan have collectively astonished the world with their accomplishments, and each in its own way is preparing for another decade or two of further success. One characteristic they share is bountiful investment in the rest of Asia, including China and India. In terms of influence over the developing economies and markets of the Eastern Hemisphere, the Tigers rank with Japan. As Asia grows in the years ahead, the Tigers will continue to growl.

The stripes are different on each, however. Hong Kong and Singapore are service-oriented economies; Korea and Taiwan are industrial economies. All except Hong Kong have strong, controlling central governments. But Hong Kong is the one being absorbed into China, arguably the control-freak champ of Asia. Foreign investors are welcomed with open arms in Singapore and Hong Kong; they are curtailed in Korea and Taiwan, but the trend seems to be toward opening up.

Each has its challenges, its problems to overcome. But each also has its opportunities.

TAIWAN

Taiwan was in the news a lot during early 1996, first because it conducted its first democratic presidential election, and second because China staged several rounds of military "exercises" in a crude attempt to intimidate the Taiwanese before they voted. As soon as President Lee Teng-hui won reelection, the Chinese backed off.

But the political chasm that separates Taiwan from mainland China is as wide as it ever was. Beijing has long deemed Taiwan a part of the "one China" and has made a nationalist cause of recovering it. On the Chinese Lunar New Year holiday in 1995, mainland China President Jiang Zemin delivered a policy speech that seemed to position the issue as a sweet matter of reunification rather than a vinegary demand for the return of the prodigal province. Mr. Jiang's measured softening of China's hard line on Taiwan included the statement that China is ready to negotiate an agreement officially ending the state of hostility between the two sides. He also said that China's long-standing threat to use force to prevent Taiwan from becoming independent wasn't directed at the Taiwanese, but rather was aimed at "the schemes of foreign forces" to sever Taiwan from China. In an important concession to Taiwan business executives who want greater security for their investments on the mainland, Mr. Jiang hinted at bilateral pledges to protect the "interests" of the Taiwanese in China. That move helped clear a path for billions of dollars of new Taiwan investment in the mainland.

So, a prospective investor might ask, is Taiwan a separate economic entity, or an appendage of China? Officially, most of the world takes the appendage view; Taiwan is recognized diplomatically by only a handful of African and Latin American countries. Taiwan's sense of diplomatic insecurity, however, fuels its intense efforts to build and maintain an economy to be reckoned with. So far, anyway, Taiwan holds on to its individual identity because of its economic success.

If the Taiwanese have their way, their tiger will never be caged. Indeed, Premier Lien Chan has set the ambitious goal of outpacing Hong Kong and Singapore in various rankings of competitiveness by the end of the decade. The plan, drafted by the Council for Economic Planning and Development and approved by the cabinet, calls for average annual gross domestic product growth of 6.5% through 2006. It won't be easy.

Taiwan is one of Asia's great exporting nations, but it thrives more on imitation than on creativity. According to a Taiwan Economics Ministry survey, the world's top exporting nations typically spend 2% to 3% of their gross national product on research and development. Taiwan, at 1.7%, is at the bottom of the heap. In response, the Economics Ministry has promised sharp funding boosts for research and development. But it will take a change of focus within the business community, as well. Acer personal computers and Giant bicycles are globally known brands developed by indigenous Taiwan entrepreneurs. But the majority of Taiwanese companies continue to compete mostly on price, churning out no-name products or branded merchandise on behalf of multinational companies. Even as Taiwan continues to amass large trade surpluses, there are signs that this long-standing success formula may be wearing thin. Over the past few years, those surpluses have been sustained more by slackening import demand than by export growth. Some people wonder whether it isn't time Taiwan came up with more of its own ideas.

So, there is a sense of urgency to Taiwan's push to enter the major leagues of manufacturing. "We could go for quality, as in fine Italian leather shoes, or we could go for innovation, as in cutting-edge high-tech industries. What we can't do is count on cheap, labor-intensive industries for our survival," says Chu Cheng-chung, an economist at the Taiwan Institute of Economic Research, a privately funded think tank.

Taiwan's economy grew 6.1% in 1994, 6.06% in 1995, but slipped to 5.7% in 1996. The growth rate was expected to recover to 6.2% in 1997, and maybe as much as 6.5%. Taiwan has the second-highest population density in the world. Most of its 20 million people are squeezed into a relatively small area of lowland by the steep mountains of the interior. In Taipei, the capital, more than 3.5 million people live and work without a mass transit system other than buses, which get snarled up in the impossibly heavy traffic; an ambitious railway system is way behind schedule and over budget. Commuters travel to work from the sprawling new suburbs on mopeds or in cars for lack of alternatives. Taipei's air quality is among the worst in the world, partly because the city is surrounded by hills, and partly because there are 5 million cars on the island, and the number is increasing at the rate of 10% a year. Outside of Taipei and other cities are other kinds of environmental problems. Development of the mountainous interior for quarrying, cement making, house building, and golf courses is destroying the natural forest. The heavy rains trigger landslides, massive soil erosion, and floods. Industries do not always abide by environmental regulations on pollution; if they are threatened with enforcement of the rules, they say they will relocate to mainland China.

One reason the Taiwanese environment has received such harsh treatment stems from the country's unusual history. When Chiang Kai-shek landed in 1947 with his army, it was a temporary stopping place before he returned to the mainland to defeat the Communists. The Republic of China, as Taiwan officially describes itself, didn't go in for long-term planning. Taipei was considered a temporary capital; it was designed for 300,000 people, and it has grown to more than 3 million.

The early settlers may have dreamed of going back to China, but now Taiwanese businesspeople are actually doing it—as investors. About 30,000 Taiwanese firms are registered to do business in China, and they have poured billions of dollars of Taiwanese capital into factories, power plants, and other projects on the mainland. Following the saber-rattling period of early 1996, during which investment announcements slowed, China put out the welcome mat for money, and the Taiwanese responded with a fresh tidal wave of investments. Some analysts think China's willingness to develop wide-ranging economic ties with Taiwan is an effort to make the island more dependent on the mainland. But businesspeople say closer cross-straits ties make sense: Taiwan is highly developed and industrialized, with high labor costs, while China has an abundant, inexpensive pool of labor and an appetite for computers, chemicals, and other products Taiwan churns out. Cultural ties make business smooth.

Even both governments now are encouraging links. Chinese state television runs frequent reports on ties with Taiwan, including a deal to supply water to Taiwan-held islands off China's Fujian province. Taiwan has revived a plan to develop a special trade zone from which direct transport links with China will be permitted. State oil companies from China and Taiwan even agreed to explore jointly for petroleum in undersea tracts, including zones where China was staging war games in early 1996.

But this capital outflow sometimes comes at the expense of Taiwan's domestic economy, which could hurt long-term growth prospects. For much of 1996, foreign investment into Taiwan was declining while outward investment—excluding flows to China—surged. (One destination for this capital was Vietnam, where Taiwan is the biggest foreign investor, ahead of Japan.) This situation reversed in 1997, mainly because Taiwan's improving economy attracted foreign companies to invest, mostly in the high-tech industry and financial services. Meanwhile, to curb Taiwan's overreliance on China's economy, the Taiwanese government imposed new rules to restrict indirect investment in mainland China. So far, the rules have caused a drop in China investments, but there is no guarantee the Taiwanese won't be tempted again to pump money into the limitless potential of the mainland.

To help attract more foreign investment into Taiwan, the government in March 1996 liberalized its rules for stock purchases by foreigners, including letting foreign individuals buy shares for the first time. The limit on total foreign investment in Taiwan's stock market was raised to 20% from 15% of the market's total capitalization, and foreign individuals will be allowed to buy up to $5 million of shares a year. Previously, only government-approved foreign institutions had been allowed to invest in Taiwan stocks. As a direct result of the rules change, Taiwan was included for the first time in the Dow Jones Global Indexes and the Morgan Stanley Capital International world index, which could help attract wealthy individuals and corporate pension funds to Taiwan.

However, complex rules on setting up an account will scare off some potential investors. Foreign individuals first need to open a bank

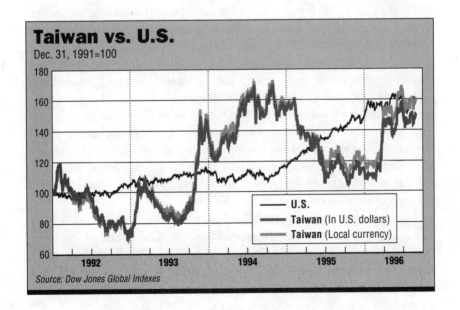

Taiwan vs. U.S.
Dec. 31, 1991=100

U.S.
Taiwan (In U.S. dollars)
Taiwan (Local currency)

Source: Dow Jones Global Indexes

account in Taiwan through an agent and deposit money with that custodial bank before being allowed to buy shares. That's a hassle compared to Hong Kong or the United States, where anyone can buy into the market directly. Moreover, these custodial fees could tack another 1% to 2% to the cost of investing in Taiwan.

Among Taiwanese stocks to consider are Acer, the personal computer manufacturer; Cathay Construction, the largest construction company in Taiwan; Far Eastern Department Stores, the biggest department-store chain; Formosa Plastic, the largest privately owned industrial group in Taiwan and one of the world's largest polyvinyl-chloride-resin manufacturers; President Enterprises, which makes food products and operates the 7-Eleven chain in Taiwan; Taipei Business Bank, which deals with individuals and small businesses; Taiwan Cement, the biggest producer in the country; Teco Electric & Machinery, which makes industrial electric motors and home appliances; and Yung Tay Engineering, Taiwan's largest elevator manufacturer.

HONG KONG

"Barren rock, with hardly a house upon it." Thus did the British foreign secretary, Lord Palmerston, sum up his low opinion of the island handed over by a chastened China at the close of the Opium War in 1841. On July 1, 1997, this war booty was returned to its original owner, though hardly in the same condition. Hong Kong is a modern metropolis and an economic wonder of the 20th century.

Hong Kong people are admired around the globe for their spirit and their success. Already, they have surpassed the average wealth of Britons (Hong Kong's per-capita GDP exceeds Britain's by more than a third), and they could overtake Americans in five years or so if present growth rates continue in both the United States and Hong Kong. With 6 million people, Hong Kong has an economy one-fourth the size of China and its 1.2 billion people. How China handles the transition will provide significant early clues as to the kind of superpower that will emerge in coming decades.

No one suspects the mainland of harboring evil intent toward Hong Kong. But the vast differences between China and Hong Kong make unintended harm a serious risk. Singapore Senior Minister Lee Kuan Yew warned about the return of Hong Kong: "As the Chinese say, when you fry a small fish, you should be careful not to overfry it. I fear that is the danger."

The gulf between Hong Kong's system and China's centrally planned, politically controlled economy could hardly be greater. Before the handover, Hong Kong has finished at or near the top of world competitiveness surveys because, while imperfect, it has been viewed as a model of unfettered capitalism in a capitalist age. It practiced free trade. Its civil servants were honest, perhaps partly because they had such little regulatory power that their influence was hardly worth trying to buy. Hong Kong's legal system was so fair and quick that lawyer jokes fell on deaf ears. (Will Hong Kong's bewigged barristers and judges remain immune to outside pressures when the new Court of Final Appeal is answerable to China's National People's Congress?) Its low and flat income tax, with a top personal rate of 15% and top corporate rate of 16.5%, funded government budget surpluses. (Will Hong Kong be able to continue these rates when just across the border the rate is 30%?)

Hong Kong at its best was a laissez-faire system of market chaos controlled only by the rule of law. That's a long way from what's familiar to Chinese officials, who come from a system that despite economic reforms still presumes government control. Hong Kong comes under Chinese rule as a pro-market economy, while China is more of a pro-business economy. That is, Hong Kong tried to focus on a favorable environment for business, while China—along with many developed capitalist societies—routinely gives businesses favors, such as subsidies and concessions.

For its part, Beijing seems genuinely eager to maintain stability and says it is willing to respect Hong Kong's economic autonomy. Invoking pledges made in the accords governing the transfer, China's top central bankers and Finance Ministry officials swore they have no intention of taking over monetary or financial control of the prosperous city.

Not that the prospect of running Hong Kong's money isn't tantalizing. Hong Kong's foreign-exchange reserves in mid-1996 amounted to $60 billion. Adding in China's $80 billion in reserves and other money set aside in a special Hong Kong development fund, Beijing calculates the combined economies would have a staggering $160 billion in reserves—a third more than that held by Japan, the world's richest nation. Moreover, the merged Hong Kong and China suddenly become the world's fourth-biggest trading nation, after the United States, Japan, and Germany. Hong Kong's stock market is the eighth largest, and it is likely to remain the center of China's equity market for the foreseeable future. Its foreign-exchange market is the fifth biggest, with daily turnover averaging $91 billion.

While the merger's advantages for China are obvious, Chinese officials insist Hong Kong will benefit as well. Dai Xianglong, governor of China's central bank, said that while he couldn't promise noninflationary growth—"as a developing country," he said, "it isn't possible to have zero inflation"—he hoped to contain inflation to 6% or 7% annually, below what he predicted would be a long-term growth rate of 8% a year. "Sustainable growth will contribute to Hong Kong's role as a financial center," he said.

The functioning of Hong Kong's market now that China has taken over remains a cause for concern, even though the initial experience has been positive. Hong Kong had made great progress toward creating transparent and fair financial markets. But the Hong Kong Stock Exchange's ambition to be the main market for China could compromise its desire for credibility with international investors. It remains to be seen whether China will uphold the Western-style market-regulation and policing standards. If the 20 Chinese companies whose stocks were trading in Hong Kong as of mid-1996 are any indication, the prospects aren't good. The companies didn't fully comply with Hong Kong's regulations regarding a public company's obligations to shareholders; several failed to deliver on commitments to shareholders. China and its murky record books can be a convenient black hole for Hong Kong companies; valuations of Chinese assets can be fictitious because it is difficult, if not impossible, to check on them.

There is more at stake in preserving the integrity of the Hong Kong market than the jobs of a few thousand brokers. Financial services and related business account for 30% of Hong Kong's economy, as much as manufacturing. With stiff competition from regional financial centers, it will be a challenge in the years to come to keep the financial sector vibrant.

As we write this, three months after the handover, many more questions about Hong Kong's life as a Special Administrative Region of China remain unanswered. Hong Kong's new chief executive, Tung Chee Hwa, a former shipping magnate, contends that it's business as usual. In late summer of 1997, Mr. Tung made a four-day visit to the United States to deliver a simple message: Hong Kong's handover is a success. "The economy is functioning normally," Mr. Tung declared. "People's lifestyle hasn't been affected."

Hong Kong vs. U.S.
Dec. 31, 1991=100

— U.S.
— Hong Kong (In U.S. dollars)
— Hong Kong (Local currency)

Source: Dow Jones Global Indexes

He has a point. On the surface, the new Hong Kong looks just as free as the old one. Mr. Tung's critics march through the streets waving placards, unmolested by the police. Newspapers publish cartoons lampooning Chinese leaders. "Demonstrations continue—arguments everywhere," Mr. Tung said with a good-natured grin. What has changed, though, is the breadth of Hong Kong's democracy. Shortly after the midnight transfer of power on July 1, 1997, China swore in a new, unelected Hong Kong Legislature to replace the one voted into office under British-backed democratic elections in 1995. Mr. Tung calmed some concerns over that move by promising new elections in early 1998. But the laws governing those elections have provoked a new round of controversy. The most important criticism is that voting for 30 legislative seats assigned to industry groups, known as functional constituencies, has been restricted to about 180,000 people—down sharply from 2.7 million in the last election, out of Hong Kong's total population of about 6.4 million. Direct elections to fill an additional 20 seats are to use proportional representation, which guarantees seats even to candidates who come in second. Proportional representation is common among democracies in the West. But critics of Mr. Tung argue its use in Hong Kong appears aimed at restricting Hong Kong's Democratic Party—the territory's largest and most popular political group—to as few seats in the next Legislature as possible. In the previous Legislature, Democrats held 19 out of the body's 60 seats; the party and its allies controlled around half of the seats. In the "Provisional Legislature," Democrats were completely absent. Party aides estimate privately that the new laws would make it difficult for the Democrats to win more than 10 seats in the 1998 elections, scheduled to take place before June.

Mr. Tung vigorously defended the election rule changes in a speech to the U.S. Chamber of Commerce as an "interim arrangement designed to maintain balance and continuity" while Hong Kong's political system evolves over the next 10 years. "There are those who believe that the pace of democratization in Hong Kong is too slow. Others believe that it is too fast. I believe we have struck the right balance," he said. He promised that Hong Kong in seven years will have "more democracy in the Legislature than we ever (had) in 156 years of colonial rule."

Mr. Tung also assured U.S. executives that his administration has been given an "entirely free hand" in managing the city's affairs since its handover to Chinese rule. He said that China has adhered faithfully to its pledge to allow Hong Kong to govern itself in all respects except for foreign affairs and defense. He promised the executives that Hong Kong will continue to manage its economy "with the lightest and most steady of hands, sticking firm to free markets, small government, low taxes, and fiscal prudence." He said that Hong Kong will invest heavily in expanding home ownership and education, and in the infrastructure of the information age.

The Hong Kong economy slowed about a year before the handover, but then picked up steam as the conventional wisdom came around to the view that China's rule would be benign. Economic growth of 5.4% in 1994 braked to 4.5% for 1995 as the handover drew closer. In 1996, growth accelerated a tad to 4.9%, and the official forecast for 1997 was 5.5%, although growth in the first six months of the year was at an annual rate of better than 6%. Inflation expectations for 1997, meanwhile, were cut to 6.5% from 7%.

Many of the people still in Hong Kong—there was a rush out of the territory after the crackdown on pro-democracy protesters in Tienanmen Square in 1989—have convinced themselves that the Beijing regime won't kill its golden egg-laying goose. Others think China is hungry enough, and insecure enough, to do just that, even while it simultaneously proclaims that it isn't.

One doubter is Nobel Prize–winning economist Milton Friedman, who is skeptical of China's commitment to the "one country, two systems" principles of the Sino-British Joint Declaration and the quasi-constitution, or Basic Law. According to these documents, China is to keep the territory's capitalist system and way of life unchanged for 50 years after the handover. "The Chinese did say that they would keep the two systems," Mr. Friedman acknowledged in an interview with *Far Eastern Economic Review.* "What they say and what they do is different, though." Mr. Friedman does not believe Hong Kong's absorption into China's economy will be cataclysmic, but the economy "is going to change character drastically." He thinks, for example, there will be a major loss of confidence in Hong Kong as a safe haven for money.

John Greenwood, architect of the 1983 pegging of the Hong Kong dollar to the U.S. dollar, agrees that "what we'll see is a convergence to 'one country, one system,'" though he thinks it will take 10 to 15 years and that China will move closer toward Hong Kong's system than the other way around. He concedes, however, "If there's a paranoid Communist Party in charge in Beijing that's scared of being ousted, then Hong Kong is very vulnerable."

It also is vulnerable in the changing competitive landscape of Asia. One by one, the currencies of Asia's mighty "tiger" economies—Thailand, Malaysia, Singapore, and Indonesia—fell sharply in 1997. But the Hong Hong dollar, propped high on its U.S. dollar-backed perch, was relatively undisturbed by waves of speculative selling. But there is a steep price to be paid for this achievement, which Mr. Tung couldn't resist crowing about on his U.S. tour. Because rival Southeast Asian currencies have fallen against the dollar, it is now much cheaper for Americans and other foreigners to buy goods from and invest in those countries. That makes Hong Kong less cost-competitive.

Hong Kong already was a pricey place to live, work, and play. In one fell swoop, though, the economies of Southeast Asia have become 10% to 30% more competitive because of the depreciation of their currencies. Consider office prices: At $1,020 a square meter, Hong Kong office rents were already among the highest in the world. In June, those rents were 45% more expensive than office space in Singapore. Now the premium is 55%. And Hong Kong's office rents are now more than 5.5 times the rents in Kuala Lumpur, where Malaysia's government hopes to construct a world-class regional financial center. Apartment costs, too, have soared. Rent for a three-bedroom home on Hong Kong island's posh south shore can easily run $12,000 a month. Buying the same apartment can cost over $4 million.

Templeton Worldwide Inc., part of the Franklin Templeton fund group, already has moved its Asian headquarters from Hong Kong to

Singapore, in part to pare costs. Singapore also offered a "fantastic tax deal," said J. Mark Mobius, executive vice president of Templeton— better even than the 16.5% corporate tax rate that lures many multinationals to Hong Kong.

In addition, tourism is losing ground in Hong Kong, as travelers discover it is no longer the bargain center it once was. The soaring rents have forced retailers to jack up prices. June 1997, the month before the handover, was supposed to be a winner for Hong Kong's hotels. Instead, they posted average occupancy rates of 70%, sharply down from 87% the year before, according to the Hong Kong Tourist Association. Visitor arrivals to Hong Kong in June fell 14% from the year before.

Hong Kong doesn't compete head-to-head with the rest of Southeast Asia in manufacturing. Hong Kong mainly sells services, such as insurance, fund management, and tourism. Still, much of Hong Kong's services revolve around China's manufacturing exports. And those exports became less competitive, too, because China's currency, the renminbi, didn't fall much during the Southeast Asian currency rout.

Hong Kong's currency troubles aren't over. A widening deficit in goods and services trade would in turn put downward pressure on the currency. But even as the cost mounts for keeping Hong Kong's currency pegged to the dollar, the horror of abandoning the peg remains deep-seated. "I would not even venture a speculation that we should devalue," says Henry Y. Y. Tang, a Hong Kong textile manufacturer and senior policy adviser to the new post-British government. "This link, for economic and political reasons, has a stabilizing effect on Hong Kong." Still, Mr. Tang admits to worrying about competitiveness, which he says Mr. Tung, the Hong Kong chief executive, wants to tackle: "We cannot just sweep it under the carpet."

While many investors are taking China's reassurances at face value, some companies have exited. Five of the Jardine Matheson group of companies delisted from the Hong Kong Stock Exchange in 1994 and 1995 because of the approaching transfer of power. Two of them, Jardine Matheson Holdings Ltd. and Jardine Strategic Holdings Ltd., had been among the most actively traded stocks in Hong Kong, with Jardine Matheson accounting for a little more than 2% of the Hong Kong market's capitalization and Jardine Strategic for slightly more than 1%. (The Jardine companies are incorporated in Bermuda; their primary listings are in London, with secondary listings in Singapore, Australia, and Luxembourg.) The companies said they were delisting because Hong Kong regulators refused to bend on certain takeover rules; however, the companies are believed to have bad relations with the Chinese government. Few other companies have followed suit, however, and trading volume on the Hong Kong Stock Exchange rose significantly as investors in mid-1997 became enamored of "red chips"—Hong Kong-based companies that either are owned in large part by mainland Chinese entities, or which do more than 35% of their business in China.

The biggest companies on the Hong Kong Stock Exchange are real estate developers, banks, and conglomerates. Among the Hong Kong–based stocks worthy of investors' attention are Bank of East Asia, which has interests in many financial-service operations, including insurance; C. P. Pokphand, which has a group of agricultural and industrial businesses ranging from running the Kentucky Fried Chicken outlets in Shanghai to forging steel, making motorcycles, and running a big animal feed mill in Thailand; Great Wall Electronics, which is a big producer of audiovisual products; Hang Lung Development and Henderson Land, which are major real estate developers in both Hong Kong and China; Hongkong Telecommunications, which is already benefiting from the increased phone traffic to and from China; Oriental Press Group, which is Hong Kong's largest Chinese-language newspaper and magazine publisher; Peregrine Investments, which is big in investment banking, securities dealing, and investment management; and Swire Pacific, which has interests in airlines, real estate, oil, shipping, and insurance.

Among the Class H shares of Chinese companies listed in Hong Kong are Harbin Power Equipment, which makes and exports power-generation equipment; Chengdu Telecommunications Cable, a maker of copper and fiber-optic telecommunications cable; Shanghai Haixing Shipping, China's second-biggest shipping company, mostly hauling coal and crude oil in China; and Yizheng Chemical, which controls almost half of China's polyester production.

SOUTH KOREA

Economists 30 years ago all but wrote off South Korea. It was backward. It had hardly any resources. Per-capita income was only $87. Meaningful economic development was, ahem, ahem, likely to be slow and limited if it happened at all.

So much for economists' forecasts. In 1996 Korea accepted an invitation to join the Organization for Economic Cooperation and Development (OECD), the world's exclusive club of industrialized nations. It has grown to be the 11th-biggest economy and 12th-largest trading nation in the world. Its per-capita income in 1996 surpassed $10,000, and its economy grew a brisk 9%, fueled by a 30% increase in exports and spectacular domestic demand for capital investment. The general upsurge kept factories humming at close to 90% capacity and pushed unemployment down to 2.2%, a record low. Inflation has hovered around 5%.

Korea doesn't plan to rest long upon its economic-bootstrapping laurels. "I will definitely make this a period when South Korea can be the center of the world," President Kim Young Sam promised in early 1995. "I have this possibility of turning this country into a proud nation in the 21st century." The government-funded Korean Development Institute has drafted an ambitious policy program calling for South Korea to grow its economy tenfold to $4.8 trillion by 2020. If it succeeds, South Korea would surpass Great Britain among the industrialized nations.

Koreans may hate the Japanese, who occupied their land off and on over the centuries, but they are following Japan's road to economic development. Indeed, they now are poised to outdo Japan. Korea already leads in shipbuilding; it matches Japan in semiconductors; it is rushing to catch up in steelmaking; it is in overdrive to be a major automaker; and it is developing ambitions to be a high-flying aircraft manufacturer.

It is making noteworthy progress on the financial front, as well. South Korea has "graduated" as a World Bank borrower, taking its last two loans in the late winter of 1995. By stepping back from the bank's lending window, South Korea will join the ranks of four other Asian-Pacific countries that have completed such a passage. Australia was the first in 1962, followed by Japan in 1967, New Zealand in 1972, and Singapore in 1975. A World Bank borrower becomes a candidate for graduation when its per-capita income exceeds a certain level and can gain access to other capital markets at "reasonable terms." South Korea has passed both tests.

However, this economic success story stands at a crossroads that promises to make the coming years as much of a challenge as the ones just completed. The price of admission to the OECD will be a profound change in the way South Korea conducts its business at home and abroad. The development of South Korea's political and economic organizations hasn't kept pace with its material achievements. In recent years, the government has come under more and more pressure from trading partners and has begun to open the gates to foreign investment. The changes are gradual, but the process appears to be moving forward. By 2000, about 97% of South Korea's economy will be open to foreign investment, claims the minister of trade, industry, and energy.

There's also strong pressure at home for leaders to keep up the fight against corruption and to curtail the power of the huge business organizations that still dominate the economy. The sensational—and traumatic—graft trials of former Presidents Chun Doo Hwan and Roh Tae Woo transfixed the public, but the anticorruption drive has reached much deeper. More than 5,000 civil servants—from cabinet members to legislators in the national assembly—have been dismissed or imprisoned on graft convictions.

But Mr. Kim's crusade is falling well short of his goal, which may have been an impossible task in the first place. Corruption has been endemic in Korean society for decades, and it may be unreasonable to think one man could abolish it in four years. Mr. Kim has instituted reforms that make bribing government officials more difficult. But in 1997 another scandal surfaced, showing there are still enough shenanigans in Korea to rattle the economy and shame the government.

"Hanbogate," as Koreans call the affair, began unfolding in January 1997, when Hanbo Steel Industry Co. filed for court protection from creditors after amassing 5 trillion won ($5.8 billion) in debt to build a steel mill. In February, prosecutors indicted 10 businessmen and politicians, including two men close to President Kim. One of Mr. Kim's former aides was charged with pressuring banks to extend loans to Hanbo, and a cabinet minister was indicted for allegedly taking bribes from Chung Tae Soo, Hanbo Steel's founder.

The bankruptcy filing burdened Korea's troubled banks with additional bad loans, boosted the rates they must pay for financing in world capital markets, and threatened the existence of hundreds of small companies. Some people worry there may be more Hanbo-style collapses waiting.

The cost of Mr. Kim's failure to meet his ambitious anticorruption goals could be high. If he had succeeded at rooting out corrupt practices, the Korean economy could become more efficient, more open to imports, more attractive to much-needed foreign investment, and more likely to avoid crises that could drag down economic growth. Meanwhile, the public is growing disenchanted with Mr. Kim. A poll after the Hanbo scandal broke said Mr. Kim and his party found approval with less than 20% of citizens, down from 80% in 1993.

The Hanbo crisis was only the latest blow to Mr. Kim in his last full year in office. Nationwide strikes went on for nearly a month to protest a labor reform law that gives big business more power to fire workers. The law was passed in late December 1996 by Mr. Kim's ruling New Korea Party in a predawn, surprise session of the National Assembly, in the absence of opposition parties. Mr. Kim's government and business leaders say the law is necessary to make the Korean economy more competitive, because wages have risen sharply in recent years. But many Koreans lost faith in Mr. Kim after his government threatened to arrest labor leaders and sent baton-wielding riot police to break up rallies. To mollify critics, the law went back to the National Assembly for an overhaul; the revised law still severely restricts a company's ability to fire workers.

Though Mr. Kim is far more democratic than his predecessors, he has sometimes employed methods reminiscent of the decades when the military ruled Korea. Mr. Kim's supporters say his methods have been necessary to push through reform. And to give Mr. Kim his due, he has scored some great successes. After his inauguration, he required senior government officials to disclose their personal finances. Huge fortunes were exposed, and hundreds were forced to resign. In perhaps his boldest move, Mr. Kim in 1993 banned financial accounts held under false names. The accounts were seen as fueling corruption, because they made it easy to move money secretly. The change helped investigators unearth a bribery scandal in 1995 that centered on former President Roh Tae Woo, who amassed $650 million from many prominent businessmen, including Kim Woo Choong, the chairman of Daewoo Group, Lee Kun Hee, chairman of the Samsung Group, and Hanbo's Mr. Chung. The conviction of Mr. Roh and former dictator Chun Doo Hwan for treason and corruption in 1996 signaled that the country was putting authoritarianism behind it.

Many Koreans hope the next president, to be elected in 1997, will extend the reforms begun by Mr. Kim, who is barred by the constitution from serving another term. Politicians say history may prove Mr. Kim to be a transitional figure between Korea's authoritarian past and a more democratic future.

One aspect of the Korean economy that already has begun to change, and surely will change further, are the big business groups, called *chaebols*, that have led the drive for economic success. With almost all owners of the country's top 30 conglomerates facing trial for their alleged contributions to the Chun and Roh slush funds, these mighty corporate organizations are as politically vulnerable as they will ever be, and many of them are in financial dire straits as well

Ironically, the *chaebols* were nurtured by the government to be the primary engines of Korea's economic growth. However much Korean bureaucrats may fret about them now, they created the superfirms by feeding the *chaebols* with cheap credit and bailing out any activity that threatened to fail—sometimes by passing it along to a rival. This is how the Daewoo Group, which started out in textiles, found itself with a machinery company, an auto venture, and finally a shipyard. When businessmen depend on government for credit, political connections become more important than market merit. Graft inevitably follows. The public is well aware of this relationship, which explains why Koreans remain so antagonistic toward the very businesses that built their country. The owners of *chaebol* companies are often criticized for running their firms by whim and freely using company funds without approval from their boards.

Several of these gargantuan *chaebols* say they plan to slim down voluntarily, before the politicians do it for them. If they deliver the recent slide of these engines of the Korean economy, which are now suffering from rising labor costs and other ills, could be reversed. Many *chaebols* are developing plans to sell assets, reduce debt, trim staff and costs, and bring focus to their expansive empires. Economists and stock analysts hope that restructuring catches on, resulting in greater efficiency, higher profits, and increased competitiveness.

In Korea, scaling back has long been perceived by management as a retreat and a blow to corporate pride. Problems such as low productivity and profits and escalating debts were swept under the rug, which was easier when the economy was growing rapidly. But as Korea's economy slows, some of the *chaebols* can't hold out any longer. The economy was expected to grow at less than 6% in 1997, down from 9% in 1995. Although this is still strong by world standards, in Korea the slowdown is practically a recession. In 1996, the net income of Korea's 30 largest *chaebols* fell by 90% from 1995, according to the Daeshin Economic Research Institute in Seoul.

The *chaebols* were counting on asset sales to help finance their re-

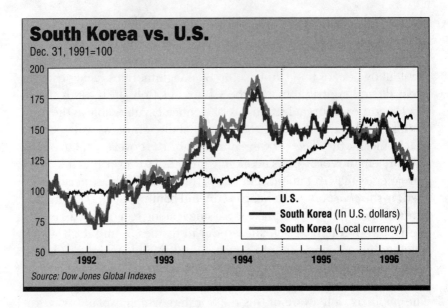

South Korea vs. U.S.
Dec. 31, 1991=100

Legend:
U.S.
South Korea (In U.S. dollars)
South Korea (Local currency)

Source: Dow Jones Global Indexes

structuring efforts, but unfortunately the weak property market in 1997 was hampering such plans. Commercial property values could tumble 30% to 40% through 1999, one study estimated. Such declines seemed impossible during Korea's boom years. But by 1992, as Korea's economy began to slow and the supply of commercial property increased, the market began to turn. Property values fell more than 1% in 1992, another 7% in 1993, and less than 1% in 1994 before recording neglible rises in 1995 and 1996.

Now, however, many corporations are desperately trying to unload land. The problem is that there aren't that many potential customers in Korea wealthy enough to buy it. The *chaebols* control much of Korea's property, but it is these same *chaebols* that hope to sell, leaving no one around to buy. The *chaebols*, in many cases, either can't sell their real estate or are dumping it at reduced prices. Meanwhile, much more land is still coming on the market.

The real estate market also is pinching Korea's banks. Most lending by the banks is secured almost entirely by property. According to an official of Cho Hung Bank, one of Korea's largest, commercial property claimed from bankrupt enterprises is receiving only about 75% of its appraised value at auction.

As this struggle proceeds, the *chaebols* are investing overseas at a manic pace. They are building cars in Poland and India, making refrigerators in Vietnam, and producing television sets in Mexico, among many other projects. Foreign direct investment by South Korean companies topped $3 billion in 1995, more than triple the amount in 1990. "We see globalization as a survival strategy," says an executive director at South Korea's largest conglomerate, Samsung Group. Because the South Korean market is gradually being opened to foreign competitors, the *chaebols* can no longer count on fat profit margins at home to subsidize low-priced exports and help them grab market share overseas. Low costs, the main weapon South Korean companies have used in international battles for market share, can't be taken for granted, either. Average South Korean wages have nearly quadrupled in the past 10 years; in the electronics industry, South Korean wages are twice the level of those in Great Britain.

Nonetheless, many South Korean products still can't match the best global technology and quality. So, the *chaebols* are focusing most of their international investment on developing countries. Daewoo Motor, for example, is undertaking more than $5 billion in auto and auto-parts manufacturing projects, and 95% of the money is heading into developing countries. South Korean businesspeople think they will have more success selling their less-sophisticated products in developing countries with potentially large consumer markets and not so much competition from Japanese and U.S. companies. Vietnam and Eastern Europe are at the top of this list.

South Korea has another major problem: North Korea. This dictatorship, intent on building its nuclear capability, dreams of becoming a tiger itself. Despite this ambition, many South Koreans think the two halves of the peninsula will never go to war again, no matter what rhetoric is spouted or however far the North gets with its nuclear weapons program. The North realizes, they argue, that such combat would be suicidal. However, war isn't the only possible scenario. North Korea's isolationist regime might crumble, forcing South Korea to take on the burden of a sudden reunification. By one estimate, it could cost $1.2 trillion over several years to bring the North Korean economy up to the level of South Korea's. To forestall this frightening possibility, the South Korean government began providing food aid to the North— a long-running food shortage has forced many North Koreans to live on one meal a day—and approving more investment projects by South Korean companies. North Korea's economy has been shrinking in the 1990s because many of its former trading partners, such as the Soviet Union and the Eastern Bloc, have disappeared.

The South Korean stock market is opening further to foreign investors. Starting with 12 companies in 1956, the Korea Stock Exchange today lists 700; more are on the way, thanks to tax advantages and other related benefits to corporations going public. The Korean market was opened to foreign investors via investment funds in 1981, and for direct investment on January 3, 1992. To preclude the possibility of foreign investors taking control, the government limited foreign ownership of South Korean companies to 12%. That limit was raised to 15% in 1995, to 18% in the spring of 1996, and was to be widened to 20% later that same year. Thereafter, the foreign stock ownership cap will be boosted by three percentage points each year until it reaches 29% in 1999. Then, in 2000, the government said it will consider abolishing the limit altogether.

The stock market is capitalized at approximately $170 billion, about half as much as Korea's gross national product in 1994, which was about $350 billion. The difference is partly because many Korean companies are still private. To the degree and at the rate they make initial public offerings, prices of already-listed stocks could be depressed. The government decided in 1996 not to regulate the pace of stock offerings anymore, following the arrest of the head of the securities watchdog agency for taking bribes from businesspeople who wanted to list their companies on the exchange.

Besides Daewoo, the big industrial *chaebols* include such names as Hyundai, Goldstar, and Lucky. They so dominate certain industries that smaller companies have found it difficult to compete. As these big industrial groups restructure, there will eventually be more smaller stocks for investors to choose from. Meanwhile, most foreign investors concentrate on big names with global status, such as Samsung Electronics, Korea Electric Power, Hyundai Motor, and Pohang Iron and Steel.

SINGAPORE

Singapore is a city-state. Officially the Republic of Singapore, it has nearly 3 million people jammed onto 225 square miles of Singapore Island and about 60 islets off the Malay peninsula. Low-lying Singapore Island is fringed by mangrove swamps. The city of Singapore is one of the world's largest and busiest ports. Not a likely setting for one of the strongest and fastest-growing economies of the world, never mind Asia, but that's what Singapore is.

During 1991–93, Singapore's gross domestic product grew an average of 7.5% a year, according to the Monetary Authority of Singapore, which is a central bank in every respect except that it doesn't issue currency. The authority forecasts potential growth in gross domestic product for the Singapore economy through 1998 at 6% to 7% annually, exceeding the Singapore government's long-term growth target of 4% to 6%. If past experience is any guide, the authority's prediction will be on the conservative side. It predicted 1994 economic growth of roughly 8%; instead, it grew by 10%. Unemployment is less than 2%. At 47% of gross domestic product (GDP), Singapore has the highest gross domestic savings rate in the world. In no small part because of this fact, its currency also is very strong.

Of course, Singapore's economy couldn't keep up the pace forever. In 1996 and the first half of 1997, Singapore limped through its worst economic slowdown in a decade. Along with several Southeast Asian neighbors, it suffered nine months of anemic exports and stunted economic growth, at least by this region's lofty standards. But by the third quarter of 1997, Singapore appeared to be marching out of the slump more quickly and strongly than other countries in the region, demonstrating the resilience of its economy. Although Singapore was one of the first regional economies to be hit by the downturn, it was weakened less than some of its neighbors. Throughout the nine-month slump in exports and manufacturing, Singapore's role as a regional center for financial services, transportation, and communications provided alternative sources of income.

But Singapore never rests easy. In his annual National Day Rally speech in August 1997, Prime Minister Goh Chok Tong warned that the city-state must redouble its efforts to remain competitive globally, and suggested that more openness in government thinking might be needed to do so. "For key sectors of our economy, like finance and banking, and SIA [Singapore International Airlines, the state-owned carrier], the issue is not just a few new competitors in the region, but a new global competitive environment," Mr. Goh said. He criticized examples of protectionist thinking, as well as a mindset "that instinctively shuts off challenges to the existing status quo." He also said Singapore needs to pursue sound fiscal and monetary policies, as this gives the country a "firm foundation for a stable economy." Singapore must live within its means and be "prudent in our spending," he said.

Singapore's leaders worry about another threat: What if its young people don't buy into the country's intensely focused work ethic? Senior Minister Lee Kuan Yew, who ruled Singapore for 31 years and took it from a sleepy Asian backwater to a thriving financial center, warned in an early 1995 newspaper interview that Singapore's economic progress could be wrecked if the younger generation aped the West and the government pursued populist policies. Singapore's wealth could vanish, the former premier warned, if the government pursued such policies as subsidizing transportation and utilities, or paying welfare benefits to unmarried mothers and their children, and to the unemployed. "Then soon we go into deficit. Then we start borrowing, then the Singapore dollar starts sinking, then we put up interest rates, then the economy slows down."

This is the country, you may remember, that caned an American teenager for spray painting an automobile. The point to remember for investment purposes, however, is that in Singapore, as in most other Asian countries, the economy and the way of life are intimately intertwined. While business thrives, individuals must pay a lot for everyday things. For the price of a private apartment, you could buy a vineyard in Italy. For the price of a 1994 Certificate of Entitlement to buy a car—about $67,500—you can acquire a three-bedroom home in some parts of the United States. (In Singapore, the car itself costs extra.) In an economy at full employment, most middle-class women work—which is possible partly because of poorly paid foreign maids who live in tiny back rooms. Building activity is performed by construction workers who live in Third World–style shantytowns at the sites.

Singapore's ruling People's Action Party (PAP) is well entrenched; the opposition remains fragmented. But Singaporeans are world-class grumblers. On their own, complaints about specific government policies don't add up to much when the economy is growing so fast. However, the ruling party is having broader problems connecting with increasingly assertive voters, and its share of the vote has declined, albeit usually in small steps, over the past several elections. "The decline is likely to continue without a considerable modification of the PAP's paternalistic 'we know best' style of government, which no longer sits well with a population that is increasingly better-educated, traveled, and self-confident, even arrogant," says Liak Teng Kiat, a fellow at the Institute of Southeast Asian Studies at the National University of Singapore.

The economic growth, however, gives the party plenty of ammunition for election contests. And the leadership aggressively defends its program against any and all critics, wherever it may find them. In January 1995, for instance, an unflattering article in *The Times* of London drew this response:

From the High Commissioner for the Republic of Singapore

> Sir,
>
> In his article, "Singapore opens debate on dissent in a nanny state" (January 12), Christopher Thomas describes Singapore as "the ultimate nanny state" where the people are treated "rather like errant children". Can nannying Singapore workers produce a world-competitive airline like SIA? Beri (Business Environment Risk Intelligence), a US organisation, ranks the Singapore workforce in 1994 as the number one in the world.
>
> The Geneva World Economic Forum competitiveness report, 1994, ranks Singapore as the second most competitive economy after the USA. Has the Singapore Government been wrong to get Singaporeans to achieve standards of excellence that have made Singapore competitive internationally?
>
> Christopher Thomas said many Singaporeans are weary of the Government's "hectoring, patronizing and pervasive presence in their lives". Eight times in the last 36 years, at four to six-yearly intervals, Singaporeans could, in free and fair elections, have changed their government. They chose to re-elect it. Could not this be one reason why Singapore has moved from "squalor to become a world economic power in three decades"?
>
> *Yours sincerely,*
> ABDUL AZIZ MAHMOOD,
> Singapore High Commission,
> 9 Wilton Crescent, SW1.

The foundation of Singapore's economic success is capital investment. It keeps climbing the technology ladder, adding design and service value to products and boosting productivity. The goal is to keep getting more sales out of fewer workers and battling low-cost competitors such as China and Vietnam with a reputation for quality.

A cornerstone of Singapore's economic strategy is "regionalization," the push for Singaporean companies to invest in Asia to help ensure the island state's long-term prosperity. During the past few years, Singapore companies have invested billions of dollars in manufacturing and property-development projects throughout Asia, making Singapore a leading investor in several countries. The Singapore Economic Development Board has been active in promoting foreign investment and assisting companies to take the leap. Lim Swee Say, managing director of the development board, discussed the policy and its effect on the domestic economy in an April 1995 interview with *The Asian Wall Street Journal:*

> As the Asian-Pacific region continues to expand, it will offer Singapore companies and Singapore-based companies the opportunity to participate in the growth of the regional economy. In addition to attracting companies into Singapore, we can also capitalize on and optimize the resources available in Singapore to invest in the region and thereby contribute to GNP growth. GDP and GNP growth should as far as possible reinforce each other. . . . Promoting GNP growth at the expense of GDP growth is not sustainable. In the case of Singapore, to ensure the continued growth of GDP, we have and will continue to invest in infrastructure . . . and upgrade the skill profile of our work force to ensure that Singapore will continue to have a pro-business environment to attract high-value-added industries. . . . We would like to see Singapore companies participating actively in economic growth in the region, and at the same time contributing to industrial modernization in the region. . . . A prosperous Asia-Pacific is good for Asia and good for Singapore, too, bearing in mind that Singapore is a small country. We are of no threat to any economy. We don't see ourselves competing with these economies.

Foreign investors are not entirely enamored of the Singapore market, however. For years, international investors in companies deemed to be of national strategic value have been restricted to buying "foreign shares." Because these shares are limited in number to ensure that control of the companies remains in Singaporean hands, a hefty premium has developed—more than 100% in some cases. The separate listing of certain stocks into local and foreign tranches was introduced in 1988 as a more transparent and equitable way to limit foreign shareholding in companies that have strategic value, such as banks, finance houses, and companies in the aviation, publishing, and defense sectors. Market participants long have argued that a dual-listing system isn't the best way to prevent foreign control of local companies. Ensuring that local shareholders maintain a controlling stake in major companies or issuing nonvoting shares to foreign investors would achieve the same objective, without creating abnormalities in stock valuations, they say.

Because foreign investors typically provide a sizable share of the liquidity in the Singapore market, locals-only shares tend to trade sluggishly. Some foreign investors complained they were paying too high a premium for foreign shares fundamentally similar to local shares. At the same time, holders of local shares felt they were penalized by the lower liquidity and prices of their stocks.

Some analysts and senior banking executives also worried that the system was an unattractive symbol of the pace of financial liberalization—even as Singapore has sought a role on the global stage as a financial center. Yet changing the system has proved tougher than it might have seemed at first, in part because separate laws define the limits on foreign ownership. The Banking Act and the Finance Companies Act stipulate foreign ownership limits of 40% and 20% for banks and finance houses, respectively. The Newspaper and Printing Presses Act restricts foreign ownership in newspapers to 49%. So, even if the local and foreign share tranches are merged, foreign investors would still face restrictions if current shareholding limits remain.

For several weeks in mid-1997, it appeared that the foreign shares policy might be changed because several companies began merging

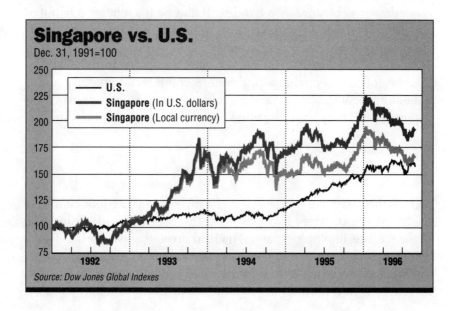

Singapore vs. U.S.

Dec. 31, 1991=100

Legend:
— U.S.
— Singapore (In U.S. dollars)
— Singapore (Local currency)

Source: Dow Jones Global Indexes

their domestic and foreign stock tranches. Immediately, the foreign-share premiums started to shrivel, which meant international investors endured several weeks in which the value of their foreign shares plunged while shares available only to local investors were surging. Some international fund managers became quite angry, fearing that their holdings of foreign shares would continue to drop. It took repeated reassurances from Singapore's central bank that the foreign share policy wasn't changing to assuage the market, coupled with denials from the remaining companies that they planned to merge their shares into one tranche.

Among the blue chip possibilities in Singapore, stocks with foreign-ownership restrictions rank high: Development Bank of Singapore, Overseas Chinese Bank, and United Overseas Bank are attractive bank stocks. Singapore Airlines consistently gets high marks for service. Singapore's biggest company is Keppel, which repairs and services ships and has diversified into several other ventures, including telecommunications. Among smaller stocks are Far East Levingston Shipbuilding, Keppel's oil rig subsidiary; Singapore Technologies Shipbuilding; Malayan Credit Ltd., which is in property investment and development; and taxi-fleet operator Comfort Group and Singapore Bus Service, both of which benefits from Singapore's high automobile prices. Other possibilities: Robinson & Co. is a major retailer of clothing and other department store merchandise. Inchcape is a retailer, too, but of Rolexes, office machines, Keds shoes, industrial equipment, Toro irrigation sprinklers, and Toyota automobiles. Cycle & Carriage deals in Mercedes-Benz and Mitsubishi vehicles. Straits Steamship Land, a member of the Keppel group, develops commercial property and is benefiting from strong demand for office space in Singapore. And Singapore Press Holdings is the city-state's big newspaper publisher.

THE TIGER CUBS

Among the objects of the Tigers' Asian investments are four countries on the verge of Tiger-like growth in the years ahead. Indonesia, Malaysia, the Philippines, and Thailand are today where the Tigers were maybe a decade or so ago. They are in far better position to take the Tiger model to heart than are China or India. If your taste in Asian investments runs toward the adventuresome, but with some assurance of seeing a payoff in five years or so, you will want to consider the Tiger cubs.

By the time you read this, in fact, the timing might be about right. For all four of these cubs were hit hard in 1997 with currency crises, plunging stock prices, and economic mayhem. The rout started in Thailand, which has the most debt—most of it from foreign sources—as a percentage of gross domestic product of any country in Southeast Asia. All four countries had currencies tied to the U.S. dollar, but currency traders believed such lofty valuations weren't justified by the countries' debt-heavy economies. They attacked, and the central banks of these countries defended. But in the end, the ties to the U.S. dollar were severed or loosened. In one fell swoop, these economies suddenly became a lot more competitive. They will take advantage of this condition in the years ahead.

INDONESIA, at first glance, shows the most promise of maturing into a full-fledged Tiger. It is the fourth-largest nation in the world, half of whose 197 million people are 21 years old or younger. It boasts an economic growth record of 7% a year between 1990 and 1996. The multi-island nation is rich in natural resources, primarily timber, oil, and natural gas.

But there are some flies in Indonesia's ointment of success. It is too dependent on foreign aid, which amounts to 2% of the country's gross domestic product and undermines Indonesia's ability to stand on its own economic feet. Moreover, Indonesia's economy is relatively closed. International trade amounts to 22% of gross domestic product, compared to 50% for all of East Asia. Much of that international trade, furthermore, is in raw materials to which very little value has been added. Increasingly, Indonesia will find itself competing against newly emergent nations such as Myanmar (formerly Burma) and Vietnam, which can export their raw materials more cheaply.

Two reasons explain why such conditions exist. One is that Indonesia's labor market gets 2 million new workers a year, and the government is scared of pricing them out of the very basic jobs that match their equally basic skill levels. Another reason is that too many heavyweight political vested interests want to maintain excessive and monopolistic profit margins in out-of-date industries. "Restrictions to domestic competition remain pervasive, hobbling the growth of progressive, efficiency-seeking entrepreneurialism," according to a paper written for an April 1995 conference by a World Bank economist. "Such restrictions take the form of cartels, price controls, entry and exit controls, exclusive licensing, public-sector dominance, and ad hoc interventions by government in favor of specific firms and sectors."

While Indonesia in the past could boast more-sanguine economic data than many of its neighbors, the deep-seated problems of protectionism and unrestrained foreign borrowing by private companies left it no less immune than Malaysia or the Philippines to investors' reassessments following Thailand's financial shake-up.

Indonesians hope 76-year-old President Suharto will seize the opportunity to push through badly needed reforms. First, though, the government has to deal with the stunning blow to economic confidence created by the rupiah's more than 20% plunge during the currency crisis. The cure for a sinking currency, of course, is higher short-term interest rates; but such a move threatens to choke economic growth. Bankers say that allowing the rupiah to float probably was Bank Indonesia's best move in the face of massive speculative pressure. But the economic shock it created widened quickly into a broader political concern about the need for stable political leadership. President Suharto's failure to anoint a clear successor has become even more problematic in the face of a potentially destabilizing economic slowdown. "The market is finally facing up to the fact that Indonesia has the biggest political risk in the region, more than Thailand," said the head of foreign exchange trading at a bank in Singapore. "We've ignored it for a long time, but now the market is saying you have to pay for having this huge succession question."

Mr. Suharto gained power in the wake of a 1965 abortive coup attempt that he blamed on the then-strong Indonesian Communist Party. He solidified his power amid one of the Cold War's bloodiest anti-Communist purges. His success at uniting the disparate nation behind the goals of tolerance and development—and then delivering roughly 7% annual economic growth for three decades running—is one of the great political feats of this century. A publicity shy man who keeps his own inner circle guessing at his every move, Mr. Suharto quietly transformed Indonesia into a darling of foreign investors and the World Bank. Pragmatic to the bone, Indonesians say, he rules along simple lines: authoritarian control to preserve stability; free markets to attract capital, technology, and jobs; and unlimited presidential power to keep everyone in check.

Even some Suharto admirers say the system has worked too well:

It has sown the seeds of public resentment that now threaten to destroy it. As the economy opened up and grew, enormous business opportunities and wealth flowed to the people best equipped to exploit the new prospects: Indonesia's military officers (Suharto is a former general), ethnic Chinese traders, and other insiders. These groups, combining the wherewithal and capital, the foreign contacts and local connections to get things done, modernized large parts of the archipelago in recent years, uprooting age-old, local economies in their wake. Anger and envy followed.

The 75-year-old president's sixth term ends in 1998, and he hasn't announced whether he will seek a seventh. Whenever he departs the scene, the transition of power is likely to be messy—which his increasing authoritarianism seems to be foreshadowing. In July 1996 a crackdown on an opposition party provoked the worst political violence in Jakarta in 15 years, as rampaging young Indonesians attacked and burned several government buildings and businesses owned by ethnic Chinese Indonesians, who have prospered under Suharto's rule. During parliamentary elections held in 1997, more than 250 people died in election-related riots, clashes between competing campaigners, and traffic accidents, as rowdy teenagers fell off vehicles joining lawless convoys.

A great deal of the anti-Suharto sentiment stems from repeated favoritism shown to his children. His daughter Siti Hardiyanti Rukmana, better known as Tutut, received the toll-road concession and now heads the operating company, Citra Marga Nusaphala Persada. Tutut's younger brother Bambang Trihatmodjo heads Bimantara Citra, a holding company with 26 different businesses, including telecommunications, television, and petrochemicals—all of which benefit from cozy ties with the government. Suharto's most controversial handout came in February 1996, when the government awarded a package of tariff and tax breaks to PT Timor Putra Nasional, an auto venture owned by Hutomo Mandala Putra (Suharto's youngest son, who goes by "Tommy") and Kia Motors Corporation of South Korea, for purposes of building a "national car." Not only did this deal's nepotism turn people off—Tommy is regarded as a lightweight businessperson who probably couldn't make it without family connections—but also the venture seemed inherently foolish: The "Indonesian" car actually will be imported from South Korea. While many other projects were put on hold following the currency crisis of mid-1997, this one went ahead—adding another rupiah of resentment about the president's nepotism.

Another troublesome issue for Indonesia is its dwindling earnings from oil exports. Price levels play a role, of course, but the main problem is that the country is running out of oil to export. Indonesia is a founding member of the Organization of Petroleum Exporting Countries and home to some of the world's largest oil reserves. But with oil production stagnating and domestic consumption rising by about 7% annually—as quickly as the economy is growing—Indonesia will someday become a net oil importer to cover its own industrial needs. That could be as soon as 1998 or between 2005 and 2010, depending on how quickly new oil reserves are found. But foreign oil companies aren't very interested in looking for more because Indonesia keeps its domestic prices low through government subsidies. In Indonesia, a liter of diesel fuel costs about 16 U.S. cents, compared with an average of 68 cents in Japan, 34 cents in Singapore, and 24 cents in Vietnam. Indonesia has an ambitious target for raising non-oil exports such as plywood and textiles.

Foreign investors dominate the Indonesian stock market, accounting for about 70% of all trades on the Jakarta Stock Exchange; in Thailand and Malaysia, by comparison, trading by foreigners is less than one-third of stock market activity. Until more Indonesians participate, that means the Jakarta market is apt to be susceptible to the movement of markets elsewhere, particularly the United States. The brighter side of that coin is that eventually there will be a buoying of share prices as

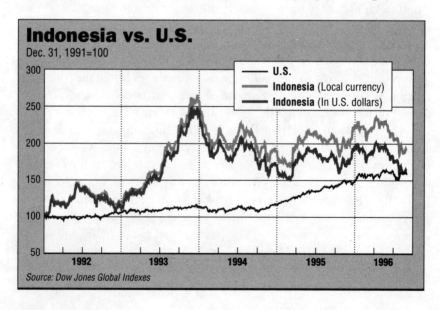

Indonesia vs. U.S.
Dec. 31, 1991=100

U.S.
Indonesia (Local currency)
Indonesia (In U.S. dollars)

Source: Dow Jones Global Indexes

Indonesians start investing themselves. Considerably less than 1% of the population owns stock, compared to 15% for Taiwan and Korea and 20% for Japan.

Foreign investors may hold up to 49% of issues listed on the Jakarta Stock Exchange. The market is growing rapidly but it isn't very liquid, except for the very biggest companies. American depositary receipts are available for PT Inti Indorayon Utama, which produces pulp and rayon fibers for the paper and textile industries; Tri Polyta Indonesia, a chemicals maker; and Indonesia Satellite, the country's long-distance telephone monopoly. Other major companies with stock listings include Barito Pacific Timber, the largest plywood producer and exporter; Gadjah Tunggal, which makes car and motorcycle tires for the Indonesian market; Gudang Garam, the largest maker of clove cigarettes; Modern Photo Film, which makes and sells Fuji brand cameras and film; Polysindo Eka Perkasa, the largest integrated textile producer; and Unggal Indah, one of the world's biggest producers of key raw materials for making detergent.

MALAYSIA, which had been on an economic roll since 1988, has taken to expressing its growing wealth and ambitions with gargantuan buildings. As we wrote the first edition of this book, developers in Kuala Lumpur were putting the final touches on twin 1,492-foot office towers (now the world's tallest buildings), and an aggressive Malaysian tycoon was winning government approval to construct the world's longest multiuse building: a ten-story, tubelike structure that will snake along for 1.24 miles above the Kelang River in Kuala Lumpur, with office towers, condominiums, and shopping malls subsequently to be built along it and on top of it. Among the attractions in the project, called KL LinearCity, will be a Rollerblade arena and an artificial rain forest populated with robotic dinosaurs. One method of getting around in the building will be an indoor canal running through the seventh floor, 80 feet above the ground.

As we write this edition, the LinearCity project is suspended, one of the victims of the Southeast Asian currency typhoon of 1997. It typified the Malaysian scene in more ways than one. It was conceived as the nation of 19.7 million people was enjoying the ninth consecutive year of inflation-adjusted economic growth averaging more than 8% annually. Also, LinearCity joined a growing list of megaprojects that are a source of pride to Prime Minister Mahathir Mohamad and that typify the "first come, first served" privatization policy of his government. Malaysia happily entertains unsolicited proposals from developers who want to acquire state assets or the rights to use them. If the government likes an idea, a deal may be struck without competitive bidding from other would-be investors. Many beneficiaries of privatization have been people and companies linked to senior officials of the country's dominant political party, the United Malays National Organization.

Complaints are heard, but nothing much comes of them because everybody is riding the longest growth cycle in the country's postindependence history. The Federation of Malaya became an independent state within the British Commonwealth in 1957; in 1963 it formed the Federation of Malaysia with Singapore, which withdrew in 1965. Waves of foreign and local investment—mostly in manufacturing and infrastructure projects—have transformed a country once dependent on commodities into a mini-industrial dynamo.

Before the currency storm blew in, the Malaysian government predicted that gross national product, the total output of goods and services, would grow at a heady inflation-adjusted 8% a year for the rest of this century, compared with 8.7% in the previous five years. If that target is achieved, Malaysia's GNP by 2000 would be more than 70% greater than it was in 1995. The problem with such heady growth is that imports of goods and capital are far outstripping Malaysia's exports, which are themselves growing rapidly. Such conditions are partly what

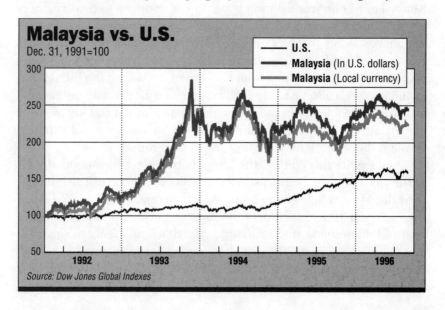

Malaysia vs. U.S.
Dec. 31, 1991=100

U.S.
Malaysia (In U.S. dollars)
Malaysia (Local currency)

Source: Dow Jones Global Indexes

attracted the currency speculators in 1997, ultimately forcing Malaysia to abandon the peg of its ringgit to the U.S. dollar.

Prime Minister Mahathir did not take the currency turmoil gracefully. He lashed out harshly and publicly at foreign hedge funds in general and at George Soros, head of the Quantum Fund, in particular, though it subsequently turned out the Quantum Fund was buying ringgit during the sharp decline rather than selling. With Malaysia's Kuala Lumpur Stock Exchange Composite Index down 32% for the year in local currency terms, the Kuala Lumpur Exchange abruptly introduced restrictions on selling stocks in order to rein in short-sellers, who were blamed for the market's downfall. Short-sellers borrow shares in the hope of buying them back later at a lower price. The authorities banned short-selling in Malaysia's top 100 blue-chip stocks, and made it compulsory for sellers to have stock in hand when they actually sold. The response was dramatic, but not as intended: The Malaysian market sank 14% during a week of heavy selling. Finally, Prime Minister Mahathir was forced to scrap the restrictions on short-selling. On the following day, Kuala Lumpur's market soared 12%.

But Dr. Mahathir (he was trained as a physician) didn't leave the market alone, even at that point. Early in September 1997, he stunned investors by announcing plans to create a 60 billion ringgit ($20.15 billion) fund—equal to 43% of Malaysia's gross domestic product—to prop up the stock market, which by that time had lost a third of its value in two months. The Malaysian market promptly plunged again, to its lowest levels in more than four years, as foreign funds dumped their holdings. Foreign investors said they had lost confidence in Malaysia as a place to invest. Though details of the share-purchase plan weren't spelled out, Dr. Mahathir said 30 billion ringgit would be raised from Malaysian funds, including the national pension fund, and the remainder would be raised through bonds issued by Malaysia's powerful state investment agency, Khazanah Holdings. Some economists and investment analysts said the move could inflict heavy damage on the country's financial system and the economy. One motivation for the share-purchase plan may be government fears about the effects of falling stock prices on the viability of some Malaysian banks and companies. Many companies have pledged their holdings of shares as security for their bank borrowings. As the market value of those shares tumbles, bankers say, some of the companies face demands that they provide more collateral.

Eventually—perhaps by the time you read this—Malaysia will

climb back on the growth track, and foreign investors will be trolling the Kuala Lumpur market again.

Stocks that are a play on Malaysia itself include Amalgamated Steel Mills, whose interests also include retailing, automaking, and tire production; Bandar Raya Developments, a property developer; Kuala Lumpur Kepong, whose plantations grow oil palms, cocoa, and rubber; Perlis Plantations, which raise oil palm and sugarcane and run movie theaters; and Resorts World, which holds the only casino license in the country. Big Malaysian conglomerates with as many or more interests outside the country as in it include Genting (hotels, plantations, transportation, property development, and half of Resorts World); Malayan United Industries (property, construction, manufacturing, hotels, education, insurance, and media); and Sime Darby, the largest conglomerate (plantations, heavy equipment, auto assembly and distribution, and property development).

THE PHILIPPINES, many Asians thought, would never rise into the ranks of East Asia's tiger cubs. Bypassed by the region's economic boom, this island nation was long called "the sick man of Asia," diseased by corrupt politics. In a 1992 speech in Manila, Lee Kuan Yew, then Singapore's prime minister and now its senior minister, asserted to his hosts: What economic development required was more discipline and less democracy.

"But we decided to do it our way," says Roberto De Ocampo, the Philippine finance minister, who, with the nation's economy recently rivaling Singapore's growth rate, is feeling his oats. "We are dedicated to formulating a new model of Third World economic development that combines growth with equity, modernization with environmental consciousness—all in the context of democracy."

The Philippines is proving that democracy and economic development need not be mutually exclusive in Asia. Under President Fidel Ramos, trade and investment are soaring, electronic products have replaced coconuts as the leading export, annual per-capita income has burst through the $1,000 mark, and, for the first time in a decade, gross national product was expanding more than 7% in 1996, bucking the Southeast Asian downtrend.

Clearing the way for takeoff, Mr. Ramos, a career soldier, pacified the corrupt military, made peace with Muslim secessionists, calmed territorial disputes with China and Malaysia, and tamed a highly contentious political culture. "We got lucky," says Peter Tan of Hambrecht & Quist Philippines Inc., the Manila affiliate of the San Francisco investment bank. "Somehow, a guy who nobody thought would get elected or do anything in office has turned everything around." When Singapore's Mr. Lee advised a clampdown in 1992, the Philippines was mired in its second year of zero economic growth. President Corazon Aquino, after surviving six coup attempts, had just left office; power shortages were making manufacturing nearly impossible. Subic Bay and another big U.S. outpost, Clark Air Base, lay deserted and covered in ash from a volcanic eruption in 1991.

Mr. Ramos, though elected with less than 30% of the vote, said everything must change. A social outsider catapulted to the top of the Philippines' ruling elite and a Protestant at the helm of a Catholic country, he took aim at one of the nation's most endemic problems: powerful families' choke-hold on the economy.

Working with the Philippine Congress, Mr. Ramos abolished tariffs and other preferential treatment that had long enriched the leading clans. Most notably, he opened the banking sector to competition, helping drive down interest rates, and broke the telecommunications monopoly controlled by former President Aquino's own Cojuangco clan, helping expand phone services. He also recruited foreign investors to solve the national power crisis—in just 18 months. "The root causes of our problems were never in the jungles," where Communist guerrillas have waged a rebellion for decades, says Gen. Jose Almonte, Mr. Ramos's national security adviser. "Our problems were in Makati," Manila's business center.

The Ramos overhaul isn't complete, of course, and there isn't any chance he can see it through. Mr. Ramos's six-year term ends in 1998, and one is all he gets under the constitution. One of the possible candidates to succeed him is Vice President Joseph Estrada, a beloved movie star with little credibility in the business community and close ties to old cronies of former dictator Ferdinand Marcos. Prominent Filipinos have called for a constitutional amendment to let Mr. Ramos run again, but the 69-year-old president has said he isn't interested. Rather, Mr. Ramos and his aides say the Philippine renaissance will continue without him. Unlike past economic booms, they note, this one is being led by productive investments and exports, not consumer spending. "Even if a chimpanzee becomes president," General Almonte says, "there's a growing constituency for reform that won't care."

But in 1997, economic growth slowed a bit from its previous torrid pace, and the currency crisis blew in from Thailand. All of a sudden, the Philippines looked to foreign investors less like opportunity
and more like trouble. Loan growth in the Philippines has been extraordinarily high. Banks were stifled for years, but thanks to economic
liberalization in the 1990s, their lending growth has taken off. "For 10
years we stagnated; we're now playing catch-up," said Rafael Buenaventura, chief executive of Philippine Commercial International
Bank. He argues that the Philippines isn't another Thailand; for one
thing, Thailand's economy grew strongly for a decade before trouble
arrived. By contrast, the Philippines has enjoyed strong economic
growth for only the preceding couple of years. However, while the
Philippine economy was growing at about 5% to 6% annually, loan
growth soared 42% in 1996, on the heels of a 43% jump in 1995, according to Moody's Investors Service. "The risk is that the Philippines'
banks (and corporations) may end up paying the same price of excessive growth and leverage that some other Asian banking systems are
paying—notably Thailand, Korea, and Japan—after the bubble economy bursts," Moody's said in a report.

President Ramos did what he could to contain the impact of the
currency crisis in his country. "The Philippines is different from Thailand," he said in a speech. "With due respect to them, we feel our

Philippines vs. U.S.
Dec. 31, 1991=100

— U.S.
— **Philippines** (In U.S. dollars)
— **Philippines** (Local currency)

Source: Dow Jones Global Indexes

macroeconomic fundamentals that we have put in place are very, very sound." He added that the property sector "has been forewarned about not overdoing it; our banking community likewise has been warned about overheating by no less than the governor of the (central bank)." But winning back investors' confidence could prove extremely difficult.

Longer term, the Philippines can count among its natural riches a workforce with a reputation for quality. In a survey of expatriate managers by Political & Economic Risk Consultancy Ltd. of Hong Kong, Filipinos ranked fourth in the world in terms of labor quality, cost, availability and stability. (Only Indians, Australians, and Britons ranked higher.) Filipino workers got especially high marks for technical skills, mastery of English, and willingness to do factory and middle-management jobs that many comparably educated Southeast Asians shun. About 20% of Filipinos employed in foreign-owned factories are university graduates, the survey found.

In establishing itself economically, the Philippines stands to benefit from its participation in the ASEAN (Association of Southeast Asian Nations) Free Trade Area, which aims to remove the tariff of all goods traded among the six-member countries. "In about eight years, the whole of ASEAN will reduce tariffs to zero," Trade Secretary Rizalino Navarro said. "That means if European companies invest here and put up their factories here, they will have access to a market of 350 million." Among the European firms already in the Philippines are the British-owned Pilipinas Shell Petroleum, Swiss-owned Nestlé Philippines, the Dutch-owned Unilever Philippines, the German-owned Bayer Philippines, and the Norwegian-owned Aboitiz Jebsen Bulk Transport. An airport and cement-company projects supported by the European Investment Bank in the southern Philippine province of Davao also are expected to attract more funds from Europe, as is the Netherlands-based ING Bank, which was one of the ten foreign banks recently granted licenses to operate up to six branches in the Philippines.

The Philippine Stock Exchange was formed out of two predecessor stock exchanges and still operates two trading floors, one at the Tektite Towers in suburban Ortigas and the other at Makati, the country's financial district. Last year, the two floors were connected by computer, which pleased investors because it produced uniform opening and closing stock prices. Total stock market capitalization stands at around 1.3 trillion pesos ($50 billion). In the exchange's composite index, commercial and industrial issues have the heaviest weighting at 80%; property stocks are at 17%; mining shares at 2%; and the oil issues at less than 1%. The movement of the index, however, is dominated by the stocks of six companies: Petron, Ayala Land (real estate development), San Miguel (food and beverages), Philippine Long Distance Telephone, Metropolitan Bank & Trust, and Manila Electric. Ayala and San Miguel have both "A" and "B" shares: "A" shares can be traded only by local investors; "B" shares are for foreigners.

Philippine Long Distance has a built-in currency hedge that may interest you: The company receives about three-fourths of its revenue in U.S. dollars. A relatively new listing that caught investors' attention is Bankard, which issues credit cards to consumers; credit card use is soaring in the Philippines.

THAILAND has been red hot for too long. After a year of tight-credit policies imposed by Thailand's central bank to wrestle inflation into submission, the country's once sizzling economy is cooling considerably. For a decade, GDP growth averaged more than 10%. But in 1996, the central bank said annual growth had braked to only 7.8%, falling below 8% growth for the first time since 1986.

Thailand needed to cool off. Its debt was rising fast, inflation remained high, and a growing gap between the rich and the poor threatened to tarnish its reputation for social stability and sound economic management. Foreign investors, who had been fretting that the economy risked boiling over, may be pleased by this turn of events in the long term. But in 1996 they started to get out of Thailand as fast as they could. They turned out to be prescient. In 1997, the Thai currency, the baht, came under attack as currency traders swarmed to profit from the discrepancy between the weakening economy and the baht's peg to the U.S. dollar. By July, the government was forced to cut the baht's dollar ties and let it float. By then, though, the Thai economy had been thrown into disarray and the country had no choice but appeal to the World Bank and others for a bailout, a $16.7 billion credit package extended by Asian central banks, the World Bank, and the Asian Development Bank.

The trouble started in the giddiness of torrid economic growth, to which the Thais naively saw no end. The expansion was more than the Thais could afford on their own, so they turned eagerly to foreign capital to fill the gap between domestic savings and the investment needed to sustain the economic growth. Poorly supervised banks and finance companies borrowed heavily in U.S. dollars—and too much of that was in short-term loans. Then they turned around and foolishly lent the money (in Thai baht) for real estate. When the devaluation came, they were devastated.

Some people saw the crisis coming. In February 1995, credit-rating agency Moody's Investors Service issued a stern warning on Thai banks, saying rapid lending growth had put the sector at risk of loan defaults should the economy falter. "Vulnerable sectors of the loan portfolios include tourism, especially in the luxury hotel sector, golf courses, and prime office space in Bangkok," Moody's said. "There is the risk that a real estate and/or stock market bubble is forming and that the banking system may face a period of asset deflation after the acceleration in property and financial asset values."

To restore investor confidence, Thailand must get its financial house in order. The $16 billion bailout package of course comes with a list of economic reforms, some of which are quite unpalatable to the Thais, who don't like foreigners telling them what to do. Thais have almost absolute faith in the "Thai luck" factor—that somehow they always land on their feet.

Indeed, some investors wasted no time after stock prices and other valuations collapsed to hop a plane to Bangkok and hunt for bargains.

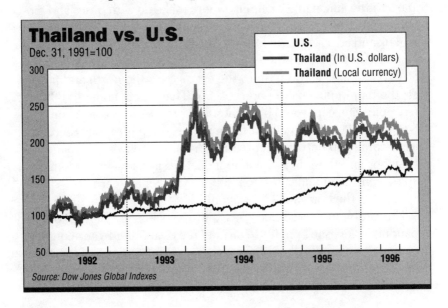

Thailand vs. U.S.
Dec. 31, 1991=100

— U.S.
— Thailand (In U.S. dollars)
— Thailand (Local currency)

Source: Dow Jones Global Indexes

"Medium to long term, Thailand is a very good investment opportunity," said Gary Stead, head of mergers and acquisitions in Asia for Merrill Lynch. Merrill Lynch found several large Thai companies that, while overextended, appear to be basically sound, Mr. Stead said. The hard part is persuading the companies' principal shareholders to sell equity stakes at today's prices, he said in September 1997. "Valuations have been wiped out. It takes time for the new reality to sink in," he said. Another active U.S. firm is Goldman Sachs & Co., whose proprietary investment arm is seeking to multiply its $100 million or so of Thai investments by some five to 10 times, said Henry Cornell, Goldman Sachs's partner for Asian direct investments. "We take a five-year point of view," Mr. Cornell said. "We want to be part of what we think will be the inevitable recovery of Thailand."

Unfortunately, Thailand has some social problems that need to be addressed, too. One of them is the widening gap in income distribution, which is being made worse by the successful industrialization of the past decade. Despite occasional bursts of rural infrastructure spending, the gap is growing as the metropolis moves from low-value-added industries to increasingly capital-intensive manufacturing or high-value services. Thailand is the largest car market in Southeast Asia, yet 60% of the cars are sold to residents of Bangkok and its environs, who comprise only about 15% of the population. The capital has become a traffic jam, while Thais elsewhere make do with buses and motorbikes, and often with bicycles and buffaloes. The result is that Bangkok and adjacent areas, with about 13 million people, account for about 56% of GDP, and the figure is rising. Household income in the metropolitan area is three times the average for the north and northeast; the dry, impoverished northeast of Thailand is home to 30% of the people. The gap would be greater but for the money sent home by migrants working in Bangkok. Even within the metropolis there is a huge income gap between those in high-value services and manufacturing jobs and those in sweatshop industries and low-wage domestic employment. Nationally, the top 20% of the people earn 56% of the income, and the bottom 40% earn only 11.5%.

This problem doesn't become explosive as long as the economy is expanding; everyone benefits to one degree or another from economic growth. It's when recessions inevitably come that social problems boil over. Economic downturns in the 1970s and 1980s led to dangerous instability. Attempting to fix the problem necessarily would involve the government investing more in the boondocks, shifting agencies out of Bangkok, and so on. But social programs such as this one, or for education and training, may be curtailed while Thailand gets its economy back into shape.

Thailand also faces a severe shortage of skilled workers, which places a limit on rapid economic growth. Rising wages have eroded the competitiveness of Thailand's labor-intensive industries, and a lack of educated workers is slowing the shift to higher value-added production. The failings of the educational system are also at the root of the growing income gap between city dwellers and the provincial poor. Many rural children lack the resources to go beyond the six years of compulsory schooling. And those with only a primary school education are increasingly excluded from the higher-paying jobs in the manufacturing and service sectors.

Foreign investors can't own more than 25% of Thai banks, or more than 49% of any other company. If you want to get into a stock that already has reached its foreign-investment limit, you must buy from other foreigners. With a rash of mergers expected as part of the fallout from the currency crisis of 1997, the stock scene is likely to change markedly in the next year or two. As of this writing, however, investment considerations should include Bangkok Bank, which is the nation's largest and which also is in mutual fund management and securities brokerage. Finance One is the largest nonbank financial-services company, and it, too, is in the securities business. Charoen Pokphand Feedmill supplies feed to animal and fish farms and also has its own prawn operation. Hana Microelectronics is a semiconductor maker, with more than half its sales made to the United States. International Cosmetic distributes and sells a wide variety of brand-name consumer goods in Thailand, which include, along with the product line suggested by its name, clothing, personal computers, and beer. Shinawatra Computer & Communications markets computers and telecommunications equipment, and it offers cable television and radio broadcasting. Siam Cement mostly makes cement, but it manufactures other building products as well. Matichon Newspaper Group publishes Thai-language newspapers and magazines.

CHAPTER XIII

The Awakening Giants

CHINA and India are huge countries, both with expanding middle classes offering enormous consumer potential and both opening up to foreign investors. One is the world's largest democracy, the other is the world's largest Communist power. When foreign-stock ownership was first allowed, in 1992, professional money managers flocked to the dictatorship, China. But by 1993 and 1994, as China's shortcomings shuttled into the spotlight and its achievements grew less surprising, the money managers looked more favorably (or was that hopefully?) on India. Then India careened into a period of political upheaval. In truth, it will take years, maybe decades, for either of these giants to stumble toward economic adolescence, much less maturity. But their sheer size—China has 1.2 billion people, India 920 million—makes their growing pains immensely important to the rest of the world. That includes your portfolio.

China was everybody's nominee for the most likely to become an economic superpower. It had started in the 1980s to move toward lowering the bamboo curtain and allowing foreign businesspeople in to establish footholds. By the early 1990s, China boasted Western-built hotels, modern airlines, and two brand-new stock exchanges. To outsiders paying only cursory attention, it must have seemed that the People's Republic was almost capitalist. By contrast, India was the ugly duckling that appeared unable to get its act together; also, it erupted sporadically with ancient religious and ethnic violence. In time, though, perceptions changed. Markets like political stability, and China's started coming unglued. With the old leader dying, the next generation of Communist leaders started jockeying for power, a black ritual of backstabbing that sends disquieting ripples through the politicized society. The economy, top-heavy with flabby state-owned companies and fueled by high-octane injections of foreign capital, overheated into a high rate of inflation. As this unpleasantness was sobering up the foreign investment community, India's economic reform program—begun only in 1991—started to bear fruit. Among emerging-markets investors, India was hot through much of 1994; China wasn't. Foreigners lapped up $4.6 billion of new Indian equity-linked paper that year but only $2.7 billion in new Chinese shares, according to figures from the Bombay Stock Exchange and Credit Lyonnais Securities (Asia).

Who's the Fairest?

	India	China
Savings Rate[1]	24.2%	35.8%
Female Literacy Rate[2]	33.7%	68.1%
Debt Service Ratio[3]	29.2%	13.0%
Average GDP Growth 1988–93[4]	5.3%	8.9%
Average GDP Growth 1995–2000[5]	6.0%	7.8%
Population (in millions)	846.3	1,172
"Economic Freedom" Ranking[6]	86	87

(1 = most free)

Notes:
[1] 1993–94 for India, 1992 for China; Asian Development Bank.
[2] 1990 for both countries, Asian Development Bank Estimates.
[3] Credit Lyonnais.
[4] 1995 Estimate, Credit Lyonnais Securities.
[5] Estimates.
[6] Heritage Foundation.

Yet, judged on fundamentals, the competition between India and China is no contest, as the accompanying table shows. China's economy is growing twice as fast. China's savings and literacy rates are more than half again higher. Foreign debts and government red ink drag down China's economy far less than they do India's. Moreover, China's lead in the foreign-investment sweepstakes—the direct kind, in factories rather than stocks—remains enormous. In 1994 alone, foreigners sank well over $30 billion into operations in China, compared with less than $2 billion in India. In a 1995 Ernst & Young survey of 230 multinational companies, 57% saw China as a "priority country" for future investment; just 17% gave that nod to India.

India has a lot of catching up to do. Though the reforms may have restarted India's economy, they haven't solved the seething ethnic and class divisions, done away with the corrupt and inefficient bureaucracy, or cleared city streets of beggars. But with the headaches, there are opportunities. For example, India has a huge middle class whose buying habits are well chronicled, unlike in China, where dependable marketing statistics are rare. The Indian government-supported National Council of Applied Economic Research periodically surveys samplings of up to 500,000 Indians. Its 1992–93 survey indicates that 550 million Indians lived in households where at least one member owned a wristwatch; that 33% of nail polish was bought by households with a monthly income of less than 18,000 rupees ($574); and that southern India accounted for 77% of the country's purchases of coffee.

India's cadre of skilled scientists and software engineers is winning international recognition. Motorola, Texas Instruments, and other foreign investors have turned Bangladore into one of the world's software-writing capitals. China still sets the pace in setting manufacturing-efficiency standards in plants operated with or by foreign companies, but India is coming on strongly enough to presage keen competition on this front.

Foreign firms can find well-managed private companies in India to do business with. In China, the potential partners for foreign investors are mainly state-owned companies, and the potential stock plays are all recent listings. The 120-year-old Bombay Stock Exchange, on the other hand, in 1994 had almost 4,450 listed companies, more than any other exchange in Asia. The people who run many of these companies have far more in common with many global executives than do their Chinese counterparts. In everything from their attitude toward profitability to their understanding of how a contract dispute should be resolved, they are far easier to work with, many foreign multinationals find. India's legal system is based on the Western philosophy of jurisprudence. The rule of law is well entrenched, if cumbersome. In China, by contrast, the first commercial laws weren't written until the 1980s.

Some Indians could barely restrain their glee as a spate of loan-payment problems and contract disputes tarnished China's business image in 1994. That was the year Beijing ripped up McDonald's lease on space near Tienanmen Square because officials got a better deal for constructing an office building on that site. But experienced foreign investors know that India also can pose frustrations. Democracies can't always pursue reforms as single-mindedly as the investors would like. While India has slashed tariffs and tackled its government budget deficit, it has balked at more painful measures, such as privatizing government enterprises or allowing imports of many foreign consumer goods. If it turns out that democracy does restrain India from developing as fast as China, some analysts say it also gives India a stability that transcends its occasional outbursts of communal violence. "Think of India as a wide, shallow-bottomed boat," said one official at the U.S. Embassy in New Delhi. "It's easy to rock but very difficult to tip over."

Investing in either country isn't a piece of cake. India has far greater experience with securities trading; the Bombay Stock Exchange is not "experimental," as Chinese Premier Li Peng terms China's two exchanges in Shanghai and Shenzhen (which is across the border from Hong Kong). India first allowed foreigners to invest directly in Indian stocks only in September 1992, and that was limited to institutions, each of which must apply for permission. "We only want long-term investors who have relevant experience" in emerging markets, an official told *The Wall Street Journal*. "If we let in just everyone, then we would be letting in both the men and the boys." Also, there are many restrictions and stiff capital-gains taxes on shares sold within one year of purchase. Receipts representing shares of only a handful of Indian companies trade outside India, and ownership of those is limited in some countries to institutions. Foreign individual investors have access to India only through mutual funds or a few closed-end funds.

China isn't much different. Eighty-two mainland companies have issued "B" shares, those available to foreigners; "A" shares are for Chinese citizens, though the distinction between the two already is starting to blur. For the most part, "B" shares, which trade on Shanghai and Shenzhen exchanges, are owned by institutions. But China has one big advantage India lacks: Hong Kong. The colony's thriving stock market lists 21 "H" shares—stock listed in Hong Kong—of mainland Chinese companies. Hong Kong also provides a crucial, albeit indirect, link for billions of dollars to flow into China's burgeoning economy, especially from Chinese investors in Hong Kong who still have strong connections to the mainland. "In Hong Kong, you have a credible stepping stone for investment into China," says Timothy Love, a portfolio manager at Marinvest, a New York–based subsidiary of Hongkong & Shanghai Banking Corporation. "That is enhanced by an English-speaking investment management community in Hong Kong, which has good links to Wall Street." In addition, the Hong Kong market is more efficient than the Bombay market.

To some extent, China basks in the aura of the other thriving nations that surround it. India's neighbors, by contrast, are less developed than it is. China's neighbor-nations have been not only profitable for investors but also politically less rambunctious than India. "There is a kind of Asian political model that the world has come to tolerate, a notion of a sort of benign dictatorship," says William L. Wilby, a vice president at Oppenheimer Management Corporation. "You see it in nearly every country in Asia, including South Korea, Singapore, and Thailand." In contrast to that stability, India in the past 45 years has had two political leaders assassinated, suffered deep-seated religious strife, and fought three wars with neighboring Pakistan. It also has a well-entrenched bureaucracy that for years controlled imports and exports, companies' foreign-exchange holdings, and corporate expansion, and it is now reluctant to surrender power. India's stock market may be old, but it sometimes acts like it was born yesterday. In early 1992, Indian stocks soared in a speculative frenzy prompted by the expected opening of the stock market to foreign investors. By late spring, the market was crashing in a $1.3 billion securities-dealing scandal that led to numerous arrests of brokers, bankers, and government officials and the suspension of trading on the Bombay exchange for five weeks.

"At some point 15 years from now, we may look back to places like India and say these were the greatest countries in Asia because they went through their political transitions early," says Mr. Wilby of Oppenheimer. "They're going through the difficult throes of the transition to democracy that many other Asian countries, including China, may have to go through in the next 10 to 15 years. The real question for Asia is whether the benign dictatorship is a stable model."

So, there are many more questions than answers about China and

India, as you will see as we take a closer look at the economies and investment opportunities of each country.

THE MIDDLE KINGDOM IN A MODERN AGE

The trouble with giant countries is that while the opportunities are giant, so are their problems. China's economy is no exception. On the positive side, it is growing nicely—nearly 10% a year for the past 17 years. Moreover, it is likely to keep growing at an above-average rate for the next decade or more. One reason for this prediction is demographic; another is socioeconomic.

Virtually alone among the world's big economies, China stands to benefit in the coming decade from a surge in the proportion of its population that is working and a tandem increase in both savings and spending. In Japan, Europe, and North America, the number of citizens outside the workforce—retirees, youngsters who haven't yet started working, or other dependents—is a troubling economic burden. In China, by contrast, a huge population bulge is just entering the workforce; 45% of the country's 1.2 billion people are under age 26. Many were born amid Mao Tse-tung's exhortations to build strength through population. The philosophy died with Mao in 1976, and Beijing now enforces a one-child-per-couple policy that in a few decades will create a major economic problem, with each child forced to support two parents in retirement. For now, though, working offspring with parents to support have a light burden.

So far during China's economic renaissance, wages have outpaced price rises. Although millions of Chinese are jobless or underemployed, wages continue to climb. J. P. Morgan & Company economist Joan Zheng predicts incomes will grow an average of 7% a year during the next decade. That, in combination with the masses entering the workforce, may form a bulwark against the pressures from any economic slowdown.

Her hope is pinned on China's frugality. As a nation, the Chinese save an astonishing 4 of every 10 yuan, about 48 cents of every $1.20, that they earn. China's 40% savings rate lags behind only the 40%-plus rate in Singapore, where state planners compel the citizens to save for retirement. Communist China used to compel savings, too, by assigning government-paid accommodations and denying its population any consumer choices. Nowadays, though, people have bought many of the consumer goods they want, and thus they can both spend and save.

Why do Chinese save so much? One reason is that many people don't pay for things like housing or education. Because the Communist system supplied housing and many families still share quarters, housing as a percentage of household expenditures is below 5%. With economic reforms marching ahead, many Chinese foresee a day when they will have to purchase or pay market rents for homes, so they are saving money. They also save because China's so-called iron rice bowl— the state's assurance that it will look after its citizens if they become unemployed or retire—has been discontinued.

Though such thrift gives individuals a financial cushion, the high savings rate isn't the boon it could be for China. Too little of the money is recycled into productive investments, and too much of it is stashed under people's beds. One of China's challenges is to channel that money into the economy, where it can fuel growth and finance badly needed infrastructure investment.

On the negative side, China has 102,200 state-owned businesses, the vast majority of which are poorly managed, uncompetitive, money-losing, or all three. These enterprises survive because they employ 100 million people, and the government doesn't want these folks out on the streets with the other 200 million unemployed or underemployed. Meanwhile, the government subsidizes loans to these companies through banks that are seldom repaid in full. Awash with these bad loans, the banks have slashed lending, which basically hurts those private-enterprise companies that have a chance to build viable businesses. The anti-inflation austerity program that began in 1993 has left the state sector in dire straits. Losses and stockpiles of unsold goods at state-run companies have mounted, and even the largest enterprises are running short of cash to cover working capital and pay wages. About 40% of the state-owned companies lose money. Two out of three state factories in China's industrial northeast have stopped or curbed production.

In a sense, the state companies are holding pens for excess workers until the private economy can grow large enough to absorb them. Foreign investment is rapidly building up the modern, efficient part of China's economy, but it isn't nearly big enough yet to absorb the millions who would be displaced by shutting down or restructuring the state-owned companies. The governement is unwilling to fling open its markets and allow imports to push down inflation, because such foreign competition might force the premature closing of the inefficient Chinese companies. By charging import tariffs averaging 35%, keeping customs requirements vague, and providing large subsidies to state industries, China's central government has maximized exports to earn the hard currency it needs for investment while strictly controlling imports. So, the government tinkers, alternately printing money to keep inefficient state firms alive, then easing off to curb inflation and the consumer anger it breeds.

For all its size, China's business economy has generated few big companies that can benefit from the country's large scale. Central planning and bureaucratic turf battles left the nation with hundreds of small companies making identical products. China still has more than 120 television manufacturers, 700 beer companies, and 30,000 rubber belt makers. Most sell products to just a tiny fraction of China's population. So fragmented is the marketplace that few companies have been able to take advantage of China's size and become real giants. The businesses that most effectively knit the market together are foreign newcomers, which aren't burdened by China's statist past.

Now, though, the state is willing to surrender control over parts of the economy. The resulting mergers and acquisitions—by one measure, 1,100 company mergers were expected to take place in 1997, up 33% from 1996—are transforming the economic landscape. In essence, the government is authorizing the creation of Chinese equivalents of Japanese *keiretsu* or South Korean *chaebol* conglomerates, developing a class of industrial powerhouses in beverages, autos, electronics, and textiles.

Beijing has tried limited reforms of the state sector. It has let companies go bankrupt—nearly 2,000 in 1995, almost double the 1994 total—but has kept a lid on the number for fear of sparking social unrest. By keeping the austerity squeeze on, it is pressuring state enterprises to introduce modern company structures and accounting as ways of coping with chronic shortages of capital. Some progress is being made, but it is slow and riddled with setbacks. In 1995, the State Council selected 100 large state-run enterprises in which to implement modern enterprise systems and shareholding structures by 1997. But the program bogged down with "unexpected complications," such as disagreements between managers of the concerns and the government over valuation of companies' assets; the lack of a complete social-security system that would provide a security net for laid-off workers; and the absence of a solution for dealing with state enterprises' mounting bad loans.

Part of the answer to breaking this gridlock may come from China's hinterland. Zhucheng, a modest city of 1.04 million in the northeastern province of Shandong, has taken matters into its own hands. It is, among other things, leasing some state firms to entrepreneurs and turning others into shareholding companies. It even gave away one marginal concern. Before reforms began in 1992, two-thirds of the city's 282 state enterprises were in the red or breaking even. Now all of the 272 that were reformed make a profit, with some companies' profits doubling each year, city officials say. The rest of the city has benefited, too, with economic output surging 87% between 1992 and 1995, and tax revenues jumping by 140%.

Led by a stable of reform-minded civic leaders, Zhucheng resorted to a variety of methods to fix its state sector, such as leasing out some enterprises, merging others, and allowing hopeless ones to go bankrupt. But the main strategy, applied to three-fourths of Zhucheng's state firms, was to sell the government's holdings in the enterprises to employees or to other companies, through share issuances.

One reason Zhucheng's restructured enterprises have flourished is that the changes have helped workers. Consider, for instance, Star Insulation Materials Company, which makes electronics parts. It was sold by Zhucheng to employees in 1993, and subsequently Star's earnings and workers' wages soared. "Before I used to come in late and chat a lot during work, and no one cared," says Wang Shurong, who has worked at Star for 28 years. "Now I sometimes come in early. I feel like the factory's mine."

Zhucheng has proved it can make money even when it gives away an enterprise. Year after year, the Zhucheng Vehicle Factory barely turned a profit making pickup trucks. Zhucheng officials wanted to modernize the plant, but they didn't have the money needed and didn't think anyone wanted to buy it. So they gave it to the Beijing United Automobile and Motorcycle Manufacturing Company, which invested in new production lines. In its first year of operation, the renovated factory produced 10,000 trucks, five times its former volume, and paid Zhucheng back the cost of its gift through taxes.

China's economy is as far along as it is because of Deng Xiaoping, China's leader for 20 years. In the late 1970s and early 1980s, Mr. Deng undertook rapid, sometimes chaotic, capitalist-oriented market reforms as a way of tackling the economic problems and of realizing China's huge economic potential. The West applauded these moves as the great opening-up of China, but not all the Chinese were enthusiastic. The opposite philosophy was embodied in Chen Yun, a proponent of enlightened central planning. Mr. Chen was, like Mr. Deng, a founding revolutionary of the Chinese Communist Party. He set up China's economy after the Communist Revolution in 1949 and thereafter had steadfastly advocated step-by-step development under careful guidance, though he allowed a role for market economics as well. He allied himself closely with Mr. Deng in the late 1970s, but Mr. Chen later grew disenchanted with Mr. Deng's capitalistic experiments, particularly when they led to inflation or a loss of control for the central government. Whereas Mr. Deng proclaimed, "To get rich is glorious," Mr. Chen promulgated "cage" economics: "The bird should be allowed to fly, but only in the cage. If there is no cage, the bird will escape." After the 1989 crackdown on dissent in Beijing, when Mr. Deng was perceived as being at the weakest point in his rule, Mr. Chen led a conservative revival against what he called "decadent capitalist ideology." As a behind-the-scenes master of the party apparatus, Mr. Chen helped select a younger generation of top leaders. Among them is Li Peng, the premier, who was named to his position in 1987 at Mr. Chen's behest. (According to constitutional rules, Mr. Li, who was closely linked with the brutal crackdown on democracy protests in 1989, must step down in spring 1998 when his second term expires.) Mr. Chen also backed the promotion of Jiang Zemin to become China's president and the chief of the Communist Party. The Jiang-Li government is inclined toward a slower pace of economic development than Mr. Deng had sought. The "moderately tight" economic policy that Mr. Li endorsed about a month before his mentor succumbed in April 1995 "is 100% the thinking of Chen Yun," said one Chinese analyst. "You could say that he died with a smile on his face."

Four months earlier, in November 1994, Li Peng granted an interview to *The Wall Street Journal* in which he revealed more of his go-slow approach. The advantages of stock markets, he claimed, are "obvious" in that they "attract funds for technological upgrading of industries at low or no cost." But he was mostly negative about markets. He repeatedly referred to China's stock markets in Shanghai and Shenzhen as "experimental" and insisted Chinese people aren't yet accustomed to taking risk. "If people suffer losses, they will go to the government because they think loss isn't normal," he said. Indeed,

Premier Li, like many Chinese officials, seemed to regard China's 10 million shareholders as a potentially destabilizing force rather than as risk takers helping to finance China's modernization. With stock markets so volatile that share prices rise and fall 40% in a single afternoon, Beijing ordered the local news media to report market information only if it was released by the stock exchanges.

This distrust has led to heavy-handed controls, which in turn have prevented China's stock markets from maturing. China's markets have been roiled by regulatory maneuvering since they were opened to foreign investors in 1992. For example, Beijing regularly restricts new stock offerings to drive share prices higher and then suddenly lifts the ban, permitting a bunch of new issues at once. This tactic is intended to take advantage of the market's higher level, but before long it drives prices lower. Rule changes and arcane penalties—trading suspensions for companies that post losses, for example—also have reduced foreign investors' confidence in China's stock exchanges.

China's listed companies have not been spared the pain of Beijing's austerity drive. Their profits have withered and share prices have dropped. Class B shares, which are earmarked for foreign investors, have been hurt the most. In June 1996, the Shenzhen stock exchange decided it was time to give the B shares a boost. The exchange offered loans to Shenzhen's biggest brokers, encouraging them to buy stocks, several brokers said. The exchange also relaxed rules barring Chinese from buying B shares. Within a week, Shenzhen's Class B index rallied more than 40%. Daily turnover, which had rarely topped $1 million, shot up to $65 million. In Shanghai, trading in B shares also perked up, as investors anticipated similar action there. But there was little long-term investing going on. Foreigners sold stocks they had been stuck with for years, while Chinese bought for short-term gains.

Alarm bells went off in Beijing. Regulators had long looked the other way as some Chinese investors traded in B shares. But Shenzhen's rally opened a breach in the carefully guarded exchange controls: Capital was pouring out of the country. Worse, the B-share market's fragile foundation of long-term capital was quickly eroding, replaced by the shifting sands of speculative local money. China's securities regulator tried to plug the hole, warning that Chinese nationals' ownership of B shares was illegal. The state-owned press reported a freeze on new B-share accounts. The regulatory commission said existing accounts had to be "rectified" and "regulated." Fear of a crackdown swept local investors, and the B-share rally soon turned to a rout. The episode left foreign fund managers, already tired of China's immature markets, wary of intervention.

When China's markets opened in 1992, foreign investors eagerly bought anything that was listed just because it was Chinese. Now that the honeymoon is over, security analysts are trying to apply their techniques to Chinese companies. But corporate disclosure is very weak in China. To help circumvent this problem, securities firms with Hong Kong offices are increasingly hiring Chinese analysts in Shanghai to cover China stocks and feed the growing demand from overseas investors for information about Chinese companies. Mainland Chinese analysts know who to call to get figures and who to call to arrange for an interview; they can visit more companies than their Hong Kong counterparts. However, many mainland analysts are weak in analyzing, because China's educational system discourages independent thinking, and stock analysis is a new field in China. The best China analysts are still the more experienced hands from Hong Kong and overseas who have strong analytical skills and a global investment perspective.

One of the things these analysts look for is debt—not so much what the companies themselves have borrowed but how much their customers owe them. China's clamp on credit means many Chinese companies that sell to cash-strapped state enterprises are seeing their profit margins squeezed because they have trouble collecting payments. The analysts pay particularly close attention to accounts receivable, or money owed by customers, and to inventory. Chinese manufacturers under pressure to keep their production lines running often face a painful dilemma. If customers can't pay, manufacturers can stop delivery of goods, but the result is bloated inventory, which ties up precious capital. The alternative is to continue delivering products and hope the customers will pay later, which expands accounts receivable and raises the possibility that the manufacturer might have to make bad-debt provisions. The state may own these enterprises, but it doesn't guarantee their debts.

If you are a stock picker, stick with American depositary receipts. China allows only its better firms to seek capital abroad, so having an ADR is a good litmus test in a situation where there is precious little data on which to base investment choices. In fact, disclosure is quite decent from those companies with ADRs on the New York Stock Exchange. In October 1996, there were five Chinese ADRs traded on the Big Board. One of them is Shandong Huaneng Power Development, formed in 1994 for the purpose of owning power plants and selling its stock to investors. It was the first Chinese utility to list on the Big Board, but there undoubtedly will be more because tremendous amounts of capital will be needed to boost China's electricity-generating capacity by more than half by the year 2000. China hopes foreigners will pick up at least $20 billion of the roughly $100 billion tab.

The first two China-play stocks available to non-Chinese investors aren't operating companies at all but rather offshore holding companies with interests in Sino-foreign joint ventures. Brilliance China Automotive Holdings owns 51% of Shenyang Automotive. Shenyang was once totally dependent on Japanese parts to build its vans, which it sells to government agencies and to industry. But the company is switching as quickly as possible to domestic parts because the combination of weak Chinese currency and strong Japanese currency is eating into profits. Shenyang is forbidden by the Beijing government to make private passenger cars. Ek Chor China Motorcycle owns, through five offshore subsidiaries, four motorcycle plants. Motorcycles are a popular form of transportation in Asia, and Ek Chor is one of the few companies available to foreign investors with an exposure to mainland Chinese consumers. Both Brilliance China and Ek Chor are Bermuda-based companies whose stocks trade not in China but only on the Big Board in New York.

If you are going to own Chinese stocks, be prepared for the unexpected. In April 1995, Tsingtao Brewery Company's shares were temporarily suspended from trading in Hong Kong and Shanghai because the Chinese company seemed to be operating more as a bank than a brewery. The company lent more than 600 million yuan ($71.2 million) to cash-strapped companies in China at rates reaching 20% a year, according to analysts. That money, raised through public stock offerings in Shanghai and Hong Kong, was supposed to be spent on expanding the company's Shandong breweries. The analysts worried that Tsingtao was left with little cash to run its business. Tsingtao issued a statement saying it had plenty of working capital, and trading in the stock subsequently resumed, but the point is this: With Chinese stocks, you never know what will happen next, or how it might affect your investing plans.

By the way, the practice of lending money was neither new for Tsingtao nor unusual in China. Because credit is tight due to Beijing's austerity program, many companies with cash on their books have opted to lend money out at premium rates rather than invest it in their businesses. But many intercompany loans in China have gone unpaid, creating a chain of bad debts. Analysts and investors feared that Tsingtao was caught in such "triangular debt." Anheuser-Busch Companies of St. Louis owns 5% of Tsingtao.

Before we move on to India, we leave you with the assessment of one Richard Rainwater, who managed the wealth of the Bass family of Texas into one of the biggest private fortunes in the United States, and now, on his own, has built his personal fortune to roughly $700 million. Speaking to a business breakfast in Fort Worth, Texas, in late winter 1995, he was peppered with questions from the audience about India and Mexico, but Mr. Rainwater said the country to bet on is "China, China, and China. And China after that." He pointed out that China's investment appeal goes beyond its own companies. For example, Mr. Rainwater asserted that growing demand from China and other developing nations will boost petroleum demand faster than supply can keep up. "For the first time in our lifetimes, the price of oil and gas will be decided by supply and demand, not by men, not by OPEC," he said. He expects Texas and other petroleum producers to benefit, while "for people who use natural resources, it's going to be terrible"— which is why he recommends buying stocks of companies with big reserves of crude oil. China's emergence as a world economic power, Mr. Rainwater predicted, also will drive a prolonged, global surge in demand for metals, lumber, and other commodities. And that, he warned, may not be good for stock and bond markets, recalling the natural resources boom of the 1970s, which sparked inflation and a recession. Also, China "will be the most compelling adversary" in business, he said. "China is Japan with a zero added on." He acknowledged that the recovery of the American automobile industry shows the United States can compete. But most Americans don't appreciate how difficult the coming years could be, he said. While a relatively wealthy America grows increasingly polarized as it grapples with social problems exacerbated by slower economic growth, he added, "the world is competing against us, very steely-eyed, just trying to get indoor plumbing."

PASSAGE FOR INDIA

During the decade following India's independence in 1947, the foreign-trained economists who packed the committee rooms of New Delhi designed an economic system that ended up being the worst of socialism and of capitalism; it suppressed growth and failed to deliver the

level of social welfare that even Communist systems provided. Five
decades later, that system is being dismantled—but slowly. One reason for the measured pace is that people who did well under the old
ways are resisting changes. Another reason is that the poor and op-
pressed people of this highly stratified society are demanding their
share of progress.

The old system constrained the private sector's growth by allowing expansion only when the government permitted it. Foreign trade
was stunted by quotas and high tariffs. Access to foreign exchange was
limited. There were controls on land use, on trade in farm products,
and more. This approach worked as long as India paid its debts, kept
budget deficits reined in, and kept inflation low, which is pretty much
how it was for 30 years, through the 1970s. In the 1980s, however,
India's governments began to push for growth by borrowing money on
the grand scale favored in Latin America, not by unshackling the private sector. By the end of the decade, India's debt-to-GDP ratio was
nearly twice its level in 1980. In 1991, with barely two weeks of foreign-
exchange reserves left, the government went to the International Monetary Fund for a bailout.

The crisis was resolved quickly, as these things go. The budget
deficit, which had bloated to 8.4% of GDP in the fiscal year ended
March 1991, was reduced to 5.7% two years later. Some of that shrink-
age came through well-deserved cuts in such things as export subsidies, but some was at the expense of legitimate government concerns,
such as education and health. All in all, though, India seemed to come
through the crisis fairly well. While the economy was under repair during fiscal 1992 and 1993, GDP grew just 1.1% a year; but in fiscal 1994
growth jumped to 4%, and then to 6.2% in fiscal 1995. Mexico had a
similar, but far more severe, debt crisis in 1982, and it took almost ten
years for its economy to start growing again.

India's economic liberalization took root during this crisis period,
as reformers took advantage of the situation to push through some important changes. For instance, some areas of the economy that had
been once closed to the private sector were opened up: electricity
generation, parts of the oil industry, heavy industry, air transport, roads,
and some telecommunications. Foreign investment, formerly allowed
only grudgingly and subject to arbitrary ceilings, was welcomed. These
days, foreign equity stakes of up to 51% in most businesses are approved routinely; stakes up to 100% aren't unheard of. Raw materials

and capital goods can be freely imported. The maximum tariff rate is down from 400% to 65%. The rupee was devalued by 24% in 1991; most exchange controls have been lifted, and the currency is now pretty much convertible. The top rate of income tax is down from 56% to 40%; the top corporation tax is now 46%, down from 57.5%. A complex system of excise duties has been replaced by a kind of value-added tax.

But very little of the benefits generated by these reforms found their way down the social ladder to the bottom rungs. India remains among the world's worst-off countries. Its literacy rate has been stuck for years at 52% (39% among women). Half of India's 200 million children don't attend school. Plumbing, electricity, and health services are scarce. The few signs of modern wealth that have begun to sparkle in major cities—Kentucky Fried Chicken outlets, mobile telephones— merely highlight the gaping disparities, many Indians say. It was only a matter of time until India's 500 million poor people—mostly members of the so-called backward castes in the traditional Hindu hierarchy and the "untouchables"—claimed a role in the world's biggest democracy.

The frustrations burst open in India's 11th general parliamentary elections in the spring of 1996. Poor, lower-caste voters abandoned the Congress Party by the millions. In power for all but 4 of India's 48 years of independence, the largely upper-caste party of Nehru and the Gandhis had become tainted by corruption and complacency. No other party won a clear majority, however. The first attempt to form a government, led by the Hindu-nationalist Bharatiya Janata Party, lasted 13 days. The next government, under Prime Minister H.D. Deve Gowda, lasted 10 months. It was a coalition of regional and lower-caste parties that vowed to spend heavily to help the poor, while continuing economic reforms. In the spring of 1997, the Congress Party withdrew its support for the Gowda government, which collapsed. But the coalition held together and put forth a new prime minister, Inder Kumar Gujral, who is in power as we write this edition.

The United Front is an alliance of 13 parties whose ideologies range from free market to Socialist. Prime Minister H. D. Deve Gowda gave the key finance-ministry portfolio to an articulate, Harvard-educated attorney named P. Chidambaram, one of the main architects of India's economic-liberalization drive over the previous five years. A former commerce minister in the last Congress Party government,

Mr. Chidambaram championed foreign investment, lower trade barriers, and the privatization of Indian industry and infrastructure. Now,
he conceded, he may not be able to move as fast as he would like: "I
have tempered my program by the fact that I am in a coalition government. I have no difficulty in saying I will faithfully implement" the
coalition's policy blueprint, which espouses "growth with social justice."
Among other things, it calls for gross domestic product to grow 7% to
8% a year in the next decade. It says India needs $10 billion a year in
foreign direct investment, up from a record $1 billion in 1995. And it
hopes to achieve annual industrial growth of 12%, up from 9% to 10%
in 1995. One of the first achievements of the new government was to
pass a budget that included personal and corporate tax cuts.

As for foreign investment, the United Front's policy blueprint
sends a mixed message. It says the new government would welcome
foreign investment in infrastructure and technology while discouraging it in low-priority sectors, which aren't specified. In the past, coalition partners have opposed foreign investment in consumer products.
Mr. Chidambaram contends this policy won't inhibit capital from flowing into the country. India will require $200 billion of investment to
build power plants, roads, ports, and telephone networks in the next
five years, he said. He expects $50 billion of that to come from abroad.
Mr. Chidambaram also said that attracting foreign investment to the
food-processing industry is essential to upgrading agriculture and creating jobs in rural areas, home to about 70% of India's population. Mr.
Chidambaram also pledged to cut the fiscal deficit to 4% of gross domestic product within five years, down from 5.9% in 1995. But reflecting the demands of leftist coalition partners, the blueprint promises
to protect jobs and to rehabilitate ailing public-sector firms rather than
sell them.

India's future will be influenced by its choice of democracy first and
capitalism afterward. Rather than unbridled capitalism, India's course
will evolve through a daily dialogue between the conservative forces
of caste, religion, and the village, the leftist and Nehruvian socialist
forces which dominated the intellectual life of the country for 40 years,
and the new forces of global capitalism. These myriad negotiations of
democracy mean that the pace of economic reforms will be frustrat-
ingly slow. It also means that India will not grow as rapidly as the Asian
tigers, nor wipe out poverty and ignorance as quickly as it potentially
could. But the stability of Indian democracy also suggests that there

might be a more balanced, peaceful, and negotiated transition into the future than, say China; that India might avoid some of the deleterious side effects of an unprepared capitalist society, such as Russia; and that it is more likely to preserve its way of life and its civilization of diversity, tolerance, and spirituality against the onslaught of the phony and fictitious global culture.

How all this will shake out insofar as investing in India is concerned remains to be seen. But Enron Corporation of Houston, Texas, had an early run-in with a branch of the new coalition government that might prove instructive. Enron was building a big, $2.8 billion power plant in the Indian state of Maharashtra, with backing from Bechtel Enterprises and General Electric Company's GE Capital Corporation. It was India's largest foreign investment and a testament to the sweeping economic reforms. But the partly built project became caught in a political swamp when the Congress Party lost control of the state government in March 1995 to the Hindu nationalists. On August 3 of that year, the new government canceled the second half of the project and repudiated the first-phase contract already in force because the project was too expensive—"Consumers can't afford the power it will produce," a senior government advisor asserted—and environmentally risky. Foreign investors were aghast. If it could happen to Enron, they figured, it could happen to them. Overnight, projects were downgraded to go-slow status or simply postponed.

To its credit, Enron correctly deciphered the political posturing as a reopening of contract negotiations, and it went back to the bargaining table to do business, not to seek revenge. Four months later, in January 1996, it had a new deal. It calls for Enron to sell power to the western Indian state for 1.86 rupees (5.2 cents) a kilowatt-hour, or 22.5% less than in the original contract. Further, the capacity of the two-phase power project will be boosted 22% to 2,450 megawatts, but the capital costs of the project will be reduced by 11% to $2.5 billion. The agreement also paves the way for the government-owned Maharashtra State Electricity Board to take a 30% equity stake in the project, reducing Enron's stake to 50% from 80%.

While balancing economic growth with social justice will not be easy, it is not an impossibility in India. Indeed, in India's only Marxist-ruled state, West Bengal, the leaders have put away their red banners and are following the lead of the rest of India in welcoming private investors. West Bengal is India's most densely populated state and one of its poorest; the Communist Party of India won power there 18 years ago. It is home to Calcutta, a synonym for filth and urban decay, an overcrowded metropolis of 13 million people where the homeless over-run the streets, traffic crawls over roads filled with holes, and tele-phones remain dead for weeks. More than any other Indian city, Calcutta resisted the economic reforms. The Communists, claiming they were upholding the rights of the working person, even refused to let computers into West Bengal government offices until the early 1990s. West Bengal looked on defiantly as the rest of the nation changed. Until 1994, that is. In September of that year, Jyoti Basu, the state's 82-year-old elected leader, jettisoned Marxism for pragmatism and ordered the communist trade union to shed militancy. Without consulting his party, Mr. Basu opened the state to private investors. A few months after this change, R.P. Goenka group, one of Calcutta's biggest companies, fired 600 workers in one day without a murmur of protest from their union; a year earlier, unions would have blocked the sacking of even the most inefficient workers. When painters white-washed over a portrait of Karl Marx on the wall of Calcutta's town hall, it made headlines because the Communist union failed to call a strike. Die-hard Marxists initially resisted these and other changes. "But we cannot remain isolated and turn our state into a desert," said Anil Biswas, who edits the Communist party's daily newspaper. "We are making policies in a capitalist society. How can we object to free mar-ket policies?"

Even with such attitudes, India has a long way to go. For instance, the country's average shortfall of electricity at peak periods is now 18%; to make up that and meet projected demand by 2002 will require a 75% increase in generating capacity, at a cost of almost $70 billion. Another example: Telephone systems in India provide only eight lines for each 1,000 people; providing phones just to the people already on the waiting lists would cost an estimated $28 billion. A bare-bones tramway system for New Delhi will take about $4 billion.

Building just the highways and bridges designated "priority" by the government will require $8 billion. Like many developing nations, India now is encouraging automaking ventures because of their po-tential to drive broader economic growth. Every job in car manufac-turing typically creates five to ten jobs in parts-supply and support industries. But also as in other developing nations, expansion of the auto industry in India raises troubling policy issues. Streets in Indian towns and cities already are overflowing with bicycles, motor scooters, pedal rickshaws, pushcarts, and animal-drawn carts. Travel times in Delhi often are double those ten years ago. Intercity travel isn't much better. India has few highways, and it's hard for even the most powerful cars to average more than 50 to 60 kilometers (30 to 37 miles) an hour on the designated national highways. At best, these highways tend to be two-lane roads without dividers, where drivers play unending games of chicken and accidents are common. Traffic exhaust has rendered cities such as New Delhi among the world's most polluted. Regulations on vehicle emissions are in the works but won't take effect until who knows when. Moreover, there is no unleaded gasoline in India. It is uncommon to see a truck or a bus that isn't belching black smoke.

As if that weren't enough, India is in the throes of a spectacular property bubble. Reforms haven't proceeded far enough to correct some severe distortions that have thrust real estate into stratospheric, even prohibitive, levels. Unlike other Asian property bubbles over the past decade in Japan, Hong Kong, and China, India's is supported not so much by a shortage of space or a rise in demand but by arcane laws aimed at protecting tenants and discouraging underground property transactions. The old laws serve to keep out development and scare owners out of renting their property, be it residential or commercial. The upshot is that while some people in rent-controlled apartments are paying small change, office rents are so high that foreign companies hoping to enter India sometimes have to rethink plans. Rents in the bustling center of Bombay are costlier than in Tokyo, Hong Kong, or Manhattan. On top of that, most landlords insist on getting one year's rent up front and a security deposit equivalent to two years' additional rent. The deposits can add up to millions of dollars, and they are returned in three to five years without interest. Many multinational companies choose to operate instead out of $250-a-night hotel rooms.

The main impediment is India's draconian Rent Control Act, which makes it virtually impossible for a landlord to evict a tenant or to raise the rent. Moreover, tenants can gain what is called statutory tenancy, enabling them *and their descendants* to remain without a lease in a property they inhabit. The other law that sets back property development is called the Urban Land Ceiling and Regulation Act. It tries to keep the development of cities under control, to avoid putting pressure on India's already-stressed roads, sewerage system, and other infrastructure. The amount of development builders are allowed to put on a site is low, making it economically unattractive to acquire expensive central sites or requiring new developments to charge astronomical rents to cover the cost of acquiring such sites. As a result of this law, a number of aging, run-down textile mills still occupy the center of Bombay, where demand for new office and housing space is monumental.

Though the numbers of India's growth potential are enticing, investors should be at least as deliberate as the liberalization process. "The message is, put India on your watch list," says a portfolio manager at Jardine Fleming India Securities. "We still think India's a good long-term play." But before you get too excited, we want to tell you a cautionary tale.

Reliance Industries is India's biggest company. It dominates South Asia's surging market for synthetic fibers. It is a juggernaut in the midst of a $3 billion plant and technology drive that, by 1998, should make it the world's eighth-largest polyester producer. Its profits in the 1990s have risen 60% a year. Its shares have plunged, however, losing roughly half their value in the 18 months from October 1994 to April 1996. Part of the slide was due to the overall decline of most emerging-market stocks in that period, but much of it stems from what Americans might consider monkey business. Indian regulators are investigating allegations that Reliance pulled such crude tricks as duplicating and switching its own stock certificates. The alleged problems have cropped up so widely that some Reliance shareholders say they are no longer certain that their shares are valid. "You never know what you get in India," says John "Dick" Breen, a Price Waterhouse consultant and head of a U.S.-government-funded project to help modernize India's capital markets. "You can wind up with a piece of paper you think is a share but is worthless." The Reliance story is the story of India: enormous assets, terrific talent, lagging ethics. But Indians are trying to clean house, making the allegations about Reliance a rallying cry for corporate and financial reform. "Reliance has become a byword for bending rules," opined India's *Free Press Journal* in an editorial headlined "The Evil Empire."

The controversies over Reliance stock would never have erupted in most Western countries, where independent firms called depositories keep track of who owns which shares. Though Western companies still issue stock certificates on paper, the depositories do the serious record keeping electronically; most Western shares now change hands only figuratively, inside computer databanks. In India, however, everything still happens on paper, which the companies shuffle themselves. So, for every stock traded on the Bombay Stock Exchange, reams of certificates are exchanged. After a trade, the seller delivers the shares to the buyer, who hands them over to the issuing company's registrar—in this case, the Reliance Consultancy Services subsidiary—which registers the serial number of every share being traded in the new owner's name; then, it ships the shares back to the buyer. Indian regulations specify some 100 different criteria that company registrars are to use in validating the required signatures. The process is not only time-consuming—it often takes weeks or even months for Indian trades to clear, compared with three days in the United States—but wide open to abuse.

Reliance got into trouble in October 1995 when it was accused of having improperly issued to its chairman's physiotherapist some 26,000 duplicate certificates for shares that the woman had already sold but claimed were lost. The alleged impropriety was revealed when a trade involving the original shares was blocked by Reliance because they had been retired after the duplicates were issued. Reliance says it acted responsibly in blocking the original shares, but the Bombay exchange found that Reliance had broken the rules by duplicating its stock. As punishment, it suspended trading in Reliance shares for three days. About the same time, in a court case concerning a 1992 stock market scandal, an investor complained to a judge that Reliance, while registering new owners' shares, had substituted different share lots for those deposited with it for registration. In several cases, the substituted shares it passed on to buyers turned out to have come from Reliance affiliates rather than from the selling investors. Critics accused Reliance of using the share "switching" scheme to evade capital-gains taxes by swapping older, company-held shares—with lower cost bases—for newer ones.

Doubts about the validity of Reliance shares and the true number outstanding pushed down the stock price and, with it, the whole Indian stock market. Reliance shares plummeted 45%, bottoming out in late January 1996 at 155 rupees ($4.30) a share on the Bombay exchange. The Bombay Sensitive Index of 30 stocks, which accords Reliance a 12% weight and usually shadows Reliance's stock, fell 21% to 2826. The market's dive, led by its mightiest blue chips, prompted

India's securities regulators to say they now are looking much more closely for all types of share abnormalities. A depositories law to simplify the nightmarish settlement and transfer procedures has been introduced in Parliament, and regulators are beginning to toughen the rules to improve corporate disclosure and accounting standards.

The scandals also have exposed another trap for unwary investors in Indian companies: insider trading. For years, Reliance has bolstered its stock by discreetly purchasing its own shares on the market through affiliated companies and brokers, local traders say. "Reliance is the only large company I know of which has played its own stock day in and day out," says M. G. Damani, a broker who in 1996 became president of the Bombay Stock Exchange. "If they were in America, they'd be behind bars." Regulators now are trying to crack down on all types of insider trading. But the share-support system, which had been legal in India, helped Reliance lay the foundation for creating the country's "equity cult" of small investors. Inspired by Mr. Dhirubai Ambani, chairman of Reliance and a Horatio Alger figure revered for his rise from humble roots, legions of ordinary Indians invested in shares for the first time. Today, Reliance, which since 1977 has raised nearly $1 billion on India's stock exchanges, claims more shareholders than any other company in the world—some 2.6 million, half of whom own less than 100 shares. It holds its annual meetings in a concert stadium. Reliance stopped supporting its stock in early 1996, brokers say, but Reliance executives contend a "cartel" of hostile brokers is trying to manipulate the company's shares downward.

But whether bull cartels or bear cartels are in ascendancy, the Indian market is largely an insiders' game. "Slowly, we are doing everything that an international investor needs to be comfortable in an emerging market," says Anil Ambani, one of two Ambani sons who now run Reliance. But, he warns, foreign investors in India better have "a far deeper understanding of this market than the fundamentals. At the end of the day, the Indian market is complicated."

Early in 1995, the Indian government increased the regulatory powers of its Securities and Exchange Board of India. Now the board can levy fines, demand information from anybody in the securities business, and take action in court without first getting government approval. These changes help, of course, but it remains to be seen if the board will actually use its powers or simply brandish them.

Because no Indian stocks are traded in the United States (just closed-end funds, so far), don't expect any help from our own Securities and Exchange Commission if something goes wrong. The SEC looked into a Bombay-based research group's claims that some Indian companies manipulated their domestic stock prices before seeking capital on international equity markets. The SEC decided the research group failed to provide specific evidence of possible unlawful trading strategies or price manipulation in Indian markets. As for the four closed-end funds listed in the United States, the SEC pointed out that their prospectuses included extensive information on the risks of investing in India-based securities.

One of these risks is the habit in India of companies lavishing discounted shares on their controlling shareholders. Such moves can push down the stock's price, and even the price-to-earnings ratio if the gift-wrapped blocks are big enough, when they inevitably come to light. Even more insidious are discounted warrant issues to promoters, which the controlling shareholders may use to effectively consolidate their hold over a company, often without paying in advance. Discounted warrants are often awarded at no cost; the holder then pays a predetermined price for the shares when he or she exercises the warrants. This exercise can cause a mushrooming of shares outstanding, which dilutes other shareholders' stakes without giving them the chance to compensate by increasing their holdings.

Another risk—common in other emerging markets, as well—is overpaying for a stock just because it, or the market it's in, has some sizzle. Happily, professional investors seem to be developing some resistance to this sort of robbery. In May 1994, India's international telecommunications monopoly postponed its offering of nearly $1 billion in global depositary receipts (GDRs). Demand was strong, but not strong enough to sop up all the shares the company wanted to sell at the offering price, which it already had cut by roughly 25%. More than two years later, the company was making an attempt to revive the offer.

By the summer of 1996, enthusiastic followers of emerging markets were being attracted by the low price to earnings (P/E) multiples— relative to other emerging markets—and strong financial performance of Indian companies. The Bombay market's average P/E multiple at mid-1996 was just 12.3 times projected 1996–97 earnings, compared with 17.3 for Thailand and 21.6 for Malaysia. But at that same time, Indian companies were, on average, reporting a 30% increase in net income for the year ended March 31.

The first private-sector Indian company to sell GDRs was Reliance Industries, in 1992. It was followed by Grasim Industries, a diversified company with interests in viscose staple fiber, cement, caustic soda, sponge iron, and rayon grade pulp. Grasim Industries is the flagship of the Aditya Birla group, which has sales of about $4 billion a year; its chairman is none other than Aditya V. Birla, who is also the chairman of Hindalco Industries, an aluminum company. The third member of the Birla group with GDRs is Century Textiles & Industries, a highly diversified conglomerate with interests in textiles, yarn, rayon, chemicals, shipping, cement, paper pulp, and tires. Its chairman is B. K. Birla, brother of the group chairman.

Tata Industries is another big group of companies, headed by Ratan N. Tata. Two of its important holdings, which also are available separately to investors, are Tata Iron & Steel Company and Tata Engineering & Locomotive Company. This latter company has a joint venture with Daimler-Benz of Germany to produce up to 20,000 Mercedes-Benz cars a year, half for the Indian market and half for export. Bombay-based Taj Group of Hotels, also a unit of the Tata Group, is India's largest hotel chain.

Here is another one: Bharat Heavy Electricals makes generating equipment; Bharat Electronics makes industrial and defense electronics equipment; and Bharat Earth Movers makes heavy construction equipment.

Even many companies that aren't conglomerates seem itching to diversify into any part of the Indian economy where growth appears likely. For example, ITC, a diversified cigarette maker and one of India's best-known companies, has a plan to move into power generation. But there also are plenty of companies that stick to related lines of business. Hindustan Petroleum Corporation, which wants to double its refining capacity by the year 2000, produces gasoline, diesel, liquefied petroleum gas, kerosene, aviation fuel, naphtha, bitumen, and more than 270 brands of lubes and greases. Mahanagar Telephone Nigam runs the telephone networks of Bombay and Delhi. Ranbaxy Laboratories, a pharmaceutical company, has some joint venture agreements with Eli Lilly & Company. Larsen & Toubro is India's leading cement and machinery manufacturer. East India Hotels is 34% owned by the Oberoi family, whose Oberoi Group is the country's second-largest hotel firm.

CHAPTER XIV

The Second Tier

MANY stock markets of the world fall between the industrialized behemoths and the emerging nations. We call them the second tier, but not to imply they are second-rate. In fact, in the aggregate they offer a great many Class A investment opportunities. You will find stocks from these countries prominent in the holdings of mutual funds and closed-end funds, and they are well represented among the ADRs traded in the United States. Among these stocks are some of the globe's corporate giants, such as Royal Dutch Petroleum in the Netherlands, Nestlé in Switzerland, and Broken Hill Proprietary in Australia. Also among them are some of the premier companies of their respective industries: Finland's Nokia and Sweden's L. M. Ericsson in telecommunications; the Netherlands' Heineken and Australia's Foster's Brewing Group in beer; and Swiss Bank and the Netherlands' ING Group in banking and financial services.

The majority of second-tier markets are what analysts call "stock specific." That is, certain outstanding stocks in these markets capture investors' interest, not the markets themselves particularly. A few of

231

these countries, such as Switzerland and Australia, have enough diversity to support broad market bets—as in a closed-end fund, for example—but for the most part, think of the second tier as the investment equivalent of à la carte.

SCANDINAVIA

Scandinavia consists of four small countries—Denmark, Finland, Norway, and Sweden—with an incredible collection of world-class stocks that either dominate their industries or are at least among the top companies globally. The countries share a couple of important characteristics. First, they regard equity financing as superior to debt financing. One consequence is that most of these companies have shipshape balance sheets. Another is that they recognize the importance of shareholders; investors are VIPs in Scandinavia. The second characteristic is that people in all four countries historically have looked beyond their borders for opportunities. The spirit of the Vikings lives today in companies that call Stockholm or Oslo home but that girdle the globe with their activities and interests. These companies are experts in foreign manufacturing and operations; they know what it really takes to sell a product in other countries.

Occasionally, the Scandinavian markets will be penalized because of some political or other problem, such as the Swedish government's financial troubles. In many instances, these selloffs provide opportunities to buy shares of companies that depend very little on their home countries for success.

SWEDEN has a big concentration of top-drawer companies. In addition to L. M. Ericsson, there are Volvo in automaking; Sandvik in metalworking and rock-drilling tools and Atlas Copco for other industrial tools; AGA in industrial and medical gases; Esselte in office supplies; Astra in pharmaceuticals; and Electrolux in home appliances.

NORWAY offers Norsk Hydro, which makes products for the agriculture, light metal, energy, and petrochemical industries; Saga Petroleum, a North Sea oil producer that also is exploring in and around Indonesia; Petroleum Geo-Services, which generates seismic data for the oil industry; Kvaerner, a big shipbuilder—it makes many of the big

new cruise ships—that also has interests in liquefied natural gas tankers; Bergesen, which also is big in tankers and other kinds of marine transportation. If for some reason you want a play within Norway, consider Orkla, a foods, consumer goods, and chemicals firm that generates more than two-thirds of its revenue in Norway.

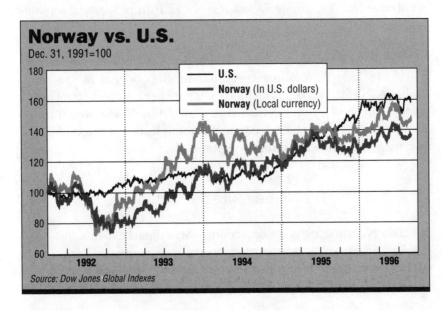

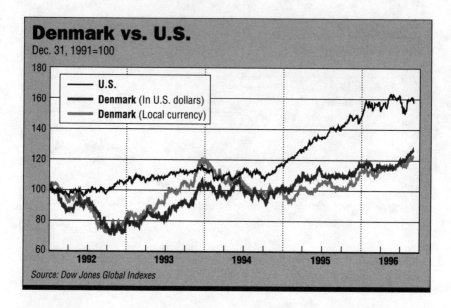

Denmark vs. U.S.
Dec. 31, 1991=100

Legend:
— U.S.
— Denmark (In U.S. dollars)
— Denmark (Local currency)

Source: Dow Jones Global Indexes

DENMARK has large shipping concerns, too, including D/S Svend-borg and D/S af 1912. Great Nordic is a telecommunications and data communications company; Novo Nordisk makes pharmaceuticals and bio-industrial products; Sophus Berendsen provides business services (such as express delivery and laundry) and makes industrial equipment; and Jens Villadsens Fabriker is one of Europe's largest roofing-felt makers.

FINLAND is largely tied to the forest products industry. Big paper-makers include Enso-Gutzeit, Kymmene, Repola, and Metsä-Serla. Huhtamäki's food products include Jolly Rancher candies in the United States. But the Helsinki market is dominated by Nokia, which transformed itself into a global telecommunications leader from a cable, rubber, data, tire, and electronics conglomerate.

THE NETHERLANDS AND BELGIUM

THE NETHERLANDS is a one-country Scandinavia, in that this small country boasts an extraordinary lineup of top-quality companies with global reputations. It also is oriented to equity rather than debt, and these companies' balance sheets are as clean as a Dutch kitchen. The

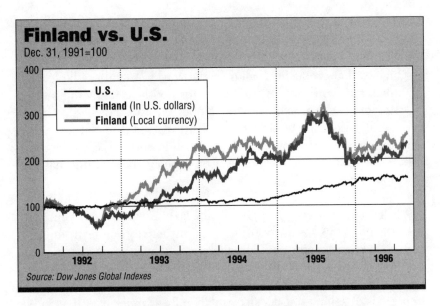

Finland vs. U.S.
Dec. 31, 1991=100

Legend:
U.S.
Finland (In U.S. dollars)
Finland (Local currency)

Source: Dow Jones Global Indexes

Netherlands has one advantage over Scandinavian markets: Its currency, the guilder, is strong, while the Scandinavian currencies tend to be weak. The guilder is managed to align with the German mark.

Royal Dutch Petroleum is the 800-pound gorilla of the Dutch market, being about 75% bigger in market capitalization than the not-

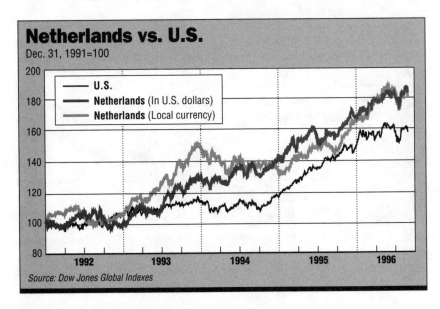

Netherlands vs. U.S.
Dec. 31, 1991=100

Legend:
U.S.
Netherlands (In U.S. dollars)
Netherlands (Local currency)

Source: Dow Jones Global Indexes

so-small Unilever, which is half British and makes food and consumer goods. Philips Electronics, another Dutch giant, is a global presence in consumer electronics. ABN AMRO and ING Group are two banking biggies that do business all over the world. Aegon is a large, full-line insurance company; Akzo Nobel, formed in 1993 by the merger of Akzo and the Swedish company Nobel Industrier, is big in chemicals; Nedlloyd Group hauls cargo on land and sea (the Netherlands is considered a key gateway of Europe, both in and out). Two big publishers are Wolters Kluwer and Elsevier, which with Reed International of Britain owns Reed Elsevier.

BELGIUM, just next door, has a small, thin market commensurate with the country's size. Most of the trading activity comes from large, conservative investment funds, which tend to be interested only in the bluest of the blue chips. As a result, Belgium is considered a defensive market by the international players, meaning it typically declines less in periods of selling but doesn't usually rally as much as others in periods of buying. Petrofina is the big oil company, Electrafina is the smaller one; you can get a stake in both with shares of Groupe Bruxelles Lambert, a holding company that also has interests in electricity (through Tractebel), insurance (Royale Belge), and banking (Banque Bruxelles Lambert). The other big holding company, Générale de Bel-

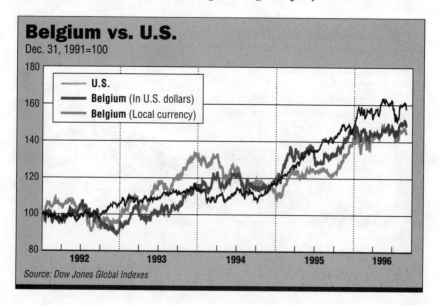

Belgium vs. U.S.
Dec. 31, 1991=100

Legend:
— U.S.
— Belgium (In U.S. dollars)
— Belgium (Local currency)

Source: Dow Jones Global Indexes

gique, owns a bigger share of Tractebel and has interests in polyurethane foam, nonferrous metals and diamonds, insurance (through Fortis AG), and banking (Générale de Banque). If you are looking for a chemicals stock, Solvay is worthy of consideration.

SWITZERLAND AND AUSTRIA

SWITZERLAND is another small country with big companies, which dominate the trading activity in Zurich. It also is a country with a very strong currency—stronger, at times, than the German mark—and a new welcome mat for foreign investors. Switzerland's new securities law, passed in the spring of 1995 and scheduled to take effect April 1, 1996, should help create a more attractive investment climate for Swiss stocks. As in many continental European nations, investor protection in Switzerland often has taken a back seat as regulators failed to curb powers of controlling families and majority holders. The Federal Stock Exchange Law aims to boost the liquidity and transparency of Swiss financial markets. It had been in the works since the 1987 global stock market crash. The law—the first to regulate the Swiss securities industry—also became necessary with the gradual disappearance of the

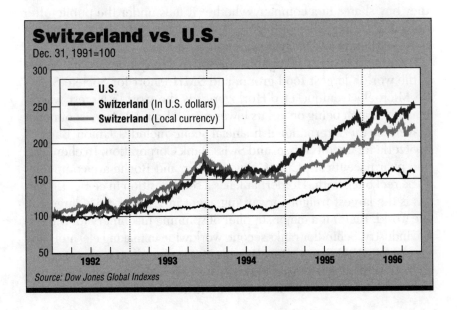

Switzerland vs. U.S.
Dec. 31, 1991=100

Legend:
— U.S.
— Switzerland (In U.S. dollars)
— Switzerland (Local currency)

Source: Dow Jones Global Indexes

regional exchanges regulated by authorities in cantons, similar to U.S. states. A nationwide electronic exchange, connecting all market trading and settlements in one computer-based network, began operating in 1996. The legislation also continues Swiss efforts to satisfy needs of international investors. Many companies have implemented internationally recognized accounting standards. Others have moved to a simpler share structure, abandoning multiple classes of stock in favor of a unitary share system.

The legislation covers all aspects of securities trading, but attention has focused on rules relating to disclosure and takeovers. The new law imposes a public-disclosure obligation when a purchaser acquires control of specified levels of a listed company's voting rights, beginning at 5%. Furthermore, the price that a purchaser pays to minority holders must be at least equal to the current stock price and not less than 25% below the highest price paid in a trade during the previous 12 months. Also, if one-third of the voting rights of a company is acquired, the purchaser must make an offer to the rest of the shareholders. But a company can bypass this requirement, or it can say that the obligation to make a public offer will occur only at 49%. Many family-controlled companies weary of inquisitive holders are expected to make use of the escape clause in their corporate statutes. The opt-out clause complicates things for investors, who should determine before they buy shares in a company whether it falls under the public-offer obligation. Companies opting out are expected to trade at a discount to those that decide to treat shareholders equally.

Among individual companies are some of the globe's giants. Nestlé is the world's largest food group, and SMH (short for Société Suisse de Microéléctronique et d'Horlogerie) is the world's largest watchmaker (Swatch being one of its lower-priced brands). Any list of major players in the international financial scene includes Union Bank of Switzerland, Crédit Suisse, and Swiss Bank Corporation. In chemicals and pharmaceuticals, Ciba-Geigy, Sandoz, and Roche are companies to be reckoned with. Holderbank has a solid position in cement. Danzas is the largest freight-forwarding agent in Europe, third largest in the world. Rieter is a major supplier of spinning machinery for the textile industry. Schindler ranks second worldwide in making elevators and escalators. BBC Brown Boveri holds 50% of Zurich-based power and industrial giant ABB Asea Boveri (Sweden's ASEA owns the other half), which has operations in 140 countries.

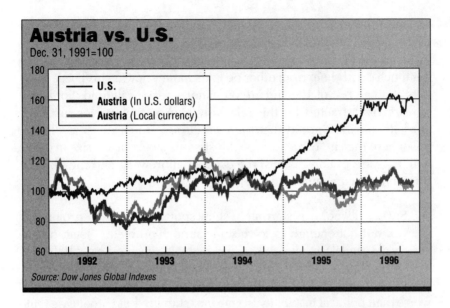

Austria vs. U.S.
Dec. 31, 1991=100

— U.S.
Austria (In U.S. dollars)
Austria (Local currency)

Source: Dow Jones Global Indexes

AUSTRIA is the prudent investor's proxy for Eastern Europe. Many of its companies have long done business in the former Communist-bloc nations, and now they are deeply involved in rebuilding these countries. The opening of Eastern Europe is giving the entire Continent a cheap labor supply with which to take on Southeast Asia and Latin America, and Austrian companies are taking full advantage of their proximity. Bonn's costly assimilation of eastern Germany is beginning to reinvigorate Europe's pivotal economy. The broadening of the European Union—which Austria joined January 1, 1995—is improving economies of scale.

Among Austria's biggest companies, and among those directly involved in reviving Eastern Europe, are construction firms (Porr and Universale Bau) and building materials makers (Perlmooser, Radex-Heraklith, Veitsch-Radex, and Wienerberger). Steyr-Daimler-Puch makes auto parts, trucks, and all-terrain vehicles. OMV, a state-controlled petroleum company, brings natural gas out of Russia.

"PERIPHERAL EUROPE"

From an investment point of view, the rest of Europe goes downhill fast after these countries. Again, we emphasize that within each country may be a stock or two, or even a handful, that are deserving of an international investor's consideration. But their home markets move into and out of favor among the investing gurus, so your picks won't get much steady help from other people's money flowing in. These markets also can be volatile and are on many occasions illiquid. Some investors are attracted by the relatively cheap stock prices in these markets, but be warned that the overall price-to-earnings levels are lower here than in "core" Europe. Most of the stocks of any size in these countries are utilities, banks, the occasional brewery, and the ubiquitous cement companies.

SPAIN'S economy is starting to show sputtering signs of prolonged growth, but not enough to solve some serious problems. That, plus a variety of scandals involving people in high places (move over, Italy and Japan), produces a degree of political instability that waxes and wanes but never seems to be fully resolved. The only thing investors hate worse than political instability is a noxious stability, but in that case they simply stay away. In Spain, they don't know whether to remain, leave, or return. The problem, in a nutshell, is that little progress has been made on structural economic reform. Rigid labor laws and highly regulated markets, such as energy and transport, contribute to above-average inflation of 4.3% and 24% unemployment, the highest rate in

Spain vs. U.S.
Dec. 31, 1991=100

Legend:
— U.S.
— Spain (In U.S. dollars)
— Spain (Local currency)

Source: Dow Jones Global Indexes

Italy vs. U.S.
Dec. 31, 1991=100

U.S.
Italy (Local currency)
Italy (In U.S. dollars)

Source: Dow Jones Global Indexes

the European Union. Economy Minister Pedro Solbes said that Spain is creating new jobs—not many, but some—for the first time ever with economic growth levels of less than 3%; the Spanish economy grew almost 2% in 1994 and 3% in 1995, fueled by a recovery in domestic consumption. This growth gives Spain the opportunity to whittle its budget deficit. But without further headway against inflation and the deficit, Spain won't meet the Maastricht treaty's criteria for joining a single European currency in 1997, an outcome that could doom Spain to second-class status in the European Union for years to come.

About 35% of the daily trading volume in Madrid—which leaps to about 50% when the market turns volatile—is in five blue-chip stocks: the semipublic telecommunications group Telefónica de España; the state-run energy concern Repsol; the state-controlled electricity utility Empresa Nacional de Electricidad SA (known as Endesa); the state-run bank Argentaria Corporación Bandaria de España, and private banks Banco Bilbar Vizcaya (BBV) and Banco de Santander. If you ever wanted to own part of a toll road, Spain has two companies in this business: Aumar, whose government contract runs out in 2006, and Autopistas, ditto in 2016.

ITALY is the only market in Europe where investors would have been better off in cash these past several years than in stocks. Italians are more debt investors than equity investors, like the Germans, but without any saving graces such as a dynamic economy or strong currency. Italy is in constant political disarray if not upheaval; the government in place as we write this—under Prime Minister Romano Prodi—is the 55th in the 50 years since World War II. Mr. Prodi, a former economics professor who appointed nine economists to his cabinet, is pursuing an economic policy aimed at reducing inflation (to 2.5% in 1997 and 2% in 1998 and 1999), lowering the debt-to-GDP ratio to less than 3% by 1999, and boosting economic growth to 2% in 1997, 2.8% in 1998, and 2.9% in 1999.

Within a couple of months of his election, Mr. Prodi had convinced many market players that Italy is no longer a basket case. But since Italian politics are extraordinarily volatile, there isn't any assurance that Mr. Prodi will be able to deliver. For now, though, he is seen as being capable of delivering, which is so far enough to declare Italy on the comeback trail as a valid economic player in Europe.

Italy at least has some world-class companies. The premier blue-chip stock on the Milan Stock Exchange is automaker and industrial giant Fiat (short for Fabbica Italiana di Automobili Torino). Others include Assicurazioni Generali, a large insurance concern with 60% of its sales outside Italy; Montedison, which makes chemicals and agro-products such as starch; Pirelli, a tire and cable maker; Benetton, the casual wear maker with the penchant for shocking advertisements; and Danieli, a global leader in building small steel mills.

PORTUGAL is the closest thing to an emerging market that there is in Europe. The country was headed for nearly 35 years by Antonio de Oliveira Salazar, who was virtual dictator of a right-wing state. Ill health forced his retirement in 1968. In 1974, a bloodless coup led by the Communist Party brought, ironically, a moderate form of political democracy but a sweeping nationalization of many businesses, particularly banks and utilities. In the years since, Portugal has seen increasing political stability. Aníbal Cavaco Silva, of the center-right Social Democratic Party, has been premier since 1985 and has overseen the rocky road to privatization.

The Lisbon Stock Exchange jolted to life in 1994 when Banco Comercial Portugues (BCP), the fifth-largest private bank, made an uninvited takeover bid for 40% of Banco Portugues do Atlantico (BPA), the biggest. But BPA's self-styled "core shareholders" said they would fight the hostile bid. The threat of a fight convinced the government not to authorize the takeover, fearing it might cause chaos in the financial sector. That move shook foreign investors, who began to wonder if the government was backtracking on its promised free-market reforms. In early 1995, BCP came back with a partner, insurer Companhia de Seguros Imperio, and went after all of BPA. This bid also met resistance from the core shareholders, led by the giant holding company Sonae Investimentos, which owned a 7.2% stake in BPA and had options to buy as much as 25% from other core holders. But the government accepted the second bid and said it would complete BPA's privatization under BCP's terms and sell its remaining 24.4% stake. Finally Sonae relented; BCP and Imperio bought 108.7 million shares, or 98.8%, of BPA for 2,800 escudos a share ($18.93). BCP is now Portugal's largest private banking group, second only to state-owned Caixa Geral Depositos in terms of assets. BCP will use BPA to expand its retail operations and will vigorously restructure the sleeping-giant bank that hadn't brought itself up to speed to compete internationally.

BCP has ADRs that trade on the New York Stock Exchange. The only other company with ADRs is another bank, Espirito Santo Financial, which was the first to be privatized in the late 1980s. Its credit operations are well run, but the interest for investors is its increasing exposure to the emerging Portuguese stock market. It formed an asset-management subsidiary when interest rates fell to uninteresting levels, and it had $2.3 billion under management by the end of 1993. It also has securities brokerage and mutual fund operations.

Privatizations aren't automatically good investments, and the governments engineering them are looking out primarily for themselves, not you. The Portuguese government was forced to yank a proposed offering of the state-owned electric utility because of the way the deal had been put together. The utility was the country's largest debtor. The government, anxious to move the loans off its own books, split it up among the 16 companies it created by restructuring the industry for privatization. Legally, each of these companies was to be responsible for the borrowings of the others. Investors rightly turned up their noses at shares with such liabilities.

GREECE is another window on Eastern Europe, like Austria. The Greek economy, however, is weak. It grew only an average 1% a year from 1990 to 1995, then accelerated a bit in 1996. That rate of growth is much lower than the European Union average. Most Greeks have seen the spending value of their income drastically reduced over the past ten years by inflation that has been running in double digits annually since 1975.

Now, however, there's a real opportunity for Greece to shake things up, thanks to a changing of the guard at the country's dominant socialist party, the Panhellenic Socialist Movement, or Pasok. Socialist Costas Simitis became prime minister in January 1996, when illness ended the reign of Pasok founder Andreas Papandreou, whose economic policies centered on generous state handouts that eventually ballooned the public debt to more than 110% of GDP. Mr. Simitis, a German- and British-educated economist and lawyer, once quit the Greek cabinet because he disagreed with Mr. Papandreou's uncontrolled spending. But he won a mandate to reform the economy when he won reelection in September 1996.

Mr. Simitis's top priority is whipping the Greek economy into shape. He wants to slash the inflation rate—whittled by previous austerity measures to 8.5% in August 1996—by two to 2.5 percentage points more. He aims to cut the general government deficit to 4.2% of gross domestic product, from an expected 7.6% of GDP for 1996. He also plans to push more private and state investments that will accelerate GDP growth to 3% in 1997, up from an estimated growth rate of 2.6% in 1996.

Selling state-owned companies also is high on his to-do list. An estimated 60% of the economy—everything from flag carrier Olympic Airways to banks and shipyards—is in the hands of the Greek state. Many of the people who work in those companies were put there by friendly socialist officials. That will make it difficult for the government to cut payroll costs and to raise cash by selling stakes in state-owned companies. But Mr. Simitis has plenty of incentive. In early 1996, the government kicked off its long-awaited privatization effort with the flotation of 6% of the Hellenic Telecommunications Organization, known as OTE. Though it took three years to organize, the stock sale was 4.5 times oversubscribed and brought the government 96 billion drachmas ($400 million). The government will use OTE as a model for selling off minority stakes in other state-controlled concerns. Oil company Public Petroleum Corporation is next in line. Then come the Bank of Crete and the Bank of Central Greece. Other flotations are expected to follow. By one estimate, these sales could raise as much as $500 million by October 1997, just in time for the next national elections.

Perhaps the biggest hurdle to a more fiscally responsible—and more mainstream—Greece lies in the country's antagonistic relationship with Turkey. If any one idea unites Greeks—from government ministers to piecework laborers—it's the belief that Turkey's territorial claims in the Aegean Sea could lead to war at any moment. And war, or even just building up for one, could wreck the carefully laid plans to put the Greek economy on sound footing.

Assuming the troubles with Turkey can be worked out, Greece is well positioned to capture much of the profitable fallout from economic reform in Central and Eastern Europe. Besides geographic advantages—the northern port of Salonika is within a day's drive of most Balkan capitals—Greek businesses are helped by the presence of ethnic Greek communities spread from Albania to Kazakhstan. Unlike their main Western competitors, predominantly European Union partners Italy and Germany, Greeks have already faced at home the bureaucratic and infrastructure headaches that plague Central Europe. One of Greece's most visible investors in the Balkans is Hellenic Bottling Company, better known as 3E. Coca-Cola of the United States selected Hellenic to form joint ventures with several Bulgarian firms to produce Coke and other soft drinks; 3E holds 75% stakes in each of five such ventures. It also owns 50% in Brewinvest, a joint venture with Dutch group Heineken, which acquired 80% of Bulgaria's largest state brewery, Zagorka. Petroleum giant Motor Oil, Greece's largest industrial group, is building a $60 million lubricant refinery in Russia and setting up a gas distribution network in Bulgaria. Motor Oil, which is part of the Vardinoyannis Group that petroleum and shipping tycoon Vardis Vardinoyannis controls, also is investing $300 million to build nine tankers in Ukraine shipyards. Intracom, which produces integrated telecommunication systems, has joint ventures to launch lottery systems in Russia, Bulgaria, Romania, and Moldova. In Russia, Intracom is setting up rural telephone networks to serve remote areas in the republic of Dagestan and in poorly developed areas around Moscow, a $20 million project; it's doing the same in Kazakhstan. In Romania, it recently won a $7 million contract to computerize the country's railway-data network, and it will supply Hungary with $1.5 million in digital systems that multiply the use of existing cables in the network so new cables don't need to be installed to serve more clients.

On a more nuts-and-bolts level are construction companies (such as Michaniki SA, Aegek, and Hellenic Technodomiki SA) and cement companies (for instance, Titan and AGET Heracles SA).

AUSTRALIA AND NEW ZEALAND

AUSTRALIA began opening up its economy ten years ago, shedding the high tariffs and restrictive government regulation that isolated it from the industrialized world. Because of its British heritage, Australia at first tried to realize its economic future in the United Kingdom and the United States. While such connections continue to be made—National Australia Bank bought Michigan National Corporation for $1.6 billion in early 1995—Australia has come to recognize the vast market on its doorstep, Asia. It's a near-perfect marriage: Australia has loads of natural resources, Asia has loads of people; Australia's exports are growing rapidly because of this Asia-Pacific alliance. Agriculture remains big in Australia, which supplies about 13% of the world's wheat and much of its wool. The country's fishing zone is the third largest in the world. Australia also is a major producer of iron ore, gold, silver, bauxite, aluminum, and diamonds, but its biggest mineral export is coal. In recognition of these resources and Asia's demand for them, the emphasis in Australia's manufacturing sector has shifted to raw-materials processing in recent years, away from such traditional industries as clothing and transportation equipment.

The Australian stock market is diverse (listings are approaching

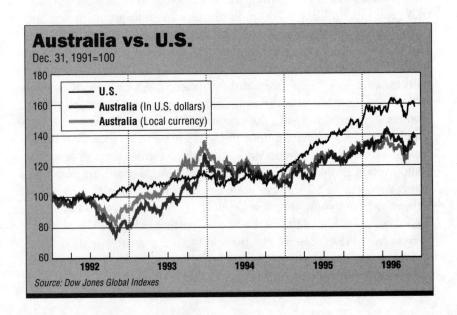

Australia vs. U.S.
Dec. 31, 1991=100

U.S.
Australia (In U.S. dollars)
Australia (Local currency)

Source: Dow Jones Global Indexes

1,200) and liquid. It is attracting both institutional and individual investors; a 1994 survey said 23% of Australian individuals owned stock, up from 16% in 1991. It also is developing into a regional equities center; the Australian Stock Exchange is creating an Asian-stock sector, beginning with a few Hong Kong–based companies, and China is showing interest in listing some of its stocks.

Many Australian stocks trade as ADRs in the United States. Among them, as in the Australian market itself, resource stocks are the most plentiful. The biggest of these—and also the largest Australian stock by market capitalization—is Broken Hill Proprietary (mining, steel, and energy). The list also includes Comalco (aluminum); Ampolex (oil and gas); CRA (iron, coal, and aluminum); North Broken Hill Peko (mining and forestry); Western Mining (nickel, gold, and other metals); Pasminco (base metals); Ashton Mining (diamonds and gold); Caltex Australia (petroleum); Poseidon Gold (guess what); MIM Holdings (copper, silver, lead, gold, and coal); and Newcrest Mining (whose gold-exploration ventures include Latin America, Indonesia, and Greece).

Australia also has important companies in building materials (Boral, CSR, James Hardie Industries, and Wesfarmers); containers and packaging (Amcor); finance (Australia & New Zealand Banking, National Australia Bank and Westpac Banking); airfreight couriers (TNT); ocean shipping (Howard Smith); and publishing (News Corporation, whose U.S. holdings include the Fox TV network, *TV Guide*, HarperCollins, and the *New York Post*). There are interesting stocks in food and beverages, too: Foster's Brewing Group has 23 breweries worldwide, with sizable shares of the Australian, Canadian, and Great Britain suds markets and two joint ventures in China. Burns, Philip & Company makes food and food ingredients; among its brand names are Fleischmann's, French's, Durkee, and Spice Island. And Coca-Cola Amatil, which is half-owned by Coca-Cola of the United States, has franchise rights in some of the fast-growing countries of Asia and Eastern Europe.

NEW ZEALAND unquestionably has an up-and-coming stock market: Volume is growing, as is local and foreign participation, and the Wild-West atmosphere of yore has been cleaned up with increased regulatory oversight, particularly in the matter of corporate disclosure. The New Zealand economy has been restructured, too, including deregulation of industry, privatization of state-owned businesses, and a stunning reduction of inflation to 2% in 1994 from a peak of 19% in 1984.

But New Zealand is a small country, which is reflected in the limited diversity of its stock listings. The biggest is Telecom of New Zealand, which was privatized in 1990; it is controlled by Bell Atlantic and Ameritech of the United States. Two forest products concerns are the next most important companies. Carter Holt Harvey makes paper, paperboard packaging, and wood products, and it manages forests in New Zealand. Fletcher Challenge is more diversified, with interests beyond paper in construction, real estate, energy supply, and agriculture. For broad diversification, Brierly Investments owns a third of Carter Holt Harvey, slightly more of Air New Zealand, and 70% of Mount Charlotte, which is the largest hotelier in Scotland and in London.

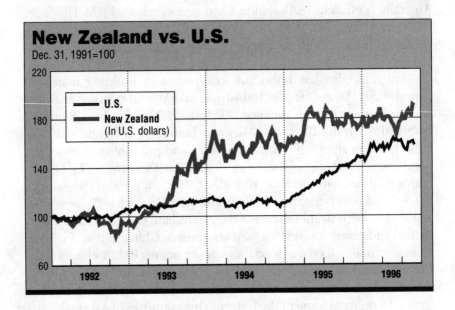

New Zealand vs. U.S.
Dec. 31, 1991=100

CHAPTER XV

Latin America

FOR years Latin America was a backwater of international investing, known best as the sinkhole into which many of the largest
banks in the United States made bad loans in the early 1980s. Plagued
by high inflation, low productivity, bad economic management, and dic-
tatorial regimes, the nations of Latin America were shunned by even
sophisticated international investors, who were much more willing to
seek profits in Southeast Asia.

But that perspective began to change in the late 1980s. First in
Chile, later in Argentina and Peru, dynamic leaders engineered re-
sounding reversals of their countries' fortunes. Ironically, the process
began with a dictator—Chile's General Pinochet—reversing the ru-
inous policies of his Communist predecessor. It continued with the rise
to power in Argentina of Carlos Menem and his economy minister,
Domingo Cavallo, and was followed by the sometimes ludicrous, yet
successful, administration of Peru's Alberto Fujimori. More recently
Brazil has joined this wave of reform under Fernando Henrique Car-

doso, who became president in early 1995 after serving as the country's finance minister.

The year 1995 also marked the beginning of the so-called Southern Common Market, or Mercosur, a zero-tariff trade zone that includes two of South America's largest economies—Brazil and Argentina—as well as Paraguay and Uruguay. Together, those four nations represent a population of 200 million. More important, economists and politicians hope to expand Mercosur to other Latin American nations, eventually creating the South American Free Trade Area (SAFTA). SAFTA is important for two reasons. First, it will clearly result in improved economic performance for its members, helping solve long-term problems of poverty and joblessness. Second, the more closely allied the economies of South America become, the less likely that any one nation can revert to old policies that resulted in hyperinflation and protectionism. For foreign investors, the move toward better economic integration among Latin American nations can only be a long-term positive development.

Sadly, not every Latin American nation is advancing in the decade of the 1990s. Venezuela has been especially disappointing. A banking crisis early in 1994 came atop already rigid foreign exchange controls and dangerously high inflation, and it isn't clear that the administration of Rafael Caldera Rodríguez, a populist politician, is making much progress with those problems.

The Mexican peso's implosion late in 1994 and early 1995 affected every Latin American market to some extent, with some seeing ominous similarities in Argentina's financial structure. (Those similarities were, we believe, convincingly denied by Argentine officials.) If nothing else, Mexico made U.S. investors wary of any emerging market, and that means every Latin American market. But as we hope this chapter points out, the long-term prospect for much of Latin America remains positive, and an American investor moving cautiously and accepting the volatility inherent in these markets can almost certainly profit from having at least some Latin American stocks in an international portfolio.

CHILE

Lost in the hype and then the furor that surrounded Mexico in the past few years, Chile has staged a decade-long economic miracle. Not only has it recovered from some of the worst economic mismanagement of any nation to become a showcase of industrial development, but it has also successfully completed the transition from a military dictatorship to an open democracy. If there is such a thing as a Cinderella among emerging markets, Chile is it.

Chile's modern economic history begins in the wrack and ruin created by Salvador Allende Gossens, Latin America's first elected Marxist president. Elected in 1970, Allende set forth an ambitious program to turn Chile into a socialist state. His nationalization program encompassed everything from banks to the nation's crown jewels, the copper mines. Not surprisingly, the results of his efforts included massive capital flight, skyrocketing inflation, and widespread shortages. Allende's disruptive regime ended in September 1973 when he was assassinated in a bloody coup that installed General Augusto Pinochet Ugarte as president.

General Pinochet has hardly been a figure of admiration. His crackdown on Allende supporters led to the imprisonment of thousands and executions of those he most feared. The long arm of his government reached as far as Washington, where Orlando Letellier, Allende's onetime foreign minister, was murdered in 1976 in a car bombing. But Pinochet was committed to undoing much of what Allende had done by creating a radical free-market economy. Economic policy was placed in the hands of several economists who had trained at the University of Chicago—they became known as "Los Chicago Boys"—who made the centerpiece of their plan a peso permanently pegged at 39 to the dollar. A fixed exchange rate, they reasoned, along with lower trade and investment barriers, would reduce Chile's inflation rate to levels more in line with the rest of the world. For several years the strong peso attracted foreign investment, giving Chile the best of both worlds: high growth rates with low inflation.

By the early 1980s, though, interest rates had risen sharply, a reflection of investor nervousness about the continued stability of the peso. The high rates hurt Chile's highly leveraged banks at the same time that the foreign lending boom that had supported the peso came to a halt. Finally, the government bowed to the increasing pressure and devalued the peso by 18%. Just as Mexico's attempt to devalue the peso gradually in 1994 failed, so did the Chilean government's efforts to take its currency lower in moderate steps; the Chilean peso plunged more than 90% in 12 months. The Chilean economy shrank 14% in 1982, one-quarter of all Chilean workers lost their jobs, wages fell to levels of a decade earlier, and soup kitchens reminiscent of the Great Depression in the United States sprang up to feed the millions of poor.

For three years Chile wallowed in confusion as five economic ministers came and went. Only after a Columbia-educated economist named Hernan Buchi took over the economic ministry did things begin to sort themselves out. Determined to balance Chile's budget, he cut pension payouts, including taking the risky step of reducing pensions to the retired military officers who supported General Pinochet. He also granted generous tax breaks to companies that reinvested their profits rather than paying them out as dividends, and he abandoned the strong peso as a hedge against inflation, allowing the currency instead to fall to a level that promoted exports.

The export play paid off handsomely in the 1980s. Chilean wines, for example, suddenly burst onto the international wine scene. Chilean fishermen developed a big export market of salmon to Japan, and machinery makers now ship equipment to the United States. Since 1982, Chile's exports have tripled and the economy has grown for 11 consecutive years. At the same time, conservative economic policy has bolstered Chile's own finances. The government in the mid-1980s instituted a pension reform plan that required all workers to save 10% of their paychecks in individual accounts managed by a private fund. With more than $20 billion in deposits, the pension fund has given Chile the ability to be choosy about the levels of foreign investment it permits. And, when General Pinochet left office, a popularly elected president was installed with barely a hitch in the economy or the Chilean financial markets. The result of all this can be seen today in the streets of Santiago, where construction cranes dot the skyline and modernist paintings decorate the subway stations.

There remains considerable distaste among many Chileans for the army in the wake of the Pinochet regime's early years of repression and torture. And it is possible that if the ill will boils up in politics and seems to pose a threat to Chile's army, the generals could once again seize power or impose civil rights restrictions. But fears of upsetting the seeming economic miracle that has taken place here make that event increasingly unlikely. While the remarkable growth rates that Chile has enjoyed for more than a decade won't continue uninterrupted forever, there is still plenty of reason to remain bullish on this most appealing emerging market.

One reason Chile remains attractive is that it is becoming the eco-

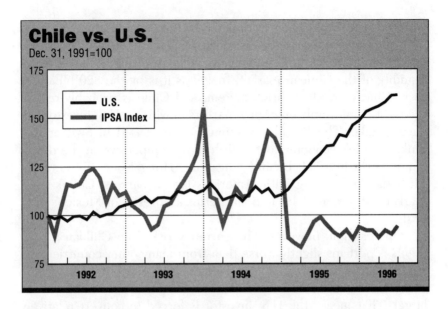

Chile vs. U.S.
Dec. 31, 1991=100

Legend:
— U.S.
— IPSA Index

(Y-axis: 75, 100, 125, 150, 175)
(X-axis: 1992, 1993, 1994, 1995, 1996)

nomic powerhouse of the region. Chilean companies are using their status as the region's most competitive to seize opportunities to make inroads in both Argentina and Peru through acquisitions and joint ventures. At the same time, Chile's exports overall are divided about equally among the Americas, Europe, and Asia, offering a degree of protection from economic troubles in any one market.

Chile's economic growth is expected to remain strong for the remainder of the 1990s. The government's current economic plan that will carry it to the year 2000 projects an annual growth rate of 5.5%, raising per-capita income by nearly half, to $4,700, and giving Chileans a standard of living just short of that enjoyed by Spain today. Chile in 1994 was invited to join the North American Free Trade Agreement, an expansion of the agreement lowering trade barriers among the United States, Canada, and Mexico. The only obvious significant economic problem lately has been Chile's inflation rate. While it is higher than the government's target of 6.5%, it appears to be responding to higher interest rates and is now running well below 10%.

Investing In Chile

Chile's remarkable ten-year rise from the scrap heap of emerging markets has not gone unnoticed, and investing in Chile isn't cheap. But with the growth rates being predicted by the government and efforts by Chile's aggressive exporters to develop new markets, long-term opportunities are almost certainly available. Add to that the excellent liquidity of the Chilean market, fueled as it is by the $20 billion or so in Chile's private pension system, and Chile is probably one of the most comfortable emerging markets in which a U.S. investor can have a stake. The World Economic Forum, based in Switzerland, ranked Chile's economy as the fifth most competitive in the developing world in 1994, behind Singapore, Hong Kong, Taiwan, and Malaysia. And among Latin America's larger markets, Chile's stock market lost a mere 3.4% in dollar terms as a result of Mexico's peso crisis.

One caution, however: The currency risk from Chilean investments is perhaps slightly worse than from many other countries, the result of a law requiring Chilean companies to distribute at least 30% of their income as dividends. In practice, the payouts are usually much larger. That means the U.S. investor is forced to convert relatively volatile Chilean pesos into U.S. dollars each quarter. And, of course, the IRS taxes dividends at a higher rate than it does capital gains.

In any developing country an investor has to consider telecommunications as a long-term growth play. Compania de Telefonos de Chile, which owns 95% of all telephone lines in the country, is the vehicle in Chile. Telefonos de Chile is controlled by Telefonica Internacional Chile, which in turn is controlled by Telefonica de Espana. Telefonica de Espana also owns stakes in Argentina's and Peru's big phone companies. Entel is Chile's best-known provider of long-distance telecommunications, its reputation solidly established after it restored service in a matter of hours following Chile's devastating 1985 earthquake. Another communications play is Madeco, a manufacturer of copper- and aluminum-based wire, plate, and coils. It owns an Argentine company that installs telephone cable and a Peruvian manufacturer that produces telephone cable.

Infrastructure investors should watch Empresa Nacional de Electridad, or ENDESA, Chile' largest and lowest-cost electricity producer. Enersis is a holding company with more than half its assets in electricity distribution. And Chilgener is Chile's principal thermal electric generator. Natural resources are a big part of Chile's economy, and Sociedad Quimica y Minera de Chile is the world's only producer of the natural nitrates used in specialty fertilizers.

Other Chilean companies to watch are Laboratorio de Chile, a pharmaceutical manufacturer well positioned to dominate Chile and to expand into Argentina; Vino Concha y Toro, a wine maker; Compania Cervecerias Unidas, the nation's largest brewer, bottler, and distributor of beer; Cristalerias de Chile, the largest producer of glass containers in Chile; and Embotelladora Andina, the country' largest soft-drink producer, with a 64% market share.

PERU

If you think of Peru at all, you probably remember it more as the country with the president, Alberto Fujimori, who had political fights with his wife, Susana Higuchi, than as one of the up-and-coming emerging markets of the world. The president tried to lock her up occasionally in the presidential palace to keep her quiet. But Ms. Higuchi invariably found a way to the media to publicize her accusations about her husband's infidelities and his attempts to sabotage her own political career (she wanted to replace him as president).

But if you can put aside the comic-opera political scene, you'll do well to cast a long-term investment eye toward this Andean nation. Judging by Peru's economic transformation in the past few years, President Fujimori was able to find time to do more constructive things than lock up his wife. Not only did he smash the Shining Path terrorist organization that had run rampant in Peru before his election, but he has also conquered the hyperinflation that was endemic to Peru's economy and turned the country into one of the fastest-growing economies in the Western Hemisphere. Although the Lima stock market's trading volume of slightly more than $3 billion annually seems minute by New York Stock Exchange standards, it represents an immense increase since the early 1990s, and longer-term investors have been able to realize substantial gains.

Mr. Fujimori, an agricultural engineer, seemingly came out of nowhere to capture the presidency in 1990. His immediate attention was focused on solving the terrorist problem that had made the countryside of Peru as lawless as the American West ever was. A concerted effort by police and army units captured many of the leaders of the Shining Path movement, and an amnesty law persuaded hundreds of lower-level terrorists to surrender. At the same time he was attacking terrorism, Mr. Fujimori also undertook a bold reform of Peru's economic policies. Bloated government payrolls were pared down, state-owned companies were auctioned off, and all restrictions on foreign investment, direct and portfolio, were lifted.

While his policies rescued Peru from the pit it had fallen into in the 1980s, Mr. Fujimori and his eventual successors still have much to do. Indeed, one concern investors share about Peru is that its success is the result of a one-man show and that a successor to Fujimori will be unable to continue his programs. Poverty is widespread throughout Peru and will be difficult to correct, especially given the nation's rugged terrain, which isolates many small communities from any real role in the nation's economy. That explains why the government's immediate goals are focused on road construction and telecommunications. Bricks and mortar for other projects can follow. Politically, the president's tough antiterrorist campaign has given his critics—particularly his vocal wife—ammunition to charge that he is running a thinly disguised dictatorship. Rumors frequently bubble up of planned military coups, and experts on Peru suggest that there are several factions within the military that could attempt to unseat the president. Early in 1995, a 50-year-old border dispute between Peru and Ecuador erupted into fighting, but a cease-fire was quickly arranged. No one expects the dispute to be resolved, but experts also predict that beyond occasional flare-ups, it will have little if any long-lasting economic effect on either country.

Investing in Peru

The U.S. investor looking to Peru as a possible play must realize two things about the country. First, its stock market is exceedingly small, with fewer than 300 listed issues at the end of 1994. Less than ten stocks account for about half of the daily trading, which takes place in three and a half hours. Second, most of the players are foreigners, who have demonstrated in other places and at other times that they can be very fickle. In short, Peru is still very much an emerging market and subject to the whims of investment opinion.

Having said that, long-term investors should be able to shop with some confidence among the natural resources and infrastructure stocks that are the hallmark plays of any emerging economy. Buenaventura mines silver and gold, Minsur has interests in tin, SPCC operates cop-

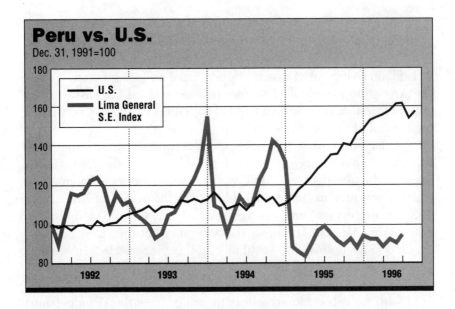

Peru vs. U.S.
Dec. 31, 1991=100

- U.S.
- Lima General S.E. Index

per mines, and Milpo extracts lead and zinc. Cementos Lima and Cementos Norte Pacasmayo are both recent privatizations that should stay busy with infrastructure projects. And Enrique Ferreyros, an importer of heavy machinery for farming and mining, will play a big role in future expansions of agricultural and mining projects.

The financial sector is expected to boom if Peru can sustain its recent growth rates for a few more years. The Banco de Credito is Peru's largest bank. Banco Wiese, the nation's second-largest bank, raised new capital in 1994 through an American depositary receipt issue on the New York Stock Exchange that was heavily sought by institutional investors.

Telecommunications investors may want to consider Compania Peruana de Telefonas. Potential consumer issues include Goodyear del Peru, which could benefit from a relaxation of import restrictions on automobiles, and Cerveceria Backus & Johnston, a big brewer.

ARGENTINA

"Argentina isn't Mexico." That was the constant refrain of Domingo Cavallo, Argentina's respected economy minister, late in 1994 and early in 1995 as the shock waves from Mexico's financial crisis knocked the

Argentinean stock market down more than 30%. Investors might be pardoned for suspecting that Argentina is a lot like Mexico. After all, like Mexico, it ended 1994 with a big current account deficit of about $11 billion that created a heavy dependence on foreign money. Also, the Argentine peso looked suspiciously overvalued, as was Mexico's peso before that government tried to ease it lower and wound up losing control of the currency's value.

But a closer look at Argentina, and the two men most responsible for its economic success in the first half of this decade—Carlos Menem, the president, and Mr. Cavallo, now the former economy minister (he was fired in 1996, widely blamed by the public for Argentina's 17% unemployment rate)—suggests that Mr. Cavallo is right: Argentina isn't Mexico. The key to the difference between the two countries lies in Argentina's Convertibility Law, engineered by Mr. Menem and Mr. Cavallo in April 1991. That legislation set the value of one Argentine peso at one U.S. dollar, fully backed by gold. That law was coupled with an extraordinary effort to bring Argentina's budget into balance through reduced spending and increased taxation and an aggressive privatization program that has opened nearly 70 former government enterprises to investment and competition. With this help, the Convertibility Law has reined in inflation (it was below 2% in 1995, by far the best performance in all of Latin America), brought down interest rates, and stemmed the flow of capital out of Argentina. At the same time, the economy grew at an average annual rate of 7% for the four years prior to 1995, when Argentina slumped into recession. More recently, economic growth has resumed, albeit at a slower pace than before. Unemployment remains a primary concern among Argentineans.

The one threat to the Convertibility Law is that Argentina's trade deficit has been growing, a consequence of cheap imports and less-than-competitive domestic industry. As the deficit grows, so do calls for a devaluation of the Argentine peso. But given the success of Argentina's economic program to date, it is highly unlikely that Mr. Menem will even consider such a move. In that respect, the 1994 constitutional reform that allows Argentina's president to seek a second term came as some reassurance to investors. Mr. Menem's reelection was followed by his request to the legislature for a grant of "superpowers" that enable him to take unusual actions in defense of the nation's economy. The grant of extraordinary powers gave foreign investors renewed confidence in Argentina as an investment target, even at the expense of undermining democratic precepts.

Investing in Argentina

Until the Mexican debacle undermined the Argentinean stock market, it had put on a sparkling display, rising 500% in four years. That performance reflects not only the country's solid growth and sound economic policies but also market reforms aimed at producing more transparent capital markets, restraining insider trading, and providing increased corporate disclosure, all of which have been reassuring to investors, both domestic and foreign.

Like other emerging markets, Argentina presents tremendous growth opportunities for telecommunications. Telefonica de Argentina was privatized in 1990, although the government guarantees its monopoly on local telephone service in southern Argentina through 1997 and perhaps until 2000. Telecom Argentina has a similar agreement with the government to continue its monopoly status for local service in northern Argentina. Another utility to consider is Metrogas, a nat-

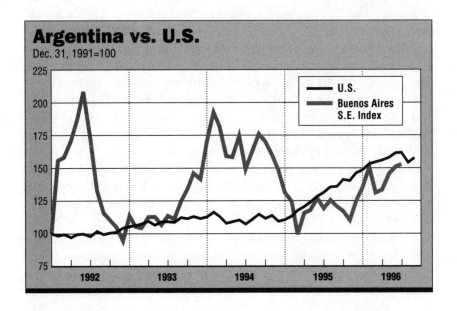

Argentina vs. U.S.
Dec. 31, 1991=100

U.S.
Buenos Aires S.E. Index

ural gas distributor that was privatized in 1994. YPF, Argentina's largest company, is an integrated oil and gas producer with big (and expensive) expansion plans. Compania Naviera Perez Companc has its fingers in oil and gas, telecommunications, power generation, and construction, and many of its assets are former government operations that the company purchased during the last four years.

Companies more attuned to the consumer include Alpargatas, a textile and footwear maker that recently joined up with Nike to manufacture and distribute Nike products in Brazil. Buenos Aires Embotelladora is a soft-drink bottler with a commanding segment of the Buenos Aires market and expansion plans in Brazil.

BRAZIL

So much promise, so little fulfillment.

Brazil is the world's fifth-largest nation, in terms of land area. With its immense natural resources and huge workforce, it should long ago have become a stellar example of all that is desirable in an emerging market. But government corruption and bureaucracy, coupled with astronomical inflation and a population crippled by low wages and poor education, left Brazil in the investment boondocks for years. The standing joke is that "Brazil is the country of the future—and it always will be."

Yet if stock markets really are leading indicators, Brazil's promise may finally be on the verge of being realized. Brazilian stocks rose nearly 60% in 1994 after effectively doubling in 1993. Mexico's meltdown in late 1994 was particularly contagious to Brazil, where stocks lost a third of their value in the six weeks following Mexico's decision to devalue its peso. But that was just another down in a history of ups and downs for Brazil's economy and markets.

Brazil's investment potential from here on out depends heavily on one man: Fernando Henrique Cardoso, the 63-year-old sociologist who assumed the presidency at the beginning of 1995. As Brazil's finance minister in 1994, Mr. Cardoso crafted what has become known as the Real (pronounced ray-AL) Plan, essentially the creation of a new currency to replace the inflation-plagued cruzeiro, which itself was Brazil's fifth currency since 1985. Backed by nearly $40 billion of foreign reserves, the real was introduced on July 1, 1994, in an operation that one economist likened to changing the engines on a Boeing 747 while in flight. The introduction of the real followed the government's adoption of a tough plan to balance its budget. The theory behind the new currency was that it would break the inflation psychology that had permeated Brazil for years. The plan was so successful that Mr. Cardoso easily won election as president, garnering well over half the vote in the first round of elections, compared to only about 25% for his closest competitor. Mr. Cardoso was so closely tied to the Real Plan that some Brazilians joked that they were electing a currency as president for the first time.

Of course, achieving power is one thing. Exercising it can be quite a different matter. Mr. Cardoso's election and the early success of the Real Plan contributed to an unusual sense of cooperation, even among his political opponents, sort of a "we're-in-this-together" attitude. More recently, though, with the price increases of goods moderating, Brazil's middle class is beginning to talk less about the success of the Real Plan in achieving economic stability and more about the pain a weak economy has inflicted.

Brazil has enormous social problems to overcome, and opinion obviously varies on how and when that can be accomplished. Some of the reforms promised by the Cardoso Administration will require constitutional changes that, in turn, hinge on his ability to hold together the coalition that supported him so strongly in the presidential election.

Investing In Brazil

Despite all the problems, the fundamentals look good for Brazil for long-term investors. If economic growth has slowed recently, so has inflation. The real is solidly backed by ample reserves, and corporate earnings are expanding strongly. Sadly, though, it isn't easy to play the Brazilian market due to stiff limitations on foreign investment. The easiest route by far is through one of two closed-end funds, Brazil or Brazilian Equity. For the investor who simply has to own individual stocks, there are several ADRs, all but one of which trade over the counter. The exception is Aracruz Cellulose, the world's largest manufacturer of eucalyptus pulp. Its ADRs are traded on the New York Stock Exchange, but analysts note that because it exports some 90% of its production, it isn't a clear play on Brazil.

As with other developing nations, the telephone utility is a good long-term bet. Telecomunicacoes Brasileiras, otherwise known as Tel-

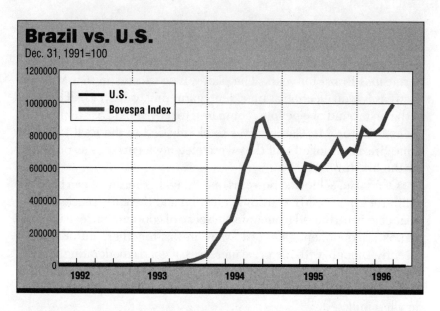

Brazil vs. U.S.
Dec. 31, 1991=100

ebras, is the last major phone company in Latin America still run by the government. But a publicly traded portion of the company is available in the form of over-the-counter ADRs. And since Brazil has one of the lowest telephone penetration rates in the world (seven lines per 100 people), the growth potential is enormous. If Mr. Cardoso continues to enjoy the popularity of his early days in office, it is assumed that Telebras eventually will be privatized.

The principal natural resource play in Brazil is Companhia Vale do Rio Doce (CVRD), a huge and well-run producer of iron ore and other metals. The Brazilian government owns 51% of CVRD, but the company nevertheless is efficient and competitive on a worldwide basis. Copene, a petrochemicals maker, has been a volatile stock, only regaining profitability in 1994 after three years of losses. Companhia de Energetica de Minas Gerais is the second-largest electric utility in Brazil. Companhia Acos Especiais Itabira is a steelmaker that sells more than 70% of its output in Brazil.

VENEZUELA

Talk about swimming against the tide. While the rest of Latin America moves forward with privatization schemes, liberalized trade and foreign exchange regulations, and more open financial markets, Venezuela is headed in precisely the opposite direction. President Rafael Caldera Rodríguez has imposed rigid foreign-exchange controls, suspended some constitutional rights, and seized 15 banks to avert their collapse. Inflation is bad, unemployment is high, and crime in Caracas, the nation's capital, has reached warlike proportions. U.S. citizens were beaten and robbed in downtown Caracas in broad daylight. Not surprisingly, the Venezuelan stock market has reflected this economic and political mess. It has been one of the world's worst investments for Americans.

Venezuela's economic situation has been deteriorating since February 1992, the date of the first of two coup attempts. The government faces a rising budget deficit and growing foreign and internal debt. To be fair, the elderly Mr. Caldera inherited a budding economic crisis when he took office in February 1994. Only a month earlier one of the country's major banks, Banco Latino, collapsed, and seven more followed it in quick succession. The ensuing government bailout of those and several others that were seized later cost the government well over $6 billion. As government spending mounted, interest rates soared. Venezuelans tried to flee the nation's currency, the bolivar, by buying dollars, sending the value of the bolivar into near free fall until the government imposed strict foreign-exchange controls. Middle-class Venezuelans, who once flew to Florida on occasional shopping sprees, found their credit cards being confiscated and cut in half at the Caracas airport. A slump in world oil prices—Venezuela is the only Latin American member of the Organization of Petroleum Exporting Countries—helped plunge the economy into a deep recession.

Mr. Caldera is a populist of the old school and had convinced many of Venezuela's poor and illiterate that his rigid controls were necessary to turn around Venezuela's failing economy. He may yet succeed. But as we write this, several economists and other experts on the region are suggesting that yet another coup attempt could result if conditions don't soon change for the better.

Investing in Venezuela

We're advocates of investing in a company or country when things seem to be at their worst. But Venezuela is stretching the point. We would

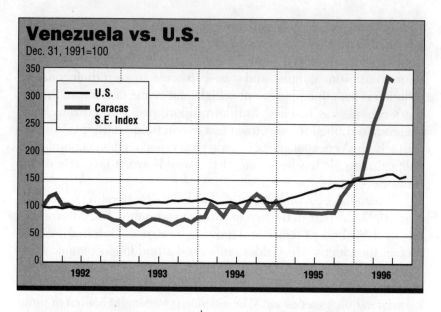

rather wait to see some indication that the government is getting its act together before rushing in. In any event, investing in Venezuela is extraordinarily difficult, given the current foreign-exchange controls. Only a few ADRs are available to individual investors. Ceramica Carabobo makes ceramic tiles and building materials and exports a large portion of the tiles to the United States. Corimon, a diversified manufacturer with operations in paint, petrochemical products, packaging materials, and processed foods, is somewhat dependent on the Venezuelan construction industry, although 40% of its revenues come from other countries. Mantex, a chemical fiber company, exports 70% of its production. It supplies cigarette filters to the growing legions of smokers in Latin America. Mavesa is a food maker that produces such staples as margarine, mayonnaise, milk products, vinegar, and cooking oil, and it has commanding market shares in several of those products. Siderurgica Venezolana Sivensa is Venezuela's premier steelmaking operation and exports about 50% of its production.

COLOMBIA

Most of us know Colombia as sort of an emerging Evil Empire, the Western Hemisphere's premier exporter of illegal drugs and the haven of narcoterrorists. But underneath that public perception lies a country with a strong democratic tradition and a steady economy that has long bucked Latin America's penchant for hyperinflation and debt debacles. Indeed, Colombia is one of only two South American nations to carry an investment grade rating from the two major ratings services (Chile is the other). Colombia's impressive record of growth is tempting, but the country's investment potential is limited by its relatively small stock market and by the total lack of any U.S.-based closed-end funds targeting Colombia alone. Only a few ADR offerings are available.

Since 1990, Colombia has taken several steps to make itself more attractive to foreign investment, including tariff reductions, decontrol of foreign exchange, and the opening of the stock market to foreigners. The discovery in 1992 of two large oil fields suggested that oil may at some point in the future displace coffee as Colombia's primary legal export. Coffee growers are mostly family concerns and offer little in the way of investment potential for foreigners. As with most other Latin American countries, unemployment, poverty, and a poor educational system continue to exert a drag on Colombia's otherwise healthy economy.

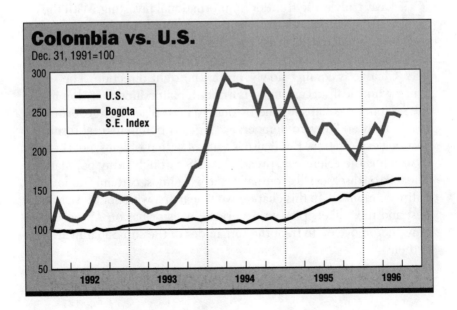

CHAPTER XVI

Africa

HERE truly is the frontier of international investing. With the exception of the relatively large and liquid South African stock market, sub-Saharan Africa is probably the riskiest, most difficult, and potentially one of the most rewarding of all the world's emerging markets. Change is coming slowly, but in the right direction. The sometimes whimsical, occasionally horrific, dictatorships that dominated the region are collapsing one by one, to be replaced by governments that at least nod toward democracy. Africa is rich in natural resources awaiting exploitation. But it also is fraught with problems, not the least of which is the relentless spread of AIDS through many populations. The toll the disease will eventually take will almost certainly undermine entire economies. In this chapter we'll deal first with South Africa, the best and most likely play an American investor has on Africa's economy, then move on to treat the remainder of the sub-Saharan area together.

South Africa

From being the world's most vilified pariah just a few years ago, South
Africa has become a probationary member of what many of us think
of as civilization. The election in 1994 of Nelson Mandela as president
marked the turning of the tide of public opinion that opened South
Africa to foreign investment, and American money managers were
eager to rush in. At least three closed-end funds are investing in sub-
Saharan Africa, and the majority of their holdings are in South Africa.
On the face of it, South Africa offers a potent combination: Its fully
functioning stock market offers modern trading practices, while the
country's economy is expected to grow at the pace of some of the most
desirable emerging markets.

But substantial risks remain. The unity of purpose that marked the
transition from apartheid to democracy broke down in 1996, leaving
Mr. Mandela opposed by both black and white leaders of other parties. The political uncertainty took a toll on South Africa's currency, the
rand, which threatens to reignite inflation. The government's target of
6% growth and the annual creation of 500,000 jobs by the year 2000
seems to be receding rather than coming closer. South Africa's economy also is heavily reliant on mining and minerals. One need only review the long list of unsponsored South African ADRs in the Bank of
New York's *Complete ADR Directory* to gain an appreciation of that
dependence: By far the majority of companies are gold or other mining concerns. Thus, it isn't surprising that the South African market
tends to track the price of gold as much as it does anything else.

Investing in South Africa

Gold is the name of the game in South African stocks. Two gold-mining
companies that trade as unsponsored ADRs in the United States are
Driefontein Consolidated and Kloof Gold Mining Company, both of
which are regarded as among the world's most efficient. Diamonds also
come to mind when discussing South Africa, and De Beers Consolidated Mines is the preeminent company in diamonds.

Among the somewhat more prosaic plays in South Africa is Anglo
American Corporation of South Africa, a mining finance concern with

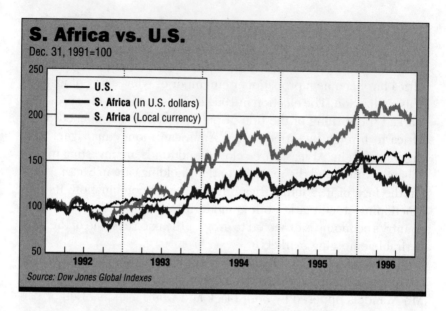

S. Africa vs. U.S.
Dec. 31, 1991=100

— U.S.
— S. Africa (In U.S. dollars)
— S. Africa (Local currency)

Source: Dow Jones Global Indexes

interests in steel, paper, and chemicals, as well. It even holds a 20%
stake in De Beers, so an investor can achieve a better diversified investment in South Africa this way than through the mining companies
themselves. With South Africa aiming at stronger economic growth,
Barlows, a diversified manufacturing company that produces or sells
steel, cement, machinery, automobiles, and construction supplies,
would be a company worth investigating. So would AECI, a chemical
and commercial explosives manufacturer.

OTHER AFRICAN MARKETS

Of the remaining 29 countries that are in the sub-Saharan region of
Africa, 15 have stock markets, although the operations of many of
them are far from what U.S. investors are accustomed to. Nigeria, the
largest after South Africa, has a market capitalization of just $2.5 bil-
lion and has about 180 stocks listed; there is no access for foreign investors, however. Zambia's stock market, the latest to open, was
formally inaugurated in 1994 and lists only seven stocks. Other markets, many of which are open only for a few hours two or three times
a week include Botswana, Cameroon, Ivory Coast, Ghana, Kenya,
Malawi, Mauritius, Namibia, Swaziland, Tanzania, Uganda, Seychelles,

and Zimbabwe. Not surprisingly, the lack of liquidity in such markets means it can take days to match buyers and sellers. The inability to leave a market quickly in times of crisis, which aren't unusual in many of these nations, compounds the already severe risk of investing there. One silver lining is that because the British colonized many of these countries, accounting standards are high—much more so than is typically found in Eastern Europe, for example.

Like South Africa, the rest of the sub-Saharan area is a commodities play. Tremendous interest was generated in 1994 when Ghana's government sold a 55% stake in Ashanti Goldfields for about $400 million. The company now has a market capitalization of nearly $2 billion, accounting for the vast majority of the $2.2 billion capitalization of Ghana's market.

CHAPTER XVII

The Fringe and Beyond

WE think you should be in international stock markets, yes, but by that we don't mean you should be in *all* international markets. If nothing else, the preceding pages in this section should have illuminated the many, many ways one might build international investment exposure by regions, countries, and stocks. There are some places, though, into which you should venture with the greatest of caution and with your eyes wide open. Still others should be avoided altogether; the risks are too great.

This position is certain to disappoint those who envision themselves as "Investment Jones" adventurers, who get a kick out of entertaining cocktail-party companions with tales of their latest foray into the exotic and the obscure. Certainly, there are some professional investors who have made or enhanced their reputations by breaking trails into uncharted markets, such as those of Eastern Europe a few years ago after the Communist bloc collapsed. It's their job to push this envelope. Heads, they win 20 times their bet. Tails, they lose their coin. If Bosnia or Haiti had stock markets, they'd be there. We expect to see

270

them in Beirut, Lebanon, where the stock market reopened in early 1996 after 20 years of bloody, devastating war. We don't expect to see you there.

Our criteria for identifying markets to avoid are excessive volatility, political and/or economic instability, and inadequate protections for shareholders. Technically, a market could be bounced if it failed any one of these "tests"—we use this word loosely because it's entirely a matter of judgment—but in our view these markets come up short on two or all three. We'll demonstrate how we judge suitability with Israel and Turkey.

Israel in particular looks like a promising investment opportunity. Its economy has expanded by nearly 7% a year from 1990 through 1995, though growth slowed sharply in 1996, and inflation seems to be waning. Because of its long-standing relations with the United States, a dozen Israeli stocks trade as ADRs, and 70 others are traded directly, typically on Nasdaq. A great many of these are in technology—Israel subsidizes research and development—and the technology sector finds recurring favor among investors worldwide. In January 1995, the government revoked a capital-gains tax.

What's wrong with this picture? Volatility and politics, mostly. The market turned frothy in late 1993, and in 1994 it sank more than 33%, from which it hadn't really recovered two years later. Some of the technology issues did even worse because they ran into fierce competition, or somebody else built a better mousetrap, or whatever; two of the worst-performing stocks during 1994 in Morningstar's ADR database belonged to Israeli technology companies. As for politics, well, where to begin? Yitzhak Rabin was assassinated; the talks with Palestine are being undermined by extremist factions; and peace negotiations with Jordan, Egypt, and Syria haven't led to anything concrete, such as a lifting of the economic embargo by the Arab League.

True, there are undoubtedly some great earnings-growth prospects among Israeli companies, and we know some U.S. investors who are snapping up shares while they are cheap. (You should, however, watch out for those that are really U.S. companies except for a Tel Aviv headquarters address; these may be valid small-stock plays, but they won't offer true international diversification.) What good will growth prospects be if the entire market is swatted down because Yasir Arafat makes some remark, or a terrorist group goes bonkers? Some of you might accuse us of being too hardhearted about the peace talks, which, you might point out, take time to bear fruit. Well, moral support is a very small item in the kind of investing we are talking about (as opposed to investing in your brother-in-law's pizza parlor); buying shares of an Israeli software developer isn't like setting a coopful of doves loose over the Middle East. Your investing behavior will *not* make a difference in that part of the world. If you really want to invest in Israel, hedge a little by also investing in some superstable country, such as the Netherlands or Switzerland.

Turkey is, if anything, on less firm footing than Israel is. The country's normally raucous politics is overlaid with a struggle between Islamists and secularists. In 1995, the secularist government under Tansu Cillar was chased from office on charges of corruption and replaced by the first Islamist government. It lasted a year. In June 1997, a new minority coalition of three rival parties took office. Their sole shared principle is dislike of the outgoing Islamists. In short order, the new government faced a vote of confidence in parliament. It won, but fistfights and name-calling with the Islamists in parliament suggested that Turkey's eighth and weakest coalition partnership in six years wouldn't have an easy time bringing calm and long-term planning to the economy.

The new minority coalition has the support of key institutions such as the armed forces, the bureaucracy, and the mainstream media. But center-right Prime Minister Mesut Yilmaz has few tools with which to accomplish his promised priority of quelling annual inflation of nearly 80%. The government has vowed to patch up the budget with $4 billion in revenue from privatizations, with big hopes riding on selling some of state-owned Turk Telekom AS. But some of the government's backers have long opposed privatization. Although Mr. Yilmaz, 49 years old, has a reputation for honesty, the coalition looks inadequate to the tasks of overcoming chronic political volatility. As prime minister in 1991 and 1996, Mr. Yilmaz chiefly distinguished himself by his failure to stay in power longer than a few months.

"The worst is over," said Yavuz Canevi, a Turkish banker who heads the country's Foreign Investors' Association. "I really think this is a positive signal. But . . . the politicians haven't learned their lesson yet. And foreign investors want to see action" on much-delayed economic reforms. The economy expanded by more than 7% annually in 1995 and 1996, but businesspeople fear that a failure to implement further reforms may hold Turkey back. The job of state minister in charge of the economy went to Gunes Taner, a cigar-smoking politician who pushed through full convertibility of the Turkish currency in 1989, but also supervised free-spending populist policies that helped create the current budget deficits.

So we can grade the political economy of Turkey no higher than C minus. We wish there were more stories like the one unfolding with the Turkish auto industry. One achievement of the Cillar government was to win a customs union with the European Union, a first step to full membership that could occur as soon as 2001. The initial reaction was tremendous fear in Turkey's automotive industry of massive layoffs, because the customs union deprived the country of steep protective tariffs. As it turned out, though, Turkey's low labor costs, a growing domestic market, and access to markets in the EU and the former Soviet Union have attracted significant amounts of foreign capital, with some $2 billion in investment since 1994. As production capacity expands faster than domestic demand, Turkey is positioning itself to become a major exporter, and is spawning a significant parts industry.

Alas, this is the only such story we know. We're not writing off Turkey forever. If it continues reforming its macroeconomic peccadilloes, if it can somehow reach accommodation between secularists and Islamists, and if it can somehow subjugate the military, then it can reap the benefits of its location as a bridge linking Europe and Asia and perhaps even the Middle East. But there is quite a way to go before such a grand vision even starts to come into focus. Invest there if you are comfortable doing so, but we see no need to tie up part of your investment portfolio waiting for Turkey to come into its own when there are so many countries far closer to realizing their destinies.

LOOKING AT THE LONG TERM

You may have noticed in this demonstration that the suitability criteria are firmly rooted in the principle of making long-term investment choices. These considerations make little sense for people trying to catch the next hiccup, which, in a volatile market, can be quite a ride in itself. But as we said in Part One, successful market timing is a matter of being lucky, not smart, and we're smart enough not to try selling you luck. We would like to sell you on common sense, though, as well as the idea of applying it even when it is out of fashion. Common Sense Corollary No. 1 is to avoid markets that aren't ready for long-term investments.

That brings us to the Czech Republic, a new country (half of what used to be Czechoslovakia) that many experts agree is well on its way to becoming one of the first Eastern European countries to reach economic respectability. The Czech Republic's mass privatization program, which placed about 80% of the country's economy in private hands, was ingenious: Citizens could buy vouchers from the state for $40 apiece, and then exchange them for shares in companies (as one-third did) or assign them to investment funds, which then converted the vouchers into stock on their behalf (as two-thirds did in 350 funds). Of the 10.3 million Czechs, more than 6.5 million directly or indirectly own shares in one or more of 1,700 companies. A long-term investor's dream, don't you think?

Eventually, yes, but meanwhile there are a few problems. The 15 biggest funds managed to acquire, in aggregate, 40% of the corporate equity. This concentration of ownership and the dominance of the funds in trading activity results in illiquidity on the Prague Stock Exchange, where daily volume amounts to only about $16 million. An estimated 80% of stock transactions are conducted "off-market" at prices that usually aren't disclosed. The other problem is that many of the biggest investment funds are owned by the country's banks, which also lend money to the companies in which the funds have investment. Will the funds act like dutiful subsidiaries of the banks or fiduciary agents of their investors? Will the funds have access to the banks' confidential information about companies? How much money would you like to put on the answers?

Lack of information with which to make investment decisions is another problem. Many of the companies are giant enterprises with dozens, sometimes hundreds, of divisions, subsidiaries, and whatnot. One of these is a company named Skoda, which isn't the automobile maker of that name but an engineering firm and manufacturer of industrial machines and tools. Technically bankrupt after the fall of Communism, the state turned it over to Lubomir Soudek, an ex-Communist industrialist. He trimmed the payroll by one-third, signed joint ventures, opened sales offices around the world, and got the dinosaur breathing heavily again. Hooray, success story. Except that Skoda's consolidated accounts in 1993 were described by the auditor as having "insufficient conservatism." And an analyst in a Prague brokerage firm declares Skoda "impossible to evaluate" because too little information about its subsidiaries is disclosed. And the finance ministry launched an investigation after 7% of Skoda's stock changed hands at a price 70% below the going market price. Prague's fund managers were the ones to complain, so it wasn't them; if they can get skinned, so can you.

Thus we arrive at Common Sense Corollary No. 2: Insist on basic protections for investors, and shun markets that don't provide them.

THE PRIVATIZATION PARADE

All these countries trying to heave themselves out of the dark ages of socialism are desperate for capital. One way to get it is to set up joint ventures with companies from industrialized nations. Another way is to sell stock in state-run or state-controlled companies to investors. This process of privatization has become common coin among the nations that are emerging and even among those still pecking at the shell. It looks so easy to the newcomers at this game; just announce that we're selling stock in the tractor plant and get out of the way so the investors don't run over you. But greed, or desperation, or both, overtakes many countries in this position, and they overprice the stock. Some countries build privatization revenue into their operating budgets, then find themselves up the creek when share offerings bring in less than expected or, in worst cases, must be pulled from the market because too many institutional investors are turning up their noses.

From the investors' point of view, the worst nightmare is a privatization that turns out to be less than advertised. That happened in 1994 in Pakistan. In August, Pakistan Telecom raised about $100 million, mainly from local retail investors, through the sale of 1 million vouchers priced at 3,000 rupees each. The success of that issue, which was heavily oversubscribed, prompted the company to tap the market again the following month, this time pitching the issue at international institutions. The deal raised a staggering $898 million as international investors clamored for a bite of Pakistan Telecom at 5,500 rupees a voucher. This money was being shelled out, mind you, for a company whose shares weren't listed, whose most recent set of audited accounts were for the year ending June 30, 1992, and which had not undergone the due diligence normally associated with global equity offerings. Investors were told that the Pakistan government would eventually set up a new company, called Pakistan Telecommunication Company, Ltd., or PTCL, which would take over most of the assets, liabilities, and operations of Pakistan Telecom. And investors were told they would eventually be able to exchange each voucher for 100 shares in the new PTCL. In short, while it was high risk with many ifs and buts, investors took the plunge because they thought it looked cheap. Their buy-in price suddenly looked very expensive, however, when it came to light that a vital piece of information on which they had based their assessments was wrong. In October, a month after the deal was done, it emerged that the company's actual number of lines in service was 1.83 million and not 2.43 million as stated at the time of the voucher offering. Since then, these investors have cursed the day they set sight on Pakistan Telecom. The voucher price has steadily declined, hitting a low of 3,000 rupees in March 1995.

As for Pakistan generally, its economic performance has been stable, although inflation is a problem, and foreigners have invested in many industries. But the society is volatile. Violence in early 1995 killed 400 people, including two U.S. diplomatic personnel, in Karachi, the country's commercial hub and main port. Islamic extremism is rising.

CHANGING POLICIES

Don't make the mistake of thinking that once a privatization program has been launched it proceeds apace until it's finished. Sometimes it starts off badly, but then gets fixed. In Sri Lanka, for instance, privatization was begun by the United National Party, which had been in power for 17 years before being ousted in 1994 by the left-leaning People's Alliance coalition. There were, among other things, too many complaints of stakes in government companies, some of which were losing money heavily, being sold too cheaply to favored businesspeople. Now, says Sri Lankan president Chandrika Bandaranaike Kumaratunga, the state will sell stock with full accountability in companies involved in aviation, transport, and insurance, plus some industrial and trading activities such as sugar, paper, fertilizer, and milk. Ms. Kumaratunga said the state would enter into long-term management leases of state-owned tea, rubber, and coconut plantations, which produce Sri Lanka's main commodity exports. The former government handed plantation management over to the private sector in June 1992 on five-year contracts. The new government will offer 99-year leases but will retain part ownership of the ventures to safeguard the interests of the nation and employees.

Elsewhere, though, privatization runs a reverse course, beginning well but then bogging down. Hungary is an example of a country where the privatization process has encountered political problems, threatening the nation's recovery. Hungary came out of the Communist era one step ahead of the pack. The Communist regime opened the door to fledgling reforms back in the 1970s, permitting small family workshops and foreign joint ventures. It was a one-party state, but Hungarians lived comfortably, earned extra money, and traveled to the West, earning their country the sobriquet of "happiest barracks in the bloc." As a result, when Communism finally collapsed, Hungary had a head start. The conservative government of Prime Minister József Antall, elected in 1990, opted for a go-slow approach, rejecting economic "shock therapy" and Czech-style mass privatization. Market-oriented privatization was the buzzword, along with generous tax incentives for foreign investors. The money flowed. Entire sectors—insurance, food processing, paper, and tobacco—were sold, largely to Western firms. Such giants as General Electric, Electrolux, and Unilever bought out Hungarian companies. From-scratch projects blossomed: Suzuki Motor, General Motors, Ford Motor, and Guardian Industries all built factories and spawned subsidiary suppliers. Marriott International bought a Budapest hotel for $53 million. The drive to sell state assets culminated in late 1993, shortly after Mr. Antall's death from cancer, with the sale of a 30% stake in state telephone company Matav to a German-American consortium for $875 million. In all, more than $8 billion of foreign money since 1990 helped the economy emerge from its post-Communist slump in 1994 with growth in gross domestic product of about 3%, the first positive result since 1989.

But the Hungarian recovery now seems shaky. A series of political blunders and policy zigzags inside the government of Prime Minister Gyula Horn has nearly derailed the country's privatization effort and still threatens to undo the hard-won gains of the past few years. Hungary must put its house in order or risk losing critical investments. As confidence in the government wanes, some have even begun to wonder whether Hungary might be headed down a slippery slope toward Mexican-style financial illiquidity and political instability. Certainly, revenues from privatization aren't likely to match expectations, or budgets. With a $28 billion debt to finance, Hungary could find itself borrowing more from capital markets abroad at ever-higher interest rates just to stay solvent. The question is, to avoid that scenario, are Mr. Horn's Socialist Party and its trade-union allies willing to slash cherished social programs—such as free health care and university education—to help balance the budget? "It's in our interest to solve the country's [financial] problems, but we have to know where society's limits of tolerance are," Mr. Horn said in an interview with *Central European Economic Review* in March 1995.

Mr. Horn's Socialist Party was elected in a 1994 landslide after promising more gentle, caring policies than the Hungarian Democratic Forum, its conservative predecessor, had provided. It was a victory tinged with nostalgia for a safer, cheaper time when jobs were secure and prices low, and when the government looked after its citizens. So, while Mr. Horn vows to stick to plans to accelerate privatization, he also wants to proceed cautiously, closely examining how, and what, the government sells from its large portfolio of about 850 companies with assets worth an estimated $14 billion. In January 1995, Mr. Horn shook up the privatization process when he personally torpedoed a $57.5 million deal to sell state hotel chain HungarHotels just days before a contract was to have been signed. He said the price was too low, and he questioned whether selling a profitable state concern was foolhardy.

Investors were dismayed by this political move, and since then they have had other occasions for concern. In October 1996, for example, the government sacked the entire board of directors of the state privatization board. The ostensible reason was a "scandal" over consultants' fees, but the move was politically inspired.

Common Sense Corollary No. 3: Privatization and politics are sometimes opposing forces.

THE MANAGEMENT GAP

In many emerging countries you will find companies so tremendously diversified that they actually are holding companies. Many countries claw their way into capitalism this way because they have genuine shortages of managerial talent. The minister in charge of facing up to reality wonders what to do with the money-losing widget factory or the technologically backward skunk works, and ends up palming them off to the already-overloaded holding companies because the only other alternative—folding them—is politically incorrect. Sometimes these behemoths survive and prosper; in other cases there comes a time of spin-offs and breakups. Management can be imported, but not in sufficient quantity to make much difference, and anyway this approach runs against national pride. For management to be homegrown takes time. During that period, investors tend to be confronted with giants so sprawling that trying to assess their performance and their potential becomes difficult to impossible.

A case in point is Elektrim, whose name beams out in electric blue from atop one of the few skyscrapers in Warsaw, Poland. A commercial powerhouse under Communism, the state-owned company was one of more than 40 foreign trade organizations that brokered trade in everything from factories to fabrics. When foreign trade was freed in 1990, Elektrim's bright light could easily have flickered out. Realizing it would not survive just as a trading agent, the company got itself privatized in 1990, later listing its shares on the Warsaw Stock Exchange. Then, helped by its contacts in the privatization ministry, it went on a shopping spree. Snapping up companies in early, low-priced privatization deals, Elektrim acquired stakes in businesses ranging from banks to a yogurt factory. Simultaneously, to shore up supplies for its traditional core electromechanical business, it bought up manufacturers it had long represented. Today, it boasts about 100 subsidiaries.

Poland was another Eastern European country marked as a comer. The radical economic reforms Poland undertook in 1989 made it a model of post-Communist transformation. The country's greatest success—its new private sector—sprang from pent-up economic energy and thrived under the government's benign neglect. Now, however, the reform initiative has slackened and the once-heralded miracle is starting to lose some of its luster. Rather than helping or even ignoring free enterprise, government policies are starting to get in its way. Entrepreneurs who saw early success with street smarts are finding that with bigger operations they need further education in business management. Without significant restructuring inside companies and reduction of government constraints on the business environment, Poland's entrepreneurial class won't be able to continue playing the dynamo for Poland's drive to catch up economically with industrialized countries of the West.

Most of the 2 million or so new private businesses that have primed Poland's economic growth since 1989 are informal family operations with small staffs. Nimble and hungry, they leap at opportunities in everything from software design to garbage hauling. They are a big part of the reason why the private sector, which now accounts for almost 60% of official employment, has nearly doubled its contribution to Poland's gross domestic product to around 55% since 1989. Estimates suggest that unregistered, "gray market" businesses add as much as 20% to total GDP. Those figures are starting to make Poland look like a Western market economy, where small- and medium-size companies provide most of the jobs and pay most of the taxes. Even the largest firms listed on the Warsaw Stock Exchange are tiny by West European standards; Elektrim, a giant in Polish terms, has a total market value of only $270 million.

But the new companies must struggle simply to survive, rather than growing into the even bigger role that many analysts say they must play if the country is to evolve from an energetic upstart to an engine of regional economic growth. Indeed, the new private sector's success could determine whether Poland gains membership in the European Union, which it wants to join in the next decade. One of the key requirements for meshing with the European Union is sufficient per-capita GDP, which small businesses have been boosting. In Poland, start-up private companies are even more important because privatization of state enterprises is moving so slowly. While the Czech Republic has sold off virtually all state companies, and even chaotic Russia has radically pared its state sector, Poland's government still owns more than 5,000 of the 8,500 enterprises it controlled in 1989. So start-ups have provided the main source of economic success. But the economic engine badly needs tuning. "We see companies increasing sales, but balance sheets worsening by the day," says Charles van der Mandele, general manager of the Polish Business Advisory Service in Warsaw, an outfit established in 1991 by a consortium of Western governments and multilateral funding institutions to assist small companies in business fundamentals. "They're not paying their bank debt, suppliers or social security . . . . So far, they've survived on wits and assets." That's no longer enough.

The lack of managerial experience has become increasingly obvious as more start-ups outgrow the mom-and-pop stage and the rising number of companies looking to expand intensifies competition. "It's a problem—how to move from the entrepreneurial level to midsize companies," says Marek Mazur, chairman of Warsaw's state-owned Powszechny Bank Kredytowy SA and a government advisor on economic issues. He says that although Polish entrepreneurs "think they're capable because they've made a lot of money, they . . . don't know how to attract customers, reduce costs or differentiate their products." The culprit is "insufficient small-business support," contends Witold Michalek, a director of the Warsaw-based Business Center Club. The 588-member organization, established in 1991 as a private chamber of commerce and business advocacy group, has emerged as one of Poland's most outspoken commercial lobbies. Mr. Michalek argues that Poland "needs small-business advisory services . . . to help [entrepreneurs] package their needs" in areas such as loan applications and business planning. A cabinet-level Office for Promotion of Entrepreneurship was underfunded and thinly staffed in previous governments; the current administration has eliminated it altogether.

Getting loans is a big problem. Companies that took out high-interest loans when banks were lending more freely before 1992 are now sinking under their debt-service burden, and many businesses that need new loans can't obtain them. Because Poland's Communist-era loan-security law gives creditors little recourse with defaulted borrowers, banks require substantial amounts of collateral; one company found it had to put up over $1 million of goods to back up a $200,000 loan. Risk aversion among banks is tremendous, and it is partly the entrepreneurs' fault. Small businesses don't know how to sell themselves to financial institutions, and many entrepreneurs don't understand how to fill out a loan application or write a business plan. So most start-ups are not even considered, especially when Polish banks would much rather finance the budget deficit than lend to entrepreneurs. The Polish government funds almost 90% of its 400 trillion zloty ($17.23 billion) domestic debt through Treasury bills and bonds. For banks, this kind of safe, liquid, and high-yield lending makes far more sense than the commercial loans they extended after 1989. Polish banks are now grappling with billions of dollars in defaults from loans made to state-owned and private firms during the past five years.

Perhaps the harshest blow to small business in Poland, coming on top of the funding and managerial problems, is heavy taxes. Corporate income taxes were raised in 1994 to 45% from 40%, while businesses already suffered a tax of nearly 50% on wages to prop up the social security system. Small businesses can't pay these levies, so they cheat. Almost no private company makes a profit officially. With two sets of books and complex employment structures, entrepreneurs deprive the government of what could be its largest tax base. According to a recent World Bank study, Poland spends 19% of its economic output on pensions, social insurance, and unemployment benefits. Portugal, with an economy twice as large, spends 11%. Attempts to make changes in the health care, education and social security systems are resisted by unions and ex-Communist leaders.

ROUGH AND TUMBLE

Some countries don't so much emerge as break the door down. One of these is Russia, and it is still too wild and woolly for individual investors. One of the hot Russian investments in 1994 was the MMM investment company, which drew millions of investors with promises of 1,000% returns. The company was the main market maker for its own shares, but it stopped quoting them when police detained MMM's president on tax-evasion charges. Share prices collapsed, burning thousands of investors.

Another problem is keeping track of who owns what, or as the pinstripers might say, the lack of adequate share-custodial arrangements. Russia doesn't have a central registry for stocks. When an investor buys or sells a share in Russia, often the buyer's name is simply listed on company books, which can be tampered with. This hazard is made clear in capital letters on the first page of the registration statement for the Templeton Russia Fund: "Russia's system of share registration creates certain risks of loss that are not normally associated with investments in other securities markets." The Securities and Exchange Commission cleared Templeton for launching the fund as long as it invests in shares of companies listed with "registrar agencies" that have contracts with Chase Manhattan Bank's local Russian subsidiary. The so-called registrar contracts require the companies to permit Chase to check on a regular basis to make sure share purchases and sales are properly entered. Better that Templeton worries about this sort of thing than you.

Not invest in Russia? Let us count the whys: Endemic corruption and crime, inflation of 100% a year, risk of anarchy or dictatorship, stock manipulation, weak market regulation, spotty financial information. The stock market is rudimentary; much trading is simply over the counter, among brokers. If you buy ten blue-chip companies, money managers say, one of them or more could well go broke, and it could be months before you know it. Several of the bigger Russian companies, such as the huge oil group Lukoil and the bank AvtoVAZbank, are negotiating with the SEC to have their shares listed in the United States as American depositary receipts. The process is taking longer than expected, but the first of these was listed on the New York Stock Exchange in the autumn of 1996. While ADRs reduce the information risk and eliminate custodial risk, they are just as vulnerable as any other investment to economic and political risk.

NOT QUITE HATCHED

In some emerging markets, the investment process starts even before there is a stock exchange, and certainly before foreign investors are welcomed in. Burma, or Myanmar, for example, has developed the beginnings of a stock market, but without a stock exchange as yet. Roughly 70 Burmese companies have issued shares to the public since 1992. Some are now trading shares, paying annual dividends and posting stock prices in newspapers. The largest of these, First Myanmar Investment Company, says it has held two share offerings and a rights issue and now has 15,810 shares outstanding with paid-up capital of 158.1 million kyats, or about $1.58 million at the unofficial exchange rate. The share price has climbed 32% since the initial public offering in 1992, and the company has paid two annual dividends, each equal to 15.5% of the IPO price. The capital has been invested in eight enterprises, including a high-rise shopping tower in downtown Rangoon, a Suzuki motorcycle dealership, an ice-cream factory, and a laundry service. Burma's transitional military government, known as the State Law and Order Restoration Council, bars foreign investment in these shares at present, and there isn't any indication of when or whether that restriction will be lifted. A team of Burmese officials has been sent to Tokyo for training with Daiwa Securities to lay the groundwork for a stock exchange. Daiwa was picked in 1994 as a consultant to Burma's stock exchange project. "In about two years' time, we can have a small stock exchange," said David O. Abel, minister of

National Planning and Economic Development. "We will legalize it, make it regulated. At present, it isn't organized, it is being done on an ad hoc basis. It is legal in the sense that ownership changes."

Vietnam also is in the process of organizing itself. It plans to create a capital-markets authority, set up a pilot stock market, and issue bonds abroad as it strives to attract foreign capital. According to a February 1994 article in the official *Vietnam Investment Review,* which is published by the State Committee for Cooperation and Investment, a recent government report estimated that Vietnam would be ready for a market by 1996 or 1997, but only if serious preparations were begun immediately. The government was focusing first on modernization and reform of the financial and banking system to fit in internationally; Vietnam joined ASEAN—an economic grouping of Brunei, Indonesia, Malaysia, the Philippines, Singapore, and Thailand—in 1995. Vietnam hopes to raise $40 billion to $50 billion in funds by the year 2000, half of it in foreign investment, aid, and loans, the rest from domestic sources. When it is organized—the projected date keeps receding into the future—Vietnam's stock market will trade shares of companies designated by the government and those going private through "equitization." Several thousand Vietnamese companies have issued stock in recent years but most are quite small. As of mid-1995, only three state-owned companies had been equitized by selling shares, mostly to workers, with the government retaining minority ownership. The stocks may be traded privately, but procedures are cumbersome. In 1996, the government expanded its "equitization" list to 200 companies.

In Romania, wannabe capitalists need only wander beneath the filthy windows of Bucharest's vast Unirea department store. "I buy shares," chant clusters of men and women, mostly Gypsies, who mill about the entry to the Piata Unirii metro stop. It's a high-risk business. What are changing hands aren't exactly shares but state-issued certificates theoretically tradable some day for shares. Valuable today, maybe garbage tomorrow. "This is a poor country," one seller says, stuffing a wad of bills into his tattered tweed coat. "Better to have money in the pocket than a piece of paper at home."

In March 1995, the Romanian Parliament approved a controversial plan under which shares of some 3,000 state companies will be sold to the public. The economy, thanks partly to a disciplined central bank, recorded 3.9% growth in 1994 and 6.9% in 1995. Inflation dropped to less than 70%, from 300% in 1993. Exports, particularly of furniture and textiles, have swelled, as have hard-currency reserves. But sustained progress will depend on clear policies, something Romania has sorely lacked since the fall of Communism. In an office overlooking the massive Victory Square, Prime Minister Nicolae Vacaroiu lights another Kent and waxes starry-eyed about his country's successes. "All the mechanisms of the free market are in place. There are no problems there," he says. "What we really need now is to obtain a proper rhythm in the pace of privatization."

For five fitful years, Romania has fought to find its rhythm, any rhythm. Leaders like Mr. Vacaroiu, often on the verge of taking decisive steps, have suddenly backed down. In the halls of government, one hears talk of bold initiatives and surefire schemes that end up taking hours to explain. "Always remember," cautions an American who has done business in Romania for years, "that this is Byzantium. Nothing's ever as simple as it seems." Nor, to be fair, is it quite as grim. Late in 1994, South Korean industrial giant Daewoo came forth with Romania's biggest foreign investment, buying a 51% stake in car maker Automobile Craiova for $156 million. Other intrepid investors include Royal Dutch Shell, which has put in nearly $65 million, Italian steelmaker Dwyer Celmag, with $22 million, and Colgate-Palmolive, with about $10 million. All told, direct investment into Romania since 1990 now tops $1.2 billion.

Still, no realistic amount of outside investment could come close to satisfying Romania's needs. The country is starved for cash; fewer than 35% of Romanians even have bank accounts. There is still only a hint of a middle class. Leadership remains weak and indecisive. Who will finance the overhaul of the hundreds of huge, unreformed factories spitting out machinery, steel, and chemicals? Of nearly 5,200 companies still in state hands, about 700 have more than 1,500 employees—and 200 of these have more than 30,000 workers. All of this, the state promises, will be sold off within seven years. In 1992, the state turned over most enterprises to a group of nominally independent funds. The State Ownership Fund, or SOF, controls 70% of each company. These assets are meant to be sold to private investors for cash. The remaining 30% is owned by five private ownership funds, whose assets will be exchanged for certificates distributed free to each citizen. Yet trial efforts of cash sales haven't caught on. Nearly all of the 800 or so state companies sold since 1990 have been small companies bought by managers and employees on long-term payment plans. In a pilot project in the fall of 1994, three profitable companies offered shares. The portion open to certificate holders was 400% over-bid, while only about one-third of the cash shares were sold. With for-eigners so far barred from bidding, experts say that Romanians simply don't have the money to spread around.

To speed the process, the new privatization plan aims to shift up to 30% of the assets now held by the SOF into the pot available to cer-tificate holders. But many, including market-oriented company chiefs, say that what is needed is capital, not shareholders. So, Romania seems bound to become a hybrid, in which most companies remain at least half state-owned, with their remaining shares spread among millions of citizens. The state shares, in theory, are to be sold gradually on an over-the-counter market named Rasdaq, which came into existence in October 1996.

Common Sense Corollary No. 4: Let somebody else lose the early money in these markets. There will be plenty of time later on, after they have matured a bit, for you to get in.

PART FOUR

Building Your Own

Now that you know why you should invest abroad, various ways to do it, and some places to investigate, it's time to start building your own international investment portfolio. Many of us will do that by seeking help from a professional, either through mutual funds or from professional money management firms. We can't recommend any particular funds or managers because we don't know enough about your own finances, your risk tolerance, or your long-term goals. But we can do two things for you. First, we can give you some background on how professionals go about building their portfolios. Don't expect any hard and fast rules, because there aren't any. No two money managers are going to see things the same way or make the same choices. But a familiarity with the basic process they use and the philosophies they espouse can help you pick a manager or fund that suits your own investment profile. If you are going it alone, knowing a little bit about how the pros think can perhaps help you better define what should and shouldn't be in your portfolio. That's the aim of the first chapter in this section.

In the second chapter, we discuss how to set up your personal international asset allocation plans based on your risk tolerance and your investment horizon. Then we create some strictly hypothetical portfolios. They aren't there for you to copy. That would be the height of folly. Instead, they are to suggest some ideas about what shape your own portfolio might take, depending on how much time and energy you want to devote to it. We move from the ultrasimple hands-off portfolio consisting exclusively of index mutual funds—which provides maximum diversification with minimum expense and trouble, but which never perform better than the indexes they follow—to more complicated portfolios that consist partly of mutual funds and partly of handpicked stocks. We create an adequately diversified portfolio out of nothing but easily purchased ADRs. And we show you how to minimize currency risks if you're the kind who can't sleep at night worrying about the value of the dollar.

Finally, we explain how to monitor your portfolio and periodically rebalance it, either to meet your changing circumstances or to take advantage of new investing opportunities as they come along. Together with our earlier discussions of foreign investment vehicles and the review of the investment potential of various countries, you should be well on your way to becoming an international investor.

CHAPTER XVIII

How the Pros Do It

PROFESSIONAL money managers, whether domestic or international, invariably have a philosophy of investing and a system to implement it. They may be growth managers or value managers, market timers, momentum players, or money-flow investors. They may do their research from the top down or the bottom up. They may confine themselves to either small capitalization stocks or large caps. They almost always use screens to identify stocks they may want to own, but they may hold a stock anywhere from a few hours to several years. They all have some method for determining when to sell.

The philosophies and systems that the professionals use have two functions. The first and most obvious one is to organize what might otherwise become a chaotic process. We've watched amateur investors drive themselves bonkers chasing the latest rumor or hot stock or even the best-performing mutual fund of the past month, completely ignoring its lousy long-term performance. We vouch for the order that systems can impose on investing.

Another reason the pros set up these elaborate guidelines and mechanisms is to have something to sell to you, the investor looking for help. By explaining to you in sometimes arcane terminology how their systems work and how successful they have been (or are going to be!), money managers can dupe you into thinking that you just can't manage all this financial stuff yourself. Never mind that many managers wind up using the same mumbo-jumbo to explain why they failed to meet the performance of an unmanaged, low-cost index. It's just a matter of time, they say, until their system proves its worth.

This chapter is intended to give you a broad acquaintance with the techniques that professional money managers use. We hope it will be useful to the great majority of you who, because of a lack of time or interest, will wind up using managers or mutual funds to do much of your investing. It should make you more comfortable interviewing a potential money manager or reading a mutual fund prospectus. But it may also be valuable to the smaller number of investors who want to make some or all of their own decisions. We think that virtually anyone with the time and interest to pursue an investment program on their own can use a mix of mutual and closed-end funds, direct investments, and ADRs to set up a very respectable long-term portfolio that effectively combines domestic and international stocks and bonds. You won't have the resources to devote to your portfolio that the professionals employ. But if you know something about how they operate, you can adapt the techniques that work for you and leave behind much of the churning and scrambling that comes from managing multimillion dollar portfolios and having your performance measured against other managers every three months.

VALUE OR GROWTH?

These are probably the two most fundamental investing philosophies. They're pretty much mutually exclusive, although nearly every growth manager claims that he or she pays attention to value, too. Essentially, a value manager looks for stocks that are selling at less than the intrinsic value of the company. He or she buys in the hopes that other investors will eventually discover this price discrepancy and bid up the stock to or even beyond that intrinsic value. Growth managers, on the other hand, look for companies that are growing considerably faster than the economy in which they operate. They are willing to pay a premium price to climb aboard that fast train and ride it until it begins to slow. In both cases, of course, the investor is assuming that he or she knows something that other investors don't yet know, and that the stock is cheaper than it should be and will be. Each camp spends considerable time boasting about the success of its system and dissecting all the flaws in the other side's approach. However, studies tend to show that over the long term both methods produce about the same results.

International investors who pursue a value approach to investing operate at some disadvantages compared to their colleagues who stick only to domestic stocks. Value investing at the professional level requires that the investor have a very good feel for what a company is really worth, compared to what the stock price says it is worth. Here at home that's relatively easy (we use that term advisedly), given the vast amount of very solid data that researchers can find. Public companies must disclose tremendous amounts of information about themselves that conform to very detailed accounting standards, and the Securities and Exchange Commission watches over the whole process with a stern eye. But as soon as you leave the U.S. borders those standards begin to wither. It's surprisingly difficult to get good information on big German companies and nearly impossible to find out much about small companies in emerging markets. So, determining what a foreign company is really worth becomes a far more speculative undertaking for the international investor. Some international value investors use price-to-earnings data as their primary statistical measure of value, but others, not trusting the way in which earnings can be manipulated in many countries, prefer price-to-book value ratios as their main tool.

Perhaps the best-known international value investor is John Templeton. The founder of the Templeton Funds, he was in the 1930s and 1940s one of the first U.S. investors to venture offshore in a big way. Mr. Templeton has no particular rule about which statistical measures are the best. His research methods incorporate many different tools, among them price-to-earnings ratios, price relative to cash flow, and even price relative to the breakup value of a company. Taking all that into account, he then measures one company against other similar companies to determine which one is cheapest. In the end, of course, he's after the same thing every other value investor is seeking: a real bargain.

Getting that bargain takes not only careful analysis but also nerves of steel, because the true value investor is buying what others are selling. Many individual investors know intellectually that the best time to buy something is when everyone else is selling it, but putting that understanding into practice takes tremendous psychological fortitude. Mr. Templeton, in the book *Global Investing the Templeton Way*, describes himself as an accommodator: "When nervous investors are selling at the bottom, I accommodate them by buying."

Value investors must also be patient. Even if they are right about an undervalued company, it can take months or years for other investors to realize the true value and bid up the price. It is tough work to hold on to a stock that sits dead in the water for two years while all around you there are reports of this or that growth stock climbing 30% or 40% in a matter of months.

But not everything about value investing is so difficult. Value can be found just about anywhere. While growth investors are often confined to smaller, less-well-known companies, value investors can search among some of the world's largest, best-known companies, as well as medium and small stocks. Thus, the potential universe from which the value investor can draw ideas is larger than that of a growth manager.

Judging by all the money managers and research analysts we have talked to over the years, growth managers don't have a good definition of what constitutes growth. At one end of the scale is a group we call the conservative growth managers, those who look for companies that are increasing their earnings 10% or so a year. At the other end are what we call the rocketeers, managers who won't touch a company that can't double its earnings in a year. That leaves plenty of room in the middle for all sorts of other managers who claim to be growth managers but who fail to better the performance of the basic indexes in most years.

The international growth investor faces some of the same problems that confront the value investor. The "growth" that these managers are buying is growth in earnings. As we already have discussed, it's much easier for foreign firms to manipulate the pace of their earnings growth than it is for U.S. companies. German companies, for example, are allowed to keep "hidden reserves" of money that don't show up on their books. Those hidden reserves come out of hiding in a bad year to boost otherwise lousy earnings and give the appearance that the company performed better than it really did. Just how important those reserves can be was evident in 1993 when Daimler Benz, to qualify for a listing of its ADRs on the New York Stock Exchange, agreed to conform to U.S. accounting rules, which don't allow hidden reserves.

Growth investing outside the United States has a different cast of characters than the same philosophy applied at home. In the United States, growth has, at various times during the past decade, included such industries as beverages, pharmaceuticals, and health care, and varying parts of the technology sector. Growth typically hasn't included utilities or industries considered to be highly cyclical, such as natural resources, petroleum, and heavy construction. But when the growth concept of big year-to-year gains in earnings is applied to less-developed countries, some of the industries that are considered staid and conservative in the United States become potential engines of growth. In many emerging markets, for example, telecommunications services are minimal, yet demand is high. That's why many international growth portfolios feature healthy doses of telephone utility companies, many of which were formerly owned by governments; the companies were sold to investors to raise money. The same is true of such boring industries as concrete. Governments in emerging economies are often intent on building their nation's infrastructure—highways, dams, and ports—as rapidly as financing can be obtained. It's the local cement supplier who is likely to get the lion's share of such contracts.

Most growth investors who take their discipline seriously are quick on the trigger. As soon as a company shows signs that its quarter-to-quarter or year-to-year growth is flagging, the stock is sold. International growth investors need to move fast. The volatility of many foreign markets, especially emerging markets, places a premium on the ability to make quick sell decisions. Growth investors in Mexico who sold their holdings at the first signal that the peso was being cut loose from its ties to the dollar escaped with far less damage than their slower colleagues who may have hoped that the market rout would end quickly or even reverse itself.

ASSET ALLOCATION

Asset allocation—the process of dividing an investment portfolio among stocks, bonds, cash, and perhaps real estate—isn't something that every money manager has to worry about. Many, for example, are mandated by their fund or firm to be only in stocks and a bit of cash. Of those, some are required to be mostly in specific kinds of stocks, such as Asian growth stocks. Still others do nothing but invest in bonds.

But for broad-line money managers who are paid to make virtually all of their clients' investment decisions, the first question is how much of a portfolio should be in each of the various asset classes. Like stocks, both bonds and cash (short-term investments, such as 90-day Treasury bills) are available in various forms outside the United States. The most ambitious money managers consider them all as potential homes for the money in their care.

The asset allocation process usually begins with an assessment of a client's long-term goals. Older investors generally look for preservation of capital foremost, recognizing that safety necessarily produces more moderate returns; a conservative portfolio would tend to have a large weighting of bonds. Younger or more adventurous investors are willing to sacrifice some of the safety to achieve higher returns; they prefer a high ratio of stocks in a portfolio. A moderate portfolio for middle-ground investors would typically be split about 65% in stocks and 35% in bonds. For those who are willing or eager to take advantage of foreign opportunities, the majority of their portfolio, say about 75%, would be in domestic stocks or bonds while the remainder would be in foreign issues. A more aggressive portfolio might be 80% in stocks and only 20% in bonds; fully half of the stock and bond choices could be outside the United States.

Once a client's risk tolerance has been taken into account, the process begins to determine which regions of the world outside the United States will be likeliest to offer the best choices. For stocks, the choices will depend heavily on whether the manager has a growth or value orientation to stock investing, as we have discussed. For bonds, though, things change dramatically. Since bonds are inherently a safety vehicle for many investors, the first criteria is to choose countries in which there is minimal credit risk, which would tend to exclude most emerging markets. Indeed, the field for conservative bond investments basically is confined to Japan and the major nations of Europe. Most money managers tend to stick to sovereign or government debt issues, although some will use highly rated corporate bonds. Research can produce lists of which countries are experiencing slower growth and expect declining rates of inflation (and consequently rising bond prices) and which countries have accelerating economic growth and therefore can be expected to encounter rising inflation, higher interest, and lower bond prices.

For more aggressive accounts, money managers will sometimes

take additional risks with the bond portions of portfolios as well as the stock portions. That typically involves buying government debt issued by nations that are less than AAA credit risks. Not only are yields on such bonds higher, but so is the price volatility. A correct bet can produce an admirable yield, coupled over time with a large capital gain. Of course, the wrong bet produces just the opposite.

Hovering over all these decisions are currency concerns. All other things being equal, higher interest rates tend to produce a stronger currency. But since things are never equal, many money managers with conservative clients tend to hedge at least part of their currency exposures. Aggressive managers are more eclectic, some avoiding the additional costs of hedging as a drag on performance, while others hedge modestly.

Take It from the Top

Once they have defined what kind of stock investor they are—growth or value—many money managers begin the process of assembling the stock portions of their portfolios by doing "top-down" research. For the international money manager, top-down research is aimed at identifying the regions or countries of the world that have the macroeconomic environments suitable to the kinds of companies and stocks that dovetail with his or her particular investment philosophy. For the value manager, that means identifying countries where markets have fallen because the economy is weak, there are political problems, or something else is undermining investor confidence. Growth managers, on the other hand, are looking for countries or regions where economic growth is accelerating. That's where they expect to find companies profiting from that growth by increasing market share or providing new products or services.

Neither approach is particularly easy. Let's take the value investor first. One big hurdle in this approach is overcoming the psychological resistance to investing money in a troubled country that other investors are fleeing. John Templeton calls it "the principle of maximum pessimism." He contends that international investors should be asking not "where is the outlook good?" but, rather, "where is the outlook most miserable?" That's where the bargains will be found.

A second related problem facing the value investor is to separate the countries or regions that have hit a temporary setback from those that are undergoing fundamental changes for the worse. While we're taking a bit of risk in this little exercise, we think Latin American nations have provided examples of the various stages of decline that a value investor should consider. Mexico's peso devaluation was a signal that the country has some fundamental problems that might not be solved for a year or two or even longer. The sharp drop in the dollar value of Mexican stocks in 1995 was tempting some of the true vultures and some of the boldest value investors. At the same time, Argentina's stock market was hit by the ripple effects of Mexico's action, even though the similarities between Mexico and Argentina were mostly superficial. Presumably, the smartest investors realized that Argentina's financial and political situation was fundamentally different—and better—than Mexico's. Thus, the Mexico-related retreat in Argentina provided a prime opportunity for even the most cautious value investors. Finally, Venezuela wasn't much affected by the Mexican rout. Its market already reflected the government's instability and the failure of its economic policies to put it on the same growth track as much of the rest of Latin America. For the most part, even the value investors stayed away from Venezuela in 1995.

For international growth investors, top-down research aims at identifying two sets of countries or regions. First, of course, are those countries whose economic growth is shifting into high gear. That's where the hot money will soon be headed and where the stock market performance is most likely to take off. The second set of countries consists of those that have enjoyed prosperity for some time and whose markets have gotten wildly ahead of any rational values. Those are the markets in which it is high time to get out, taking profits before the inevitable correction sets in. The problem is getting in and out of these markets early enough. If a manager is too late, prices will already be so high that the potential profits are mostly gone. And, given the volatility of many markets, big gains can be wiped out quickly when the corrections occur.

FROM THE BOTTOM UP

After top-down research has identified the countries or regions in which a money manager wants to shop, the really hard part begins: "Bottom-up" research basically tries to identify the specific companies and stocks that will go into the portfolio. This is the point at which many professionals use "screens," which are nothing more than filters designed to weed out companies that clearly do not fit the manager's philosophy. Various criteria can be used. Value managers might, for instance, ask their computer to identify every company on a given stock exchange that has a price-to-earnings ratio of ten or less. If they want to be sure the stocks they buy are liquid enough that they can get in and out of them easily, they might then ask the computer to take all the names of the low P/E stocks that it has identified and weed out all that weren't traded every day for the past year. Growth investors' criteria will obviously be different. They might seek out small companies that have posted 35% or better earnings gains for the past two years.

Once the screens have produced fairly narrow lists of possible investment candidates, the fundamental analysis begins. Each company is assessed individually, its performance compared to industry averages and to other specific companies in the same or similar businesses. After all, a company's low P/E might be entirely justified because its management is poor, or it might simply be the result of a temporary setback or even a contagious worry like the one that knocked down the price of many Latin American stocks when Mexico devalued its peso.

Companies that once again survive the weeding-out process now receive close scrutiny. Analysts attempt to project earnings and dividend growth (when appropriate) out three to five years using forecasting models that range from the ultrasimplistic (simply graphing a line through the past two years' earnings and extending the line another three years) to complex statistical programs that demand computer power. Once the earnings have been forecast, the manager turns to determining what investors are likely to pay to own the company that produces the earnings. The key to projecting stock prices is to remember that it isn't what you would be willing to pay that matters; it's what somebody else is willing to pay. Companies that have been identified as selling at lower prices than they are worth now and will be worth in the future enter the final cut, where only the cheapest are added to portfolios. Understand, though, that cheap is a very relative concept. Aggressive growth managers will pay many times more for a stock that they like than value managers. Yet to growth managers the stock is still "cheap" because they figure somebody else will pay them considerably more for it later than they are paying for it now. Under different circumstances—an aging bull market in which investors have bid up stock prices far beyond what the economy can deliver—this approach would be called "the greater fool" theory: It doesn't matter what I pay for a stock, because a bigger fool will come along and buy the shares at an even higher price. Investment styles require the proper environment to work properly.

Riding the "Big Mo"

Technical analysis, which in its purest sense tries to predict the direction of stock prices or markets by studying trends in buying and selling, has a substantial following in the United States. While few money managers admit to using it exclusively, many at least give it a nod, acknowledging that if two stocks appear equally desirable from a fundamental viewpoint, technical analysis can sway the decision to purchase one and leave the other alone. We've not noticed many international money managers who use technical analysis even to that extent. A lack of historical data by which to judge previous market trend patterns may be part of the reason, especially in emerging markets. But occasionally we run across growth managers who include measures of "momentum" in their portfolio decisions. Momentum is nothing more than a measure of how fast a market or stock is rising or falling, incorporating both price levels and trading volumes. Less politely, it's "hot money." At its best, momentum analysis helps a money manager choose between two otherwise equally desirable markets. The one that is rising fastest, by whatever measures the analyst takes into account, will get the nod over the one where conditions are somewhat more sedate. At its worst, momentum investing is the lemminglike behavior many money managers exhibit as they struggle to show clients that they were in the right place (although not necessarily at the right time) and have the stocks in their portfolios at the end of each quarter to prove it. It isn't a method we recommend for any but the speculators among you.

Getting Out of What You Got Into

Professional money managers like to talk all the time about their sophisticated and very successful methods of choosing stocks to buy. You don't hear nearly as much about how they determine when to sell. Yet getting out of a stock or a market is almost as important to a manager's overall performance as getting in. Of course, for a money manager, whose performance is generally subjected to scrutiny every quarter, knowing when to sell is more critical than it is to a long-term investor with a five- to ten-year time horizon. Nevertheless, it's worthwhile for every investor to think about knowing when it's time to sell.

One commonly cited rule is to sell a stock only when there is something better to buy. We think that's a little too simple. First, there's always going to be something better to buy coming along a day, a week, or a month after a manager has made his or her stock selection. But to chase the latest, greatest buy in those time frames is a sure route to financial destruction. Yet, you don't want to hang on too long to a stock. After all, the list of better buys grows longer and longer each time a poorly chosen stock sinks another point or two in price.

The most sensible money managers set targets that, once hit, trigger the decision to sell, or at least to reevaluate whether the stock still has the characteristics that made it attractive in the first place. Growth managers tend to do more buying and selling overall than do value managers. Growth portfolios often turn over entirely in the course of a year, while some value managers hold their stocks patiently for three or more years. The difference is that the growth managers are looking for spectacular rates of growth that, if they continued for long, would turn some tiny company into the equivalent of General Motors in a matter of a few years. Obviously, high rates of growth can't continue forever, or even for very long. At the first sign of a slowdown, the alert growth manager bails out of a stock. Value managers, on the other hand, think they have identified a value that no one else has seen. They are willing to wait until that value becomes apparent to other investors. Because these other investors aren't so smart (at least in the opinion of the manager who found the bargain), this process can take quite a while. The managers bide their time either carefully monitoring how a company and its stock are performing, or else merely exhibiting the patience and fortitude of a saint.

In the end, the stock is sold when some preordained event occurs: growth slows, or others recognize the value that you saw earlier. Just remember, as you talk to portfolio managers or read mutual fund prospectuses, that every purchase and sale of a stock costs money. Transaction costs can be a substantial burden to money managers with high turnover.

CHAPTER XIX

Building Your Own International Portfolio

NOW it's your turn to do some work. Your own international investments should be a reflection of your risk tolerance, your time horizon, and your ability and willingness to monitor and adjust your investments. There will come a time, for example, when what is today a ten-year horizon has shrunk to two. And if you diversify well, you're likely to find that assets devoted to one kind of investment have grown much faster than others in your portfolio, to the extent that they represent too much or too little risk. In short, over time you will have to make occasional changes in your domestic and international portfolios.

There are some fundamental points to keep in mind as you decide how much of your money you want to invest overseas and where to put it. Especially important is the concept of risk. The risk you're willing to take with your investments has to be matched to an appropriate period of time. If you will need $25,000 six months from now for a down payment on a new house or for your kid's first year in the Ivy League, don't invest that money in stocks. You want it somewhere safe, like a bank savings account. You want to minimize the risk that you won't have that money when you need it.

On the other hand, if you're laying away $25,000 as part of a retirement plan that you might not activate for 20 more years, you most decidedly do not want that money in a bank savings account. Sure, the $25,000 plus a little interest will be there when you need it 20 years from now. But during that period there will almost certainly be some years in which inflation runs higher than the interest you're earning on that money in a simple savings account. It is entirely possible that 20 years hence you will have $35,000 in the savings account, but it will be worth only $20,000 after adjusting for inflation. Your seemingly risk-free investment has wound up losing 20% of its value!

We think it's far better to invest that long-term money in a portfolio of stocks, including foreign stocks, which have historically grown at a pace of 10% or more per year. Certainly, there will be years when your portfolio doesn't grow that fast. Indeed, there may even be a year or two or even three when it actually shrinks, given the volatility of some foreign markets. But at the end of 20 years we can almost guarantee you that you'll be better off financially for having invested in stocks. So the "risk" that many people perceive in stocks, and especially foreign stocks, isn't nearly so risky measured over time. Just be sure to make the portfolio adjustments to become more conservative as you draw closer to that retirement date.

THE ASSET ALLOCATION DECISION

You should treat an international investment portfolio as part of an overall plan, not as some separate facet of your investing life. That means you must have a thorough understanding of your entire financial situation. You will almost certainly have established a domestic portfolio of some sort, whether it's something as simple as a savings account and a mutual fund or two, or a much more complex mixture of individual stocks and bonds you have picked after substantial research. Your international portfolio will become part of that existing investment program, adding diversity and, in the long run, improved performance without substantial additional risk. Unless, of course, you choose to make the foreign portion substantially more risky because your domestic portfolio is too conservative.

In any case, the first decision you must make is how much money to put to work overseas. Part of the answer will depend on whether you will be reallocating existing investments to your foreign portfolio or will be investing "new" money—that is, funds that were perhaps parked in a savings account or maybe inherited. If you are reallocating domestic investments to build your foreign portfolio, go slowly. You might think you want 40% of your portfolio abroad. But rather than do it all at once, set out to achieve that goal over perhaps four years. You don't want to be selling things willy-nilly just to raise the money to get to that 40% level instantly. Here's where the old technique of dollar cost averaging comes into play. Dollar cost averaging is a method of investing that requires you to invest a specified amount at specified periods, say $1,000 every month. By doing this, you will buy more of any given asset when its price is lower and less of it when the price has risen. That's exactly what the ideal investing equation says you should be doing: buying low.

So, what are you selling to raise that cash? Well, the other part of the ideal investment equation dictates that you should sell high. Perhaps the domestic stocks or bonds in your existing portfolio that have experienced the best price gains will be candidates for selling. But before you sell off the crown jewels of your portfolio, review it carefully for the dogs that just aren't ever going to bark. You're almost certain to have made one or two mistakes in those previous choices and you might as well admit it. Swallow your pride and dump them. There's greener grass abroad.

If, on the other hand, you just laid your hands on $25,000 of new money, you needn't be so patient. Studies have shown that putting a single large amount of money to work in the U.S. stock market, even at its peaks, usually provides better returns than dribbling it in over a prolonged period, especially when it would otherwise just be parked in a low-yielding bank account. We don't know of any such studies that address the same question in foreign markets. We suspect that if you had committed that $25,000 to Japanese stocks at the peak of that market's frenzy in 1989, you might have a hard time just getting back to even over five to seven years, which is pretty dismal. But what were you doing buying a single foreign market anyway? After all, the whole point of this international investing exercise is to diversify, diversify, diversify.

There are numerous ways to figure out how to divide your money between your domestic portfolio and your foreign portfolio. We know some aggressive young investors with plenty of time ahead of them who have invested everything they have outside the United States on the presumption that foreign markets, especially emerging markets, are almost certainly going to rise faster than our own. They have our best wishes.

Other smart investors figure that the United States represents about 40% of the world's total market capitalization, and they set up their portfolios to reflect that. There is at least some logic to that method. But keep in mind that as U.S. citizens we live most of our lives dealing in dollars, and it might be best in the long run to keep a larger proportion of your portfolio in the currency you have to live with. The counter argument is that if you own a house and car or have substantial insurance policies, you already have a very large proportion of your total assets in dollars; thus, this argument goes, you should skew your investment portfolios more heavily toward nondollar assets. We think this approach is fine only if you regard your home, car, and so on, as being among your investments; if, like us, you think of investments as primarily financial instruments, go with an allocation that keeps half or more of your investment capital in the United States.

Finally, there are those who simply don't like the idea of having much money outside the confines of the U.S. border. They are unwilling to put even 10% of their portfolios abroad. Ten percent seems to be the level that most people coming to foreign investing for the first time can be comfortable with, and that's important. If you aren't comfortable with your investments, you're going to worry and lose sleep. Nothing is worth that. We're personally comfortable with about 40% of our investment portfolios abroad, but in the end all we can really recommend at this stage is the ancient advice: To thine own self be true.

STOCKS OR BONDS?

Here at home a diversified portfolio often contains at least a smattering of bonds, and that smattering tends to grow to a larger proportion of a portfolio as an investor nears retirement. The objective in shifting money from stocks to bonds, of course, is to take a more conservative posture, relying more heavily on the sure income that flows from bonds and less on the variable returns available from stocks. Unless you have some compelling reason to seek out higher rates of interest income than can be generated here in the United States through ownership of domestic bonds, whether Treasury, municipal, or corporate, we would advise an investor new to international markets to avoid foreign bonds and bond funds. It is simply impossible to generate the kind of safe income you can earn through U.S. bonds by going abroad, because something will always be slightly out of kilter. In most cases there will be currency risk that you don't have here at home. In situations where you minimize currency risk by buying bonds issued by countries whose currencies are tied to the dollar, there's a higher credit risk since there are no countries with their currency tied to the dollar that are as creditworthy as the United States. And lest you yield to the temptation to buy a foreign bond fund, go back and look at their performance in the Great Bond Bear Market of 1994. That's the kind of performance that you buy bonds precisely to avoid.

There's the answer: Make your international portfolio a stock portfolio. Keep your safe money safe here at home.

MUTUAL FUNDS OR INDIVIDUAL STOCKS?

For most of us, mutual funds are going to be the best way to begin building a portfolio of foreign stocks. First, it's easier. Global and international mutual funds offer one-stop, one-decision shopping. If you already own a domestic mutual fund or two, chances are the company that offers it also has some international funds for consideration. If not, it's about as easy as dialing a toll-free number to get a prospectus and application.

Second, it's the only way those of us with less than about $100,000 are going to achieve the necessary kind of diversification that will make this whole exercise worthwhile. Many mutual funds let you start with minimums of $2,500 or less and add to your fund at a rate of just $100 or so each month.

Third, owning a mutual fund, while not worry-free, requires far less time and effort than monitoring the performance of a dozen or more individual stocks while at the same time studying research reports on another two or three dozen for likely candidates to replace the issues you might sell. That isn't to say that owning a mutual fund doesn't require some oversight and thought on your part; it just demands less of you than a portfolio of individual stocks.

Having said that, let us add that once you have achieved whatever minimum international diversification you have set for yourself through a mutual fund or two, there's nothing wrong with using future money to buy an individual foreign stock or two. We think it's fun to own shares in a company that we can watch progress, stumble, pick itself up, and go forward again. And a foreign company, especially one whose stock trades as a listed ADR, can be particularly intriguing. You will likely find yourself drawn into a search for more information about the politics and economies of the countries that are home to your foreign stocks. You almost certainly will take a new and more intense interest in currency values and why they move the way they do. All in all, owning a few foreign stocks to supplement your international mutual funds can be fun as well as profitable.

THE ROLE OF EMERGING MARKETS

When we first began the research for this book in 1994, we figured we would have to take some pains to warn novice foreign investors not to put all their money in emerging markets. The spectacular returns that Hong Kong and other emerging markets had enjoyed in 1993 had begun to attract millions more dollars from U.S. investors anxious to share in the loot. Then, as 1995 opened, we worried about having to warn novice investors not to avoid emerging markets altogether. Mexico's financial meltdown and the havoc it wrought on emerging markets around the globe came as a tremendous shock to the investors who had jumped into those markets so enthusiastically in 1994. Badly stung, many overreacted and came rushing back to U.S. stocks, swearing off any more risky international investing. In their greed to capture the fat returns that emerging markets seemed to offer, they had neglected to consider that skyrocketing markets can sink just as quickly.

We're big advocates of emerging markets. What has transpired over the past few years in Latin America and before that in Southeast Asia demonstrates that many of these smaller economies will, over the long haul, provide superior growth rates and better market returns than the big industrialized nations. We want to enjoy some of those gains and so should you. But you should not do so at the risk of being so psychologically shattered by the inevitable, steep declines that will occur from time to time that you flee international investing altogether. For those who find it difficult to sleep well if anything in their portfolio falls more than 25%, we suggest a minimal exposure to emerging markets, say about 10% to 15% of your international portfolio. Being the cautious type, you probably won't have more than about 10% of your entire investment portfolio overseas anyway, so your total exposure to emerging markets will be a mere 1.5%. That's enough to give your overall returns a modest lift in good years, but not so much that you have to worry in the bad years. For the more aggressive investor it wouldn't be amiss to have 40% or even 50% of your international portfolio spread among emerging markets. Since you probably would have about 40% of your entire investment program in foreign markets, that means your total exposure to emerging markets could be as high as 20%. That's big enough to produce a healthy kicker in good years, but in a bad year it might negate more modest gains elsewhere in your portfolio.

A REBALANCING ACT

Once you have achieved a well-diversified portfolio of domestic and foreign securities, the work isn't over. In either case various assets are going to perform better than others. That can lead, over a period of time, to a distortion in your carefully worked-out asset allocation plan. For example, let's assume that you want to be a little aggressive with the emerging-markets portion of your overall portfolio, putting maybe 40% of your international funds in that category. After two years of spectacular returns from emerging markets and the usual 10% or so from your investments in Europe and Japan, the emerging-markets part of your portfolio could represent 50% of your international funds. That is getting a little dicey by anyone's measure. So you would want to sell enough of your emerging-markets funds or stocks to rebalance that portion of your portfolio back at the 40% level you originally set. It's going to be hard to take money out of such a winning category, but comfort yourself with the thought that after such big gains, a correction can't be far away.

Equally difficult, perhaps, is rebalancing a portfolio to add more funds to a losing category. Again we'll use emerging markets as our bogey, since they're likely to be more volatile than other categories. If, conservative soul that you are, you had pegged emerging markets as 10% of your international portfolio and two years of subpar performance brings that category down to the 5% level, it's time to add some money to bring it back up to snuff. Think positively. After two years of bad performance, a rally is nearer now than it was before, and you want to take maximum advantage of it. In any event, just remember that you made your initial asset allocation decisions for some reason. If the reason hasn't changed (other than you have become either elated or frightened by the performance of some category) stick with your initial decision by periodically rebalancing your portfolio.

THE PORTFOLIOS, PLEASE

Now we can start to assemble some hypothetical portfolios that will demonstrate the range of possibilities available to any investor. We don't recommend any of these portfolios. They are here to give you an idea of how you can achieve international diversification given your own risk tolerance, skills, interest, time horizon, and investable funds. With few exceptions, we don't recommend any of the funds or stocks that we use to illustrate these hypothetical portfolios. They're just there as illustrations. Circumstances change constantly, and what looks like a perfectly reasonable stock or fund to own today may be something to be shunned six months from now.

The Minimum-Maintenance, Minimum-Cost Portfolio

Here's a portfolio for those of us intent on sailing away to the South Seas for a few years where we hope not to be bothered by any of the common concerns of civilization, including the ups and downs of financial markets. It should also suit those of us with jobs, kids, civic responsibilities, and hobbies that leave us little free time to monitor an investment portfolio. Finally, it should appeal to those who want to put the maximum amount of their money to work in an investment while paying the minimum amounts possible in fees, commissions, and operating costs.

The foundation of this low-maintenance, low-cost portfolio is built on index funds. As we explained in the chapter on mutual funds, index funds are designed to mimic the performance of some chosen stock or bond market index. By far the most popular domestic index funds focus on the Standard & Poor's 500-stock index, a broad measure of the performance of 500 large capitalization stocks. The advantage of index funds is that they require minimal management time and effort by a fund manager and incur very few transaction costs, since it is only occasionally that one of the components of an index is changed.

There is, as with everything else in life, a downside to index funds. For one thing, when *The Wall Street Journal* each quarter publishes its scorecard of how all the mutual funds performed, you won't find your index funds among the top 50 winners. While it is difficult and nearly impossible to predict, good fund managers can outperform indexes for a substantial period of time. Of course, you also can be sure that you won't be embarrassed by finding your funds in the worst 50 performers, either. Second, if you pay close attention to how the particular index you're emulating performed in any given period of time, you probably will find your fund fell slightly behind. We told you that management fees were minimal in an index fund, but there are some costs, and those costs come out of your performance. You can't have it all.

Let's assume for planning purposes that your entire portfolio amounts to $100,000. Knowing that you want a low-cost, low-maintenance portfolio, we'll assume that entire $100,000 is in Vanguard's S&P 500 Index Fund, where it tracks the performance of the S&P, albeit with a little bit of slippage representing the necessary management fees. To diversify this portfolio internationally, all you need do is pick up your telephone, dial Vanguard's toll-free number, and tell the customer rep that you want to move $50,000 of your total account into foreign index funds. The truth is, Vanguard makes this a little more difficult than it should be, because it offers two different index funds that, taken together, track the most popular international stock index, Morgan Stanley's Europe, Austral-Asia, Far East Index. To duplicate the EAFE, which is a perfectly rational thing to want to do, you have to split your foreign investments equally between Vanguard's International Equity Fund Europe and its International Equity Fund Pacific. Here's what your minimum-maintenance, minimum-cost, well-diversified foreign portfolio now looks like:

Vanguard S&P Index Fund	$50,000
Vanguard Europe	$25,000
Vanguard Pacific	$25,000

All you need to do from now on is put new money equally into each one of your three funds and sit back. If you want to be marginally more active as an investor, you can take a look, say once a year, at your portfolio and do a simple rebalancing act, taking money out of the best-performing fund or funds and putting it in the worst-performing, so that you always have half your money at work in an S&P fund and half at work in foreign funds.

A Slightly Jazzier Low-Cost, Low-Maintenance Approach

Now let's go back to your basic $100,000 portfolio and assume that you have been looking for a little extra oomph! without any extra work or cost. We might find a portfolio with $80,000 in an S&P index fund and $20,000 in an index fund that tracks some small-stock index, such as the Russell 2000. This gives you a play on small stocks for those times when they're hot, but you still have the basic safety of a blue-chip index fund. Let's apply that philosophy to building a low-cost, low-maintenance diversified portfolio that includes foreign stocks. Let's take half your S&P fund and put it to work just as we did in the previous example, splitting it evenly between Vanguard's European and Pacific Index funds to replicate performance of the EAFE Index. Then, take half your small-stock money and put it in a riskier kind of index fund, in this case Vanguard's Select Emerging Markets Free Index. Now you have most of your worldwide exposure to larger, very liquid stocks, with 20% of your portfolio in smaller (but far from tiny) U.S. stocks and some riskier, but hopefully more rewarding (over the long term) emerging markets. Here is the resulting portfolio, one that we think is probably the sine qua non of well-diversified, low-expense funds. This is our idea of the ideal "sail-away-and-forget-it" portfolio:

S&P Index Fund	$40,000
Vanguard Europe	$20,000
Vanguard Pacific	$20,000
Russell 2000 Index	$10,000
Emerging Markets	$10,000

There are a few other index funds from which you can choose, but the menu isn't long. At least two of the international index funds available to individuals charge loads, which seems to us the height of stupidity. What sane investor who knows anything would pay a fund company 3.5% to get into a fund that requires minimal management and promises no more than to equal an unmanaged portfolio? There must be some, but we sincerely hope you aren't one of them. Schwab has a no-load international index fund, but it tracks something called the Schwab International Index. Whoever heard of that? And where can you find it, except at Schwab? If you go the index fund route, make sure the index is one you can find readily (although the point of indexing is that you don't have to—indeed, shouldn't—look every day).

Upping the Ante: Global and International Fund Portfolios

Okay, you aren't satisfied earning what the indexes earn. You want more. To get it, you must do more and pay more. We're still assuming you don't have a lot of time to devote to building a foreign portfolio, but to get superior performance you must study the records of various funds and their managers and make some decisions about costs versus returns. As you know, we generally don't like global funds because they have the authority to invest in the United States, and we're trying to get money out of the United States. But if you like a certain global fund's record and want your life to be very simple, don't let our reservations put you off. Somebody has to like these things or they wouldn't be around. Just pick from among the ones with good, long-term records (there won't be many) and that haven't changed managers lately.

For everyone else looking for an easy solution as well as superior performance, the international funds that keep their investments outside the United States are the place to shop. You could take the one with the best five-year performance record, but you might feel more comfortable, if your resources and their minimums allow it, to choose two or more. Several international funds offer a blend of growth and value investing and have reasonable records. The EuroPacific Fund, Managers International Equity, and Wright International Blue Chip Equity all have good five-year records.

But blends aren't for everyone. We, for example, much prefer a single-malt Scotch to even the best of blends. You can pursue a pure value approach to international investing by purchasing GAM International and maybe Harbor International, two top-rated international funds (on a five-year performance basis) pursuing a value philosophy. But be wary of what you would own if you looked for the best-performing international growth funds. The way Morningstar classifies such funds, many are really just emerging-markets funds that had some spectacular years before the debacle of 1994. You may want them, but then again, you may not. Personally, if we were going this route, we'd pick one value fund and one growth fund. That way you can be sure of maximum diversification, because it is extremely unlikely that managers with markedly different styles would wind up in the same countries, much less the same stocks, at the same time.

PLAYING TO YOUR PERSONAL STRENGTHS

We've covered the ways in which those of us without much time to devote to international investing can construct some sound, long-term portfolios. Now let's move on to the next level, at which we begin to tap your own expertise in certain areas. Let's start with an assumption that you work for, say, a big U.S. chemical company with a major subsidiary in Germany. You spend a lot of time in Germany, consulting with the management of the subsidiary there, and every so often you have dinner or lunch with the subsidiary's economist. From those sessions you have developed a strong sense that the German economy is about to enter a stage of robust and prolonged growth and you want to take advantage of it. Being a wise investor, your portfolio already looks like one of those we've constructed earlier: It's broadly diversified globally. What to do about this German play you have in mind?

First, don't go crazy. Don't cash in all your chips and buy Daimler, Hoechst, and Bayer shares. That's market timing and in a market that you don't really know all that much about. Remember that in the long run you will probably do best by remaining well diversified around the globe. So we advise pulling anywhere from 10% to 20% of your total holdings, both U.S. and foreign, out of those funds and using that to make a broad-based bet on the German economy and, hence, on the German stock market. The easiest way to make that bet is to go with one of the closed-end country funds that specializes in Germany. So here's what the modified, German-weighted $100,000 portfolio looks like:

S&P Index Fund	$36,000
Vanguard Europe	$18,000
Vanguard Pacific	$18,000
Russell 2000 Index	$ 9,000
Emerging Markets	$ 9,000
Germany Fund	$10,000

You'll note that each of the funds in the existing portfolio has been reduced by 10% (i.e., S&P Index Fund's $40,000 was reduced by $4,000, the $20,000 Vanguard funds were reduced by $2,000 each, etc.) to put 10% of your total $100,000 pie in the Germany fund. Now you're following your hunch on the German stock market (remember, the Vanguard Europe Fund already has some holdings in Germany), yet you're remaining comfortably diversified for the long haul. If you're right about Germany, your portfolio will comfortably outperform the $100,000 pure index portfolio. If you're wrong, it won't hurt too much.

You don't have to limit yourself to one country, either. Let's pretend you're still a chemical executive and visiting Germany frequently. But you're also smart and know a bargain when you see one and like some emerging market that has recently taken a heavy beating. Instead of putting 10% into Germany Fund and standing pat on everything else, you take another 5% or 10% from your existing funds portfolio and buy the emerging market through a closed-end fund. Now you have increased your exposure to single countries from 10% to 20%. Fortunately, there's probably little correlation between your bedraggled but lovable emerging market and Germany's, so you're still diversified in that sense. But you can't go on doing this for every country, since it becomes almost prohibitively expensive to buy single-country closed-end funds for every country in which you should be investing.

The obverse of a strategy that is aimed at beefing up your exposure to a market that you believe will perform well is to cut your exposure to a market that frightens you. For the past few years, for example, many investors have shunned Japan. Let's say you want broad international exposure, but you, too, are worried about Japan, especially since it carries so much weight in many index funds. To avoid Japan, you can do a couple of things. First, you can significantly underweight the Vanguard Pacific Fund in your basic index fund portfolio, putting, say, just $5,000 in that fund and redistributing the other $15,000 proportionately among all your other funds. Here's the result:

S&P Index Fund	$47,500
Vanguard Europe	$23,750
Vanguard Pacific	$ 5,000
Russell 2000 Index	$11,875
Emerging Markets	$11,875

That's an easy way to do it, but note that you're lowering the foreign proportion of your portfolio from 50% to just over 40%. Another way to avoid Japan that doesn't reduce your overall exposure to foreign markets is to replace the Vanguard Pacific Index Fund with a fund that invests in Asian countries other than Japan. Examples are Fidelity's Southeast Asia Fund or Scudder's Pacific Opportunity Fund. Just be aware before you make such a move that you are substantially increasing your overall exposure to emerging markets, since most Asian markets other than Japan fall into that category. The point is, there are several ways to avoid a single country that scares you, but you have to make a conscious decision to increase your exposure somewhere else.

There are other ways to play your own expertise besides upping your bet on a country's economy. If you are involved in some way in a global industry, such as telecommunications, heavy construction, or raw materials, there are funds that give you access to companies in those industries worldwide. Play them in the same manner as we placed a bigger bet on Germany. Just remember to keep the biggest proportion of your portfolio in broadly diversified funds, enhancing their performance with 10% to 20% bets on an industry you know something about.

STOCK PICKING AROUND THE GLOBE

You may recall that in the closed-end fund chapter we pointed out that it could be fairly expensive to assemble a globally representative portfolio of individual closed-end funds. It can be done with a basic $100,000 portfolio, but we don't advise it. That goes double or even triple for trying to build an internationally diversified portfolio of individual stocks. First, it's difficult to find enough representative stocks readily available from a U.S. broker (although, we admit, the ADR list is growing by the month). Researching and monitoring all those stocks will be well-nigh impossible. And buying enough to construct a real portfolio will require hundreds of thousands, perhaps a million, dollars. But that doesn't mean you can't practice your stock-picking skills and make some money. You just have to start slowly and build a portfolio of individual stocks atop a well-diversified funds portfolio.

Not surprisingly, we recommend you start with ADRs—specifically, sponsored ADRs—to supplement your basic funds. They tend to be well-known companies with fairly liquid stocks that can be bought and sold easily. We aren't going to pretend to tell you which ADRs to buy. If you want to go the individual stock route, you don't want stale advice from us. Suffice it to say that you need to be confident of your own investment philosophy and to set aside some time to do your research. We think an investment in Morningstar's ADR reports will be well spent if you intend to be an active trader. You might also consider supplementing your *Wall Street Journal* subscription with the *Financial Times,* which is generally available on the day of publication in most U.S. cities. If you're using a discount broker, you might at least consider establishing an account at a full-service outfit such as Merrill Lynch if, in your conversations with brokers, you can convince them that you'll be doing a lot of foreign investing and want to see their global research reports.

How much of your portfolio you devote to individual stocks depends in large part on how much time and expertise you bring to the investment game. We could easily picture an active investor—retired, perhaps, with plenty of time on his or her hands—running a portfolio of $100,000 or more in individual foreign stocks, mostly ADRs, atop a basic fund portfolio of $200,000 or $250,000. But attempt this scenario yourself only if you prove to yourself over time—and we mean five years minimum—that you can really pick foreign winners; only then should you have more than 50% of your total portfolio in individual stocks. And if you can do that, you certainly don't need this book anymore. Please pass it along to a friend.

Index

Page numbers in italic type indicate charts and graphs.